Automotive Repair Service

Start and Run a Money-Making Business

Dan Ramsey

TAB Books

Division of McGraw-Hill, Inc.

New York   San Francisco   Washington, D.C.   Auckland   Bogotá
Caracas   Lisbon   London   Madrid   Mexico City   Milan
Montreal   New Delhi   San Juan   Singapore
Sydney   Tokyo   Toronto

FIRST EDITION
FIRST PRINTING

Business forms in this book were created using PerFORM Forms Designer from Delrina
Technology Inc.

All brand and product names mentioned in this book are copyright, trademarks, or registered
trademarks/tradenames of their respective owners.

© 1994 by **TAB Books**.
Published by TAB Books.
TAB Books is a division of McGraw-Hill, Inc.

Library of Congress Cataloging-in-Publication Data

Ramsey, Dan, 1945–
    Automotive repair service : start and run a money-making business
/ by Dan Ramsey.
        p.   cm.
    Includes index.
    ISBN 0-07-051363-5 (pbk.)
    1. Automobile repair shops—Management.   2. New business
enterprises—Management.   I. Title.
HD9710.A2R35   1994
629.28'72'068—dc20   93-38576
                                                                      CIP

Acquisitions Editor: April Nolan
Managing Editor: Lori Flaherty
Editor: Barbara Minich
Production team: Katherine G. Brown, Director
                Lisa M. Mellott, Typesetting
                Rose McFarland, Desktop operator
                Stephanie Meyers, Computer Illustrator
Design team: Jaclyn J. Boone, Designer   TAB1
                Brian Allison, Associate Designer   0513635

For Byron Hyun-Mo Ramsey,
who came too late
and left too early.

Contents

3 Planning for success

4 Start-up money

5 Keeping track of your money

Acknowledgments

A book is the product of many people besides its author. This book is certainly no exception. Veteran auto-repair-shop owner Rich Day provided valuable information gained from many years in the business. Adding to this book's completeness are Kimberly Tabor, April Nolan, and Stephen Moore of TAB Books/McGraw-Hill, Inc.; Jim Jackson, George Lord, J. C. Mascari, and Beatrice Dare of the Service Corps of Retired Executives, Portland, Oregon, District Office; Roy L. Fietz and Lori Capps of the Business Development Center at Southwest Oregon Community College; Steve Herman, Sandra Thompson, and Ron Hoyt of the Oregon Technology Access Program; Irene Vawter of the Bureau of Consumer Protection, Federal Trade Commission; Martin Lawson of the National Institute for Automotive Service Excellence; Valerie Rinehart Wright of Babcox Publications; and Monica Buchholz of the Automotive Service Association.

Thanks also to the U.S. Small Business Administration, Office of Business Development; U.S. Department of Commerce, Office of Business Liaison and Minority Business Development Agency; and the U.S. Treasury, Internal Revenue Service for their assistance in research. Thanks, too, to the staffs of Communication Solutions for their work on the manuscript.

Foreword

While lying on a creeper under a car, has it ever hit you how great it would be to run your own auto repair shop? To work for yourself? Be your own boss? If you were the shop owner as well as the mechanic, wouldn't *all* the labor charges be yours, not just a percentage? And wouldn't you get the shop's share of the parts discounts? What's more, couldn't you run things better than now? Wouldn't it be great?

If you've ever had thoughts like these, maybe it's time to do something. Step out on your own and make it happen. I did just that. It was a long time ago because I'm no kid, but I left a salary-plus-commission mechanic's job working on Fords and opened my own auto repair shop working on all types of cars. My shop was small with only myself and a few part-time employees doing every-day tune-ups, brake jobs, and other repairs. Although being the owner wasn't everything I thought it would be, I never once regretted the move. I learned that I was born to work for myself.

If you're like me and many others, running your own auto shop can be the route to the freedom, happiness, and success you deserve. You have two ways to go. You can start on your own, misfiring but learning as you go. Or, you can get a jump-start by reading Dan Ramsey's book, *Automotive Repair Service: Start and Run a Money-Making Business.*

Learning as I went is how I did it, and it's not the best way. Too much knocking and pinging. Too many unexpected obstacles requiring you to shift into reverse and steer around. Learning entirely through experience gets you down the road without fully seeing where you've been. I don't recommend it as a first choice.

I'd have given a line of brake jobs around the block to have had this book when I began. It has been fun reading an advance copy, and I learned a great deal. You will, too. That's because this book is designed to help new shop owners as well as established shop owners who'd like to tune up their businesses and become more successful than they already are.

As you'll see, Dan Ramsey has put a tremendous amount of know-how into this book. There's no information on auto mechanics in this book, you'll have to depend on your own background for that. What Dan *has* done is collect the other knowledge— the nonmechanical know-how—needed to hit on all fours as an auto repair shop owner. Then he wrote it in a clear, interesting, and easily understood manner. Authoritatively, too. Dan knows what he's talking about.

Those of us who want to be in business but don't have a college degree in running one will learn much of what we need to succeed. For example, what single thing is most vital to success in the auto repair business? What 15 questions should you ask yourself before you decide to start your own auto repair business? What 12 questions should you ask before you open your doors? How do you attract customers? How much can you expect to earn? What does Dan mean, "If it ain't broke, break it?"

Dan then answers these practical questions: How do you choose a successful name for the business? Where can you get capital for start-up and expansion? (Dan lists 14 sources.) What equipment should you acquire? How do you select the right business computer? When should you buy equipment and when should you lease equipment? How much should you charge for your services? (How to figure it. How to estimate.) What should you say when a customer tries to pick your brain? How can you minimize taxes? And what do you need to know to succeed in the auto repair business?

This book shows how you can say goodbye to life as an employee—forever. You'll learn how to set your own income level—as high as you wish. You'll see how you are the one who ultimately determines how much money you will make. You'll learn good ways to charge up your cash flow. How to avoid failure. You'll understand how to shift into gear and get where you want to be through strategic planning. That's the way big businesses do it.

Can you name the two secrets that make an auto repair business succeed? You'll be able to after reading Dan's book. Do you know how to manage risks? Solve problems? And how to keep one-cylinder problems from becoming eight-cylinder problems? Do you know where to get lots of help you don't have to pay a dime for? If not, you'll appreciate the scores of names, addresses, and telephone numbers Dan gives where you can get good advice.

You'll see how other professionals—accountants, attorneys, insurance agents, and temporary-help services—can benefit you. Even other repair shops. You'll learn how to get up and running fast through a franchise, with specific information included on locating worthwhile franchises.

Dan's book offers how-to information on negotiating from strength, finding and keeping good employees, expanding an existing business and, best of all, having fun doing it.

As a bonus, Dan shares great tips on writing, all slanted to an owner of a repair shop. He tells you how to write a business plan. How to write letters to customers and other people. You'll like his method for getting what you mean down on paper (or on screen), even though you've never written anything before in your life. Using Dan's method, anyone can write a letter (the example he gives is a letter explaining from the customer's viewpoint why parts didn't arrive on time) that would be understood immediately by everyone who reads it.

If running your own auto shop sounds good, *Automotive Repair Service: Start and Run a Money-Making Business* can help you be well on your way to becoming your own boss.

Richard Day

Introduction

It's a natural progression: an experienced auto mechanic decides to start his or her own auto repair business. The problem is that many are progressing toward failure. Why doesn't trade experience guarantee business success? Because knowing how to repair a car doesn't assure that it can be done profitably. There's more to know: how to deal with bankers and credit, how to purchase parts and tools at the greatest discounts, how to easily track income and expenses, how to get customers—and how to keep them coming back.

The purpose of this book—written with the guidance of dozens of successful auto repair service owners—is to help you start and run a money-making auto repair business. It clearly answers 66 questions you should ask.

- Should you start an auto repair business?
- What kind of auto repair business best suits you?
- Is there a real need for your business?
- Who will buy from you?
- How much money can you make?
- What should you name your business?
- Where should you locate your business?
- Should you incorporate your business?
- Should you buy a franchise?
- How much money do you need to start your business?
- Where can you get start-up capital?
- How much should you charge?
- How can you keep track of money?
- What about taxes?
- And dozens more!

Included are numerous forms and worksheets that you can use to make your auto repair business more efficient and more profitable from Day One.

This idea-packed book can also help current owners of auto repair services become more successful. It includes extensive information on how to reduce costs, reduce risks, and increase profits through enhanced management.

Chapter 1 starts you on your successful journey toward owning and managing a money-making auto repair service. You'll learn why some shops succeed while others fail. You'll learn what type of service offers the greatest opportunities for you. You'll learn how much money you can expect to make with your new business. And you'll start a business and marketing plan.

At the end of Chapter 1, and all other chapters in this book, you'll find your success action list. The lists give you step-by-step activities for making your dream a reality.

Chapter 2 can help you define your business, find your potential customers, select a successful business name, set up your bank account, and decide what legal form your business should take: proprietorship, partnership, or corporation. It can also help you select the right location for your auto repair service.

Chapter 3 provides valuable information on franchises, with specific names and addresses, professional associations, government resources, and helpful books and manuals. You'll learn how to furnish your office with business tools that can make you money: telephones, answering machines, fax machines, computers, and printers. Finally, you'll be introduced to the world of computer software written specifically for auto repair services. If you don't like recordkeeping, or even if you do, this information can help you automate your office and keep you profitable.

If you're not sure how much money you'll need to start your auto repair service or where you're going to get it, Chapter 4 can help you estimate start-up and operating costs as well as capital requirements. It also tells you how and where to get financing for your new business. Also important is learning how to set your rates to be profitable *and* competitive. You'll learn how to estimate a job and how to offer terms.

As you begin making money with your auto repair service you'll want to keep track of it, for profit and for taxes. Chapter 5 clearly explains records and recordkeeping, managing your bank account, managing payroll records, using outside accounting services, and producing and using financial reports. You'll also learn what you need to know about taxes, including dozens of resources that are available to you free of charge. Finally, you'll learn about budgets and the most important tool of successful auto repair services: ratios.

What do you need to know about customers? Who they are. Why they buy. Where to find them. How to get them to come to you. How to keep them happy. How to find out what they want, and how to give it to them. All this and more is covered in Chapter 6.

To profit you must increase sales and reduce costs. Chapter 7 tells you how to improve your business profits by reducing costs without reducing quality of service. You'll also learn how to improve cash flow: get money to come in faster than it goes out. You can also reduce costs with leases.

Once your auto repair service makes money, you want to hang on to it. Chapter 8 explains the many ways that you can reduce business risks. You'll discover what insurance you need and what you don't need. You'll also find out how to reduce bad debts.

You aren't paid for repairing autos, but for solving automotive problems. Chapter 9 clearly explains how to apply problem-solving techniques to ensure business success. You'll also discover the secrets of easy business communications. How to say and to write exactly what you mean.

As your auto repair service grows, you'll need to find and hire employees, without getting in trouble with all of the new laws. Chapter 10 covers all this and more. You'll learn about job applications, certifications, labor laws, interviews, policy manuals, wages, and commissions. You'll learn how to hire a profitable service manager. You'll also learn about employee-benefit plans and how to select one that can help you keep good employees as well as profits.

The final chapter in this comprehensive book tells you how to stay ahead of your competition and have fun at what you do. You'll learn what works for you as well as how to make sure it works. You'll learn how to face recessions and other rotten markets. You'll discover SWOTs and missions. Long-term business planning, time management, stress management, retirement, bankruptcy, and how to handle success are all covered.

Each chapter is illustrated with numerous charts, tables, and forms that can teach you the secrets of other successful auto repair shops. The appendix includes more than 50 forms that you can use today and every day to profitably manage your business: journals, work orders, schedules, employment application, credit application, time sheets, phone records, cash flow statement, and more. Each can be personalized in minutes and reproduced on any copy machine.

HOW TECHNOLOGY CAN HELP YOUR BUSINESS

There's one more important ingredient you'll find in this book that you'll find in no other: a simplified yet comprehensive view of how technology—computers, fax machines, modems—can give you the competitive advantage.

Technology applies science to the needs of people. A hundred years ago, technology offered us the gasoline-powered engine and great things came from it. Today, technology is using microelectronics to expand the knowledge and power of the human brain. In both cases, technology brought greater service to people and greater profits to businesses.

Auto repair services benefit from technology with new materials that make your job easier and safer. Technology can also help your business become more efficient and more profitable—if you know how to use it. This book tells you how to use technology for greater profits from your auto repair business.

1
Success and your auto repair business

Success is not a destination. It's a journey. It's enjoying what you do everyday—weekdays and weekends. Thousands of men and women have discovered their own success as owners of auto repair services. They are enjoying what they do: helping others maintain their transportation (FIG. 1-1). They are also enjoying who they work for: themselves. Sure, there is more grief for the owner than for the employee, but it's their grief and not someone elses.

A recent study of successful business owners said that 54 percent began their venture because they wanted independence, 33 percent identified a need or market opportunity, 8 percent wanted to make more money, and the rest had other personal reasons. The study also indicated that those who simply wanted to use their knowledge or experience were less successful than those who wanted their freedom. Both are necessary, but the desire to "be your own boss" was a powerful incentive to these successful business men and women.

Maybe you have considered putting your years of auto repair service experience to work in your own business but don't know where to start. You've already started. You've begun to read this book to learn how others have succeeded with their own auto repair service.

There's much to learn. In this first chapter, you'll learn the answers to many of the initial questions you have about starting your own auto repair service. Those questions might include the following:

- Should I start an auto repair business?
- What type of service should I offer?
- Is there a need for my service?
- How much will I make?
- How can I get started?

Fortunately, you have a trade that will always be in demand. And you're good at it. But maybe you don't have the business knowledge or skills to make the jump from employee to employer. You will—if you apply the learning skills you've developed in your auto service career to your new venture. You will soon be on your journey to success.

1-1 An auto repair shop owner offers a valuable service to others.

SHOULD YOU START AN AUTO REPAIR BUSINESS?

The automobile aftermarket is one of the largest of the retail trades. Total annual sales exceed more than $25 billion. The primary trade within this group is auto repair services, with more than 218,000 shops in the United States. In addition, there are more than 100,000 service stations, many of which offer auto repair services. There are also nearly 70,000 auto body repair shops, 43,000 tire dealers, and 36,000 brake services.

There's more. Serving the auto repair market are nearly 60,000 parts and supplies dealers, almost 40,000 towing services, and literally thousands of other firms.

It's no wonder that you cannot drive more than a few blocks in any town without seeing a business that depends on the automobile. And most of these firms are small businesses, often with a single owner and a staff of less than 20. The auto repair business is one of the last great frontiers of enterprise.

To start your own auto repair service you'll need a number of resources. First, of course, you'll need to have extensive knowledge, skill, and experience in the field of auto repair. Many auto technicians have at least 10 years experience before their skills are developed sufficiently to start their own auto repair service. You'll be paid very well for what you know. So the more you know, the more you'll be paid. Of course, if you have less experience you can hire key employees with extensive experience to do much of the actual work.

Experience as an auto mechanic, or in the specialty you select, can come from many sources. You can gain formal training through a college, trade school, or evening adult courses at a high school. You can serve an apprenticeship at a new car dealer's repair shop, an independent garage, or at a specialty automotive service center such as a tune-up shop or muffler shop. The broader your experience, the more ready you will be to manage your own auto repair shop.

To expand your training, the *Automotive Service Training and Job Skills Directory* published by the Automotive Parts and Accessories Association (4600 E. West Highway, Bethesda MD 20814) lists sources for automotive training materials and numerous automotive service trade schools and college programs. In addition, videocassettes on more than 30 auto repair jobs in the *New Automotive Mechanics Series* are sold by RMI Media Productions (2807 W. 47th St., Shawnee Mission KS 66205, 800-821-5480).

Should you start your own auto repair business? Ask yourself these questions, then get a friend or relative to answer them for you as well.

- Do I sincerely like people?
- Do I have self-discipline?
- Do others turn to me for help when making decisions?
- Do I get along well with others, even those with whom I don't agree?
- Do I like to make decisions?
- Do I enjoy competition?
- Do I plan ahead?
- Am I a leader?
- Am I willing to work long hours?
- Do I have the physical stamina to handle a busy schedule and heavy workload?
- Am I willing and able to temporarily lower my standard of living in order to firmly establish my business?
- Is my family or others close to me willing and able to go along with the struggle for business success?
- How much money am I willing to gamble on this venture knowing that I might be risking all of it?
- Do I have sufficient experience in this field to know what is required to be successful?
- Have I had any training in the basics of business? If not, am I willing to take some time to learn them?

As you go through this book, other questions will occur to you.

- Is there a need for this service in my area?
- Is my goal realistic and attainable?
- Who else is offering such a service in my area?
- How busy are they?
- Why will my service be of greater value to customers?
- How can I let prospects know the value of my service?
- Who will my customers be?
- What do they want?
- How much will they pay?
- How will I keep these customers happy?

- Where will I set up my business?
- How will I keep my business going when the economy changes?
- How can I make my business more profitable without diminishing the quality of my work?

Of course, you won't have the answers to all of these questions yet. The intent of this book is to help you get the right answers to these and other questions that are important to your success.

In addition to knowledge and experience, you'll need some physical assets in order to operate an auto repair service. Most are obvious:

- basic tools (sockets, wrenches, screwdrivers);
- specialized tools (depending on your specialty);
- electronic test equipment;
- up-to-date reference books.

You'll also need one important asset: cash. Most new businesses fail within a couple of years and often for the same reason—they run out of money. You don't have to be rich to go into business for yourself, but you do need some cash and at least a few assets (home equity, cars, investments) that can be turned quickly into cash if necessary. We'll discover later how much you'll need.

Another vital part of building your business will be building your credit. Even if you lack some of the cash you need, your credit can make startup easier. In fact, you'll learn how profitably to use your credit and save your cash for emergencies. So if your credit is poor or nonexistent, you will learn how to build it up to where it becomes a valuable asset to your business and your success.

Let me talk about another essential asset—one that doesn't always get discussed in business books: work ethics. Ethics are rules of conduct. So work ethics are the rules you set for yourself for performing the work that you do. If you will set— and stick to—the "golden rule" in your business dealings you will find, as thousands of others have, that gold comes to him who follows the rules. This isn't preaching. It's just good business. Treat your customers the way you want to be treated and you will be so far ahead of the "anything for a buck" auto repair services that you can't help but prosper. More important, you will feel good about yourself and what you do. Your customers will also be your friends and they will help you to prosper. Remember the first rule of good business: use money to make friends—not the other way around.

Another vital asset to your business success is related: your relatives. That is, if you have family and close friends who will help you and support you, you have already succeeded. If your family is not supportive of your business ideas, start now in your search to find common ground where you and they can be comfortable with this new adventure. Maybe they are concerned about your health, about your possibly failing, about your being away from home so much. Or maybe they are honestly jealous of your success. Take time to talk with them and get them to share their real feelings about your ideas. Don't talk; just listen. Believe me, success is so much more satisfying if you have people with whom to share it.

You might find that you have relatives or friends who want very much to see you succeed and have skills or assets they will share with you. Make them a part of your journey and your success. Maybe your spouse or a parent has business skills you might need, or can help with office duties, or has other resources that will help you build your business. Ask for participation, for ideas, for suggestions. You certainly don't have to accept all of them, but you might find just the right pieces to make this puzzle become a complete picture.

The point of this discussion is that there are many assets required to start your own auto repair service business. But don't let the lack of any of them discourage you from starting. In the coming pages, you'll learn how to make the most of what you do have and how to increase these assets until they are sufficient for success.

THE REAL REASON BUSINESSES FAIL

The statistics about business failure are enough to make you quit before you start. Many new businesses close their doors within the first year and most within five years. Why?

Not all businesses who close their doors have failed. Some actually merge with other firms, or sell their assets at a profit. But, unfortunately, too many to fail, losing money in the process.

So why do people continue to open businesses? Because most of us feel that we can beat the odds. If this wasn't so, Las Vegas would be a small desert community instead of Glitter City. The ones who win at Vegas or in business are those who know the odds, learn how to master them, and know when to quit.

Many business experts will tell you the reason businesses fail is "undercapitalization." That is, they don't have enough money to survive. But, if they're in the business of making—not spending—money, the actual problem is that they didn't *make* enough money. And how does a business—any business—make money? By supplying a product or service to those who need it. So the real reason businesses fail is that they fail to communicate the benefits that customers will receive by using their product or service. Or they fail to successfully communicate their business philosophy and ethics to all employees.

Businesses fail because they fail to communicate. Communication is the distribution of information. That information might be fact, or opinion, or emotions. To transfer information to another person is to communicate. This book communicates information to you. It does so with black marks on paper that your mind recognizes and translates into ideas. Information can also be communicated by the sound of words heard by your ears and translated into thoughts in your mind.

So what does communication have to do with an auto repair service business? There must be a source, a communicator, and a receiver in order to make things happen.

It's the same in your business. You are the source of knowledge about auto repair. In a way, your hands and tools communicate this knowledge to the job you're performing.

If you want to get prospects to know about your skills and to use them, you must communicate with your prospective customers. If you want employees to perform their jobs accurately and efficiently, you must communicate with your employees. If you want bankers to lend you money—and be glad to do so—you must communicate with these bankers.

If you want your family to be proud and supportive of what you do, you must communicate with them. Communicate what? Communicate accurate information that you want them to know in terms that they want to hear. That is, communicate "benefits." A benefit is simply an advantage or a reward that one product or action has over another or over not doing anything.

The benefit of this book to you is that, if you will put out time, effort, and money, you will learn what you need to know to be successful as an auto repair service business owner. That's the clear and understood reward you can receive for applying what you learn here.

So what benefits does your auto repair business offer that you can communicate to prospects, customers, employees, bankers, family, and others? Start thinking about them; write them down on a sheet of paper as they occur to you. We'll be discussing them throughout this book as I help you design your business, market your services, and communicate with others.

BUSINESS OPPORTUNITIES FOR AUTO REPAIR PROFESSIONALS

Maybe you've been in your line of auto repair work for many years and want to specialize in it as you become an auto repair business owner. Or maybe you want to transport your auto repair knowledge and skills into a related field such as tire sales and service.

On the next few pages, we'll summarize many of the fields that have been successful for auto repair professionals. It might confirm to you that your chosen specialty is the right one for you. Or it might give you new ideas that can lead you into a specialty that will be more enjoyable and more profitable for you.

General auto repair services

Only in the smallest communities across the United States and Canada do you find auto repair businesses that attempt to provide all automotive services under one roof. Cars and trucks today are just too complex for one shop to handle everything from power trains to paint jobs. The investment in tools, alone, is too great.

Instead, many auto repair services specialize in a general field. For example, a shop might offer auto service by type of vehicle (car, truck, 4WD, RV, farm, motorcycle), by group (foreign, domestic), by brand (Buick, Honda, Saab, etc.), or by purpose (maintenance, performance, rebuilding, repair).

For many auto repair services, purpose is the most profitable specialization. It utilizes their experience while serving a specific and easily defined marketplace. Later, we'll review how to determine local market support for your specialization.

Auto system services

Other successful auto service businesses specialize in installing, maintaining, and/or repairing specific auto systems found in nearly all vehicles. An example is a transmission shop that will work on cars and trucks, foreign or domestic, Buick or Honda, or whatever.

Auto systems that can be served by a profitable shop include: air conditioning, alarm and security systems, brakes, carburation and fuel, diagnostics and computer systems, drive line and differential, electrical, emission control, engine (gas, diesel, propane), exhaust and muffler, lubrication, radiator and cooling, suspension, tires and wheels, tune-ups, towing equipment, transmission and clutch, wheel alignment.

This list of auto system services indicates that highly specialized knowledge is required. A general auto repair service specialist might have a few hours training on diagnostics and computer systems, but a specialist in that field will need to have hundreds of hours of training in their specialty. For this reason, most auto system service shops earn a higher rate than general auto repair services.

The need for specialized information and the opportunity for greater profits has drawn a number of franchises to this trade, such as AAMCO, Big-O, Firestone, Jiffy Lube, Midas, etc. We'll cover franchises later in this book. Specialized auto system services also draw numerous independent shops into business.

Auto appearance services

Another profitable specialization for auto service businesses is built around the appearance of vehicles. Businesses have found that car owners will spend thousands of dollars on the appearance of their car, truck, or recreational vehicle. Combined, this becomes a multi-million dollar industry that many auto specialists join for long-term profits.

Auto appearance services include both the practical and the aesthetic. The most common auto appearance services are body repair (metal or fiberglass), customizing, detailing, engine cleaning, glass, painting, plating, restoration, rust proofing, seat covers, sun roofs, tops, upholstery, and van conversion. Within these specialties are micro-specializations that some shops decide to market such as painting murals on motor homes, antique car upholstery, Corvette body repair, etc.

Franchise opportunities are available, too, for those who want to specialize in auto appearance services. These will be discussed later.

Other auto services

The automotive aftermarket is extensive. Besides the above specializations, there are related services that can be profitably marketed in your area either combined with other services or as a primary service.

Other auto services include machine shop, parts, towing, and wrecking. These are large industries on their own. The auto parts business is the largest of these, and one vital to auto repair services. Some successful general auto and auto system services offer customers towing service utilizing employees or a subcontractor.

Consider these other auto services as add-on profit opportunities for your general, system, or appearance service.

IS THERE A NEED FOR YOUR SERVICE?

By now you might have narrowed the field down to one or two specialties where your knowledge, skills, experience, and interests come together. But you're still not sure which would offer you the best chance for success as an auto repair service. After all, the success ratio for a farm tractor repair service in Los Angeles or a Porsche repair service in rural Iowa is small. You're either going to have to change specialties or move. No matter what you decide to do, the next step is to evaluate the local need for your service.

The first step to measuring local need is to check the local telephone book's yellow pages under "Automobile Repairing & Service" and related headings for your specialty. Count the number of listings under each heading. Then count the number of listings that indicate by name or wording that they would be a competitor. If you are in a large metropolitan area, mark the location of each potential competitor on a map to determine if there is a geographic area unserved. Maybe there's a reason for an area to have no auto repair services. Or maybe it's a gold mine waiting to be worked. It's worth further investigation.

You can also measure potential need for your service by checking with your local business licensing agency such as your city hall. They might categorize local businesses by type of product or service. This resource can help you determine whether there are many potential competitors that are not in the yellow pages because they have opened or closed since the last phone book was printed.

Here's another idea. If you know any auto repair professionals in other regions, or know someone who could introduce you to them, interview them as well. These noncompeting auto repair professionals might give you additional information that can help you build your new business. Be aware, though, that conditions in their market might be different from yours. But any information can be useful.

WHO ARE YOUR CUSTOMERS?

Okay, you've done some research to find out if there is a local need for your service. You've studied area phone books and interviewed auto repair business owners for information and opportunities. Now let's look at the market itself.

To clearly define who your customers are, you first need to define who you are to them. That is, you have to understand what it is that you can offer them. At this point, you only have to express it in broad terms.

- "I want to own an auto repair service business specializing in one-man jobs that can be performed with minimal tools."
- "I plan to offer an auto repair service that works primarily with German-made cars."
- "I will use my knowledge of the auto field to hire specialized employees for almost any type of auto repair job."
- "I am an auto repair professional who prefers to spend my time working rather than marketing, so I want larger jobs from long-term clients, even if they aren't as profitable."
- "I am a well-known auto repair professional with extensive experience who would prefer to find a young, energetic partner who can do much of the work so I can spend time fishing."

By defining your own skills and interests, you can better define those who might hire you—your market. A recent study of automotive consumers indicates that about 35 percent do their own vehicle maintenance, 31 percent bring their vehicles to a repair garage, and another 31 percent go to a dealership for service. Of those that use an independent garage, they do so because it is less expensive (46 percent), more convenient (23 percent), or because they know the mechanic (22 percent). The other 9 percent say they don't trust the dealer. These are your potential customers.

WHAT IS YOUR "PROCESS"?

A process is a series of actions performed to get a specific result. An automotive assembly line is a process where a series of actions are performed—bodies attached to frames, doors and dashboards installed—to get a specific result: a car. Makes sense.

But did you ever think that what *you* do is a process? It is. Your process might be installing mufflers or rebuilding industrial engines. Like the automobile assembly process, it requires specific tools, materials, procedures, and knowledge. And it has a specific result. The point here is that no one gets paid unless they perform a needed process for someone else. A tailor makes suits, McDonalds makes hamburgers, Boeing makes commercial aircraft.

By now, you've hopefully decided what type of auto repair business you will operate and what services you will specialize in—general, systems, appearance, or other services. In fact, you might have two or three ideas on what type of auto repair business you will build.

To define the process you can perform, first define the end product or service you can sell to your customers. As an example, if your auto repair service specializes in Hondas, your process is to analyze and correct operating problems on that marque at prices competitive with other shops offering the same process. Clearly defining the end product can help you and your client maintain clear expectations. It can also help ensure that your business stays focused.

For an auto repair service, the process might be simple or it might be complex. But it has many things in common with other tasks performed by auto repair services—and by other service firms. Time to make some more notes.

First, an auto repair business has tools. These might be basic hand tools or complex tools, or they might simply be your hands. What are the tools you need in your process?

A process also has raw materials: engine parts, oil and filters, mufflers, etc. What are the raw materials you need in your process? A process requires skill or the application of certain knowledge. It might be the skill of diagnosing engine sounds, welding, machine work, or replacing diesel components. It's probably a combination of many skills and extensive specialized knowledge. What are the skills and the knowledge you need in your process?

Finally, how do others profit from your process? Is your process a convenience for them, or do they actually make money from it? How much money? The more someone else profits from your process, the more you will profit.

Knowing the answer to these questions can help you become more efficient—and more profitable—at what you do. You will know exactly what tools and materials you need, understand what you do to these materials, and the end result for your customer. This might sound pretty basic to you, but understanding your process helps you become more successful at it. Defining your process also helps you from getting side-tracked on jobs that really don't fit your goals and won't be as profitable for you.

HOW MUCH CAN YOU MAKE?

One of the primary motives that you have in aspiring to become an auto repair service is monetary. You want to make a profit. It's the American way! How much money should you expect to make with your successful auto repair service business?

Of course, much depends on your local market, your specialty, your capital, your time in business, your management skills, and many other factors. According to the Internal Revenue Service, a typical breakdown of costs as a percentage of net sales for a medium-sized auto repair services is shown in TABLE 1-1.

**Table 1-1
Typical expense
and profit percentages
for auto repair services.**

	Percent
Operating costs	55
Owner's compensation	8
Rent	5
Depreciation	3
Taxes	3
Advertising	1
Other expenses	22
Profit	3

That's it? You'll only receive a 3 percent profit? Yes, and be happy with it—because it is 3 percent of total sales. That is, if your firm sells $1 million in services in the coming year, your profit is $30,000. That's after paying salary to yourself and any partners. Obviously, as your sales grow and you learn more about your business, your profits will increase. But it isn't realistic to expect a net profit of more than 5 percent. In fact, most large successful auto repair service earn a net profit of much less.

As most auto repair businesses sell at least five times as much in services per year as their net worth, your capital is actually earning 15 percent or more (5 × 3 percent). If annual sales become seven times your firm's net worth or you increase profits to 4.2 percent, you can be earning 21 percent!

WHAT GOALS SHOULD YOU HAVE?

Every business has the goal of being successful. But what is success to you? Here are some goals set by auto repair service owners. Select any of those that seem to apply to you and make them yours.

- Become a well-respected businessperson in my community.
- Build an auto repair business that will furnish me with a comfortable living and an ample retirement.
- Establish a successful auto repair business that I can sell for at least $500,000 within 10 years.
- Build a successful auto repair business that I can pass on to one or more of my children when they become adults.
- See my name on the side of a dozen billboards.

- Build a large auto repair business by offering good service and eventually taking over unprofitable auto repair businesses in the area.
- Take on a partner with more marketing knowledge who can help me build this business.

Those are just a few of the goals that potential auto repair services set for themselves as they start their business. Of course, goals might change along the way. But goals give you a target to aim for.

WRITING AN EFFECTIVE BUSINESS PLAN

Your business goals, your process, and your assets all come together in a single document called a "business plan." For large corporations, a business plan might be as large as the Denver phone book. But for your new enterprise, a business plan is simply a few pages of ideas and numbers that help you focus on the future. Your business plan should include the following.

- A definition of your process that describes what you do, how you do it, and what tools and materials you require to produce an end product.
- A description of the type of business that would be most likely to purchase this service from you including their background, location, typical annual sales, association memberships, and other precise information.
- Information on your business, including name, location, required licenses and bonds, form of ownership, the names and qualifications of members or partners, and related structural information.
- A list of the assets (what you own) and liabilities (what you owe) you bring to the business including a list of the professional skills, certifications, and training you have.

Of course, you're not going to be able to complete this business plan today. However, you can start it today with a spiral-bound or loose-leaf notebook. Call it your "business notebook." Start by defining your process and your business goals as we just discussed. Then make a section for each of the other categories: prospects, business structure, and assets. As you read through this book and come up with new ideas, write them down in your business notebook and you'll soon have the first draft of your business plan.

A business plan compiles the answers to the basic business questions.

- Why am I in business?
- What business am I in?
- What is my market?
- How can I make a profit?
- How much do I need to start and operate this business?
- How can I find customers?
- Who is my competition?
- How can I sell my service?
- How can I plan my work?

- Who will do the actual work?
- What tools and materials do I need?
- Will I have employees, use subcontractors, or do all of the work myself?

A successful business plan should include the following information, as appropriate to your business.

- Description of your business and a statement of its purpose.
- Table of contents of your business plan.
- Description of the services or products your business will provide.
- Information on the location of your business and, if necessary, plans for expansion of the physical plant.
- Definition of the management structure of the business, and the job descriptions and qualifications of the managers.
- List of personnel who will initially be employed.
- Description of your business marketing plan (see the following).
- Information on your competition and market share.
- Outline of your price structure and the philosophy behind it.
- Facts on short- and long-term trends in the market.
- Discussion of quality and how you expect to obtain and retain it in your business.
- Description of the sources and requirements of funds, including inside and outside investors, and how they participate in your business.
- Include a capital equipment and capital improvement list.
- Develop an opening balance sheet for your business.
- Include a projected cash flow statement.
- Produce a break-even analysis for your business.
- Incorporate monthly income projections for the first three years of business.
- Include a list of the independent professionals hired to assist you in the establishment and management of your business such as accountants, attorneys, financial consultants, etc.

Chapter 9 covers the writing process and shows you how to turn your business notebook into a business plan.

WRITING A USEABLE MARKETING PLAN

A marketing plan is simply a description of how you plan to market or develop customers for your auto repair business. You can incorporate your marketing plan into your business plan or you can make it a separate document. That decision depends on how you use your marketing plan. If you will implement your own marketing plan, incorporate it into your business plan. If you will hire a marketing consultant or an advertising agency to implement your marketing plan, make it a separate document that doesn't require a copy of your business plan to be understood. In some cases, your banker or potential investors will want to see your marketing plan as well as your business plan. A typical marketing plan will include the following:

Executive summary Overview of the plan, short description of your service and how it differs from services offered by other auto repair services, the required investment, and a summary of anticipated sales and profits.

Introduction A full description of your service and how it fits into the marketplace.

Situation An analysis of local demand and trends for your service, laws and regulations, financial requirements, competitors, and structure of your company including key employees.

Market Describe in more specifics your target market, its size and requirements, its needs, and the problems that your auto repair service will solve for this market.

Strategy Explain how you can reach this target market, the promotional tools you will need, the image you will present, and how you will react (or not react) to competitors.

Control Specify how you expect to manage your auto repair firm to improve your services and increase your market share (your share of the available customers).

A marketing plan can be as long or as short as required by its purpose. If you are planning to bring on a big-bucks investor, you will want to develop a detailed marketing plan. However, if you are both the writer and the implementer of the marketing plan, a few pages might be sufficient. In either case, the act of writing can help you clarify your intentions and help you to visualize the outcome.

YOUR SUCCESS ACTION LIST

You're on the road to success! In this chapter, you've reviewed a number of factors important to your success—your decision to start a business, the various types of auto repair businesses, the need for your service, your process, and how much you can make. You've also begun writing your business plan. In the next chapter, you begin your business startup. Here's how to put this chapter into action.

_____ Start your own Auto Repair Service Business Plan notebook and begin making notes in it.

_____ Outline your experience in the auto repair business.

_____ List the auto repair tools that you own and estimate their replacement value.

_____ Write down the estimated value of your assets: tools, cash, home and car equity, credit card limits, stocks and bonds, whole life policy values, etc.

_____ Write down your business philosophy.

_____ List at least six types of auto repair service businesses in which you might be interested.

_____ Check local phone books to determine how many businesses are now offering the same services in your area.

_____ Talk to other local auto repair professionals about your ideas and goals.

_____ Select one or two of the potential auto repair services as the one(s) you will offer.

_____ Define the process that you will offer to your customers; write one for each of the specialties that you're interested in.

_____ Write your own personal definition of success in your business notebook.

2
Starting your business

You're on your way to owning a successful auto repair business. In this chapter, you'll move even farther along the road to business ownership. You'll better define your prospective customers, select your business name, learn how to license your new firm, and find out how to set up a commercial bank account. Finally, you'll consider what form your business should take: single owner, partnership, or corporation.

As with the first chapter, this one includes Your Success Action List to help you as you move along the road to success.

DEFINING YOUR CUSTOMERS

Who will want to hire you? Hopefully, lots of people. You're skilled, ambitious, knowledgeable, honest, brave, thrifty, etc. The more you know about those who will hire you, the more customers you will have.

Demographics is a study of statistics about people: where they live, how much they make, how they buy, their favorite brands. Retailers use census information to build demographics to help them decide where to build a store. Auto repair services can use demographics, too. You can learn who might use your services and, then, where to find them.

As an example, an auto repair service specializing in foreign car transmission repair will need to know something about people who buy foreign cars, as well as how they select a specialist to work on their car's transmission. This information and more is available from a number of sources including trade journals and magazines on transmissions, foreign cars, and automotive services. You might know of some of these sources yourself. If not, I'll tell you later where to find this information at low cost.

Psychographics is a two-dollar word that means studying *why* people buy. You might think most people buy for logical reasons. However, in many cases, even in the business world, people buy for emotional reasons and justify their decision with logical reasons. So knowing why your clients buy can help you sell to them more effectively.

Clients of a franchised lubrication service might buy because of name recognition, perceived quality, and efficiency. Price, while certainly important, might be a secondary consideration.

A side note: price isn't all it's cracked up to be. In fact, most customers who argue price with you are actually asking you to sell them value. I'll show you how to do this later in the book so you don't have to haggle prices with every customer.

Remember, too, that your customers are not just Joe Citizens who come to you for service. Your customers also include businesses, insurance companies, service contractors (such as AAA), and even other auto repair services that refer customers to you.

Back to psychographics: if you've built a solid reputation in your area as an auto repair service whose name means quality, you can sell that name. People want to go with a winner, so you will get some jobs just because people know you are involved. So learn what makes your customers buy and help them to buy from you.

PROSPECTING FOR CUSTOMERS

A prospect is someone who might become a customer. Why "might?" Because they don't know you, your services, or the benefits of becoming your customer. We'll later cover how to turn prospects into customers. But for now, let's start looking for prospects.

Once you define who your customers will be, you will have a pretty good idea of who your prospects are. If you know that your customers will be owners of late-model luxury cars with air conditioning systems, this definition covers your prospects as well. Many successful auto repair services start prospecting for clients by building a list of those who might someday purchase their services. Some state automotive registration offices sell lists of owners by marque, year, and zip code. With this list you can know who in your market owns Buicks, for example, that are less than 4 years old. This information can be augmented with data from phone calls to these prospects.

The same process can be used to build up a list of prospects for your specialty auto repair business. Prospects might be individuals, firms, or insurance companies, depending on your type of auto repair business.

We'll talk about the many uses for computers and technology in your business later in this book. One type of program you should consider for your new business is called "contact management software." These programs are available for $50 to $500 with the lower end adequate for smaller businesses. Contact management programs can help you build a prospect file or database where you can store information on prospects you gather from these sources. As you call these prospects and develop them into customers, your database can keep track of contacts you make, letters you've sent, requests made, and call-backs needed. Some contact management programs can even help you write letters, develop proposals and bids, take orders, and schedule jobs.

NAMING YOUR BUSINESS

Naming a business is much like naming a baby. In some ways, it can give direction to its growth. A well-named business will seem more successful to prospects, and will then become so.

A business name should make it clear to prospects what the firm does, or at least the industry the firm is in. If the owner or a partner is well-known in the area or the trade, his name might be incorporated into the business name. Here are some examples.

- Prairie Auto Repair Services (denotes the region and the industry).
- Bob's Auto Repair Services (identifies the industry, is personalized at the expense of sounding like a small business).
- Haskell Auto Repair Services, Inc. (sounds bigger; surnames are better than first names and Inc. implies that it is a larger firm).
- Atlas Auto Repair Service (specifically identifies the service, though Atlas isn't a modern business name).
- Smithtown Auto (unclear what service is involved).
- Quality Auto Repair Services (clearly identifies the industry and, hopefully, the owner's attitude).

After selecting a business name, many firms write a defining motto or slogan that they use on all stationery and advertisements to further clarify what the firm does.

- Specializing in Repairing Unibody Cars.
- Specializing in the 20-Minute Oil Change.
- Commercial and Industrial Auto Repair Services.
- Budget Auto Repair.
- On-call 24 hours a day.
- Since 1979.
- Your One-Stop Auto Repair Service.

In your business notebook, write out a few possible business names and slogans. Of course, check the local phone book to make sure someone else isn't already using your choice of name or slogan.

ASSUMED BUSINESS NAMES

An assumed business name is a name other than the real and true name of the person operating the business. A real and true name becomes an assumed business name with the addition of any words that imply the existence of additional owners. For example, Bob Smith is a real and true name, while Bob Smith Company is an assumed name.

In most states and counties, you must register an assumed business name to inform the public about who is transacting business under that name. Without the registration you might be fined or, worse, might not be able to defend a legal action because your assumed business name wasn't properly registered.

In many states, an assumed business name is registered with the state's corporate division. Some states also register your assumed business name with counties in which you do business. Other states require that you do so. In some locations, you must publish a public notice in an area newspaper telling all that you (and any other business principals) are operating under a specific business name.

The typical assumed business name registration requires the following information: the business name you wish to assume, the principal place of business, the name of the authorized representative, your SIC (standard industrial classification) code, a list of all owners with their signatures, and a list of all counties in which your firm will transact business (sell, lease, or purchase goods or services; receive funding or credit). The SIC for a general auto repair shop is 7538; gasoline service stations' SIC is 5541; automotive transmission repair shop is 7537; auto body repair and paint is 7532; muffler and exhaust system shop is 7533; miscellaneous automotive services is 7549.

By the way, you can learn more about the sales levels of other auto repair services in your SIC by looking them up in *Ward's Business Directory* available in the reference section of many libraries.

LOCATING YOUR BUSINESS

Next, you must determine where to locate your business: at home, from a vehicle, in a service shop, in a shopping mall, or in an auto mall? The answer depends on how much business you expect to initially contract, what your space requirements are, your budget, and whether you plan to have customers visit your place of business. Some factors you should consider as you determine the location of your business include:

- Customer convenience.
- Availability of materials.
- Availability of transportation.
- Local zoning.
- Quality and quantity of employees in the area.
- Requirements and availability of parking facilities.
- Adequacy of utilities.
- Tax burden.
- Opportunities for signage.
- Neighborhood character.
- Quality of police and fire services.
- Environmental factors.
- Physical suitability of building.
- Opportunities for future expansion.
- Personal convenience.
- Cost of rent.

Considering these factors, let's look at your options.

Home shop Many small repair service businesses begin their life at home. The entrepreneur sets up a small workshop in the garage. This is an ideal situation for new auto repair services for obvious reasons.

First, there is little or no additional rent expense. It is also more convenient for you to have all your records at home where you can review them at any time. In addition, you could have a family member, roommate, or someone living with you answer the telephone while you're out test driving or picking up cars. Finally, you might be able to deduct some of your household costs as legitimate expenses and reduce your tax obligation.

But the best reason is that it saves you time. A client can call you in the evening to ask about a specific job and you can quickly check your records or make notes in the job file without leaving your home.

If you're considering using a portion of your home as a shop or office, order *Business Use of Your Home* (Publication 587) from the Internal Revenue Service (Washington, DC 20224). It can help you determine if your business qualifies for this option as well as how to take advantage of it to lower your taxes.

Vehicle office   Another practical office that you can use instead of or in addition to your home office is a vehicle office. The vehicle might be a car, a pickup truck, a tow truck, or a van. A tow truck is preferred because it can bring you income from towing services, and can be used to advertise your business wherever you go. It offers two large surfaces on which the name of your business can be painted. Second choice is a van on which you install tools so that you can offer your customers mobile on-site service.

Keep in mind that your vehicle represents you and should be in good physical and mechanical condition. Breaking down at the side of the road or at a job site will be poor advertising for your business. If your climate doesn't require it, keep away from vehicles with air conditioning and other optional equipment that might require additional maintenance and costs. Basic is better.

If you don't plan to carry more than one passenger, a full-size pickup can be equipped with a rack on the middle seat on which you can place a briefcase or a file box for papers, contract forms, plans, and other important papers. Another option is to take out the rear cab window and build a shallow box above the bed where you can store papers from inside the cab. You can also build this office onto the two sides of the truck bed and make compartments for tools or plans. Just make sure that you have a way of locking your office.

Depending on how much you use your vehicle for personal travel, you can either list all costs of operating the vehicle as an expense or you can deduct a standard mileage rate when you file income taxes. For more information, request *Business Use of a Car* (Publication 917) from the Internal Revenue Service.

Service shop   Depending on the specialty you select and the availability of business space, you might be able to rent reasonably a small auto repair shop or garage. This becomes a requirement if you are servicing trucks or numerous vehicles that cannot be legally parked at your home. Your garage might not have sufficient room for such jobs. You might also need to keep an inventory of parts or materials.

It might surprise you to learn that the most important factor to consider when selecting a shop location is *retail compatibility*. For your small store in its first years of operation, with limited funds for advertising and promotion, locating your store near a traffic-generating business might help you survive. You'll often find restaurants grouped together for this reason. Antique stores might take over a city block. The old business adage says that the three most important factors in selecting a retail site are: location, location, and location.

The next most important factor to consider is the availability of a local merchants association. A strong merchants association can accomplish through group strength what an individual store owner couldn't even dream of. Not only can they speak as a booming voice to city planners, a merchants association can also bulk-buy advertising at lower rates and promote their own events. But make sure that you understand your responsibilities to the association before you sign up. If the site you select doesn't have a merchants association, consider starting one.

Other factors to look at include the responsiveness of the landlord, and the opportunities for negotiating a favorable lease. Make sure your landlord continues to invest in the property with regular maintenance and quick repairs. Talk with other commercial landlords in your area to ensure that your lease is the best you can negotiate.

Call your local and regional chambers of commerce before you select a business site. They might be able to give you an educated guess on what you will probably have to pay for a property that can help your business become successful.

Shared shop You might have friends or relatives who own a related service business. You could share a shop or garage with them, and reduce your costs while bringing them some rental income. Of course, don't share a shop with anyone who might, in any way, be a competitor or associated with a competitor. Prospects calling for you might be diverted. If you are specializing in a single aspect of auto repair, look for a shop-mate who might be able to bring you prospects, and vice versa. You might even decide to strike up a partnership and join forces.

Shopping mall Most shopping malls offer you the advantages described above: retail compatibility, a merchants association, active landlords, and negotiable leases. But with these features comes additional costs. Space in shopping malls, if you can get into them, is typically more expensive to rent. And rent is often based, at least in part, on your level of sales. The more you sell, the more the mall receives as rent. Here's a summary of the type of shopping centers and malls you'll find.

A neighborhood shopping center is built around a supermarket or drug store with a trade population of 2500 to 40,000 and offers 30,000 to 100,000 square feet of leasable space.

A community shopping center (100,000 to 300,000 square feet) often has a variety or discount department store as its leading tenant and serves a trade population of 40,000 to 150,000.

A regional shopping center (300,000 to 1,000,000 square feet) builds around one or more full-line department stores with a trade population of 150,000 or more.

A super-regional shopping center includes three or more department stores with more than 750,000 square feet of leasable space.

Keep in mind that most shopping centers furnish only bare space. You must then finish it out at your own expense. Finishing out includes lighting fixtures, counters, shelves, painting, flooring, merchandise racks, and related needs.

Auto service mall Larger communities are offering one-stop shopping centers for those who need automotive service. Auto service malls typically include 5 to 20 specialized shops in an area of 10,000 to 45,000 square feet. These centers typically include a diagnostics service, a few specialized services such as transmission repair and lube/tune-up, and a major auto parts store.

Depending on the mall, the lease might include fully-equipped bays with hydraulic lifts and complete compressed-air and lighting systems. Others are more basic and require an extensive investment before you move in.

Zoning laws   Your business location might be limited by local zoning laws. Before you decide where to set up your auto repair business, or even in your truck, talk to the local zoning office about restrictions. You might find that so called *cottage* or home-based businesses are allowed in your neighborhood as long as no clients come to your home and no equipment or job trucks are parked on the street overnight. Or they might not be allowed. Few auto repair services stay in residential areas very long.

Some zoning regulations might allow you to set up an auto repair shop, but not park any cars on the street under certain zoning classifications. Ask questions about zoning and restrictions *before* you set up your shop.

Americans with Disabilities Act   The Americans with Disabilities Act offers employees and customers in many firms access to business locations without physical barriers. The ADA requires that business owners offer easy access to their location that will not restrict people with disabilities. This act applies to all businesses with 15 or more employees. To learn more about ADA requirements, contact the Small Business Research and Education Council (800-947-4646).

Clients and suppliers   Here's one last, but important, question you should ask as you decide where you will locate your business: where are your customers and your suppliers located? Specifically, is your repair shop close enough to your potential customers that they will consider you to be "conveniently located?" And, if your auto repair business requires frequent runs for parts that cannot be delivered to you, is your shop close to that of your primary parts houses? If you are not close to them, consider the cost of fuel and time in your estimate of costs for the site.

LICENSING YOUR BUSINESS

Unfortunately, the licensing requirements for auto repair businesses are not universal. In some communities, all you need is a local business license. In other locations, you must apply for state, county, and local business licenses; meet professional requirements; furnish a bond; and jump through a flaming hoop on a hot day.

The best way to learn the requirements for your area is to contact your state government. Some states have a "one-stop" business telephone number where you can find out what the requirements are, or at least the phone numbers of governing offices, such as a state bureau of auto repair. You might be required to include a state license number on all correspondence, bids, estimates, advertisements, and vehicles.

STARTING A COMMERCIAL BANK ACCOUNT

Some new small businesses set up a commercial account at the bank where they have their personal account. If you have a good relationship with the bank, this is a good idea. However, some long-time auto repair businesses complain of bankers suddenly changing policy and withdrawing credit from otherwise trustworthy customers. They then begin to shop around for a new banker. The point is that the best time to shop for a second banker is when you begin your business. As your business grows, you might want to have accounts at two or more banks. Why? Because as your business becomes more successful, both will probably solicit your complete business and make you offers that you might not get from a single suitor.

One more reason for separate banks for personal and business accounts: fewer errors. Small businesses who have both types of accounts at a single bank might find that checks are deposited to the wrong account, especially deposits made to a cash machine. Doing business with two banks gives you twice as many options.

To start a business account, you'll have to have some "seed" money, typically $100 or more. Also, most banks require a copy of your Registration of Assumed Business Name form approved by the appropriate government office. If you make large night deposits, you will want a night deposit bag and key. With the proliferation of cash machines, your deposits can be made anytime and almost anywhere. You'll also need to furnish a federal ID number (discussed later) or your social security insurance number.

CHOOSING YOUR BUSINESS STRUCTURE

One of the most important decisions you can make as you start your auto repair business is the legal form it will take. Why is this so important? Because how you record expenses, how you build your business, how you pay taxes, how you treat profits, and how you manage liability all depend on the structure you give your business.

Of course, as your business grows, you'll be able to move from one type of structure to another, but sometimes there will be a cost. The cost will be paid primarily to the tax man as he decides whether you changed structure to avoid paying your fair share of taxes. One of the reasons you might later change structure is because you want to legally reduce tax liability, and that's okay. It's the abuse of tax laws that brings the wrath of the IRS.

There are three common types of business structures: proprietorship, partnership, and corporation. Each has specific advantages and disadvantages, but they must all be considered against your individual circumstances, goals, and needs. Before we consider each of them, consider the following questions.

- What is the ultimate goal and purpose of the enterprise, and which legal structure can best serve its purposes?
- What is the investors' liability for damage, injuries, debts, and taxes?
- What would the life of the firm be if something happened to one or more of the owners?
- What legal structure would insure the greatest flexibility in managing the firm?
- What are the possibilities for soliciting additional capital?
- Would one type of business structure attract additional expertise over another?
- What are the starting costs and procedures?

Sole proprietorship

The sole proprietorship is usually defined as a business that is owned and operated by one person. However, in many states a business owned jointly by a husband and wife is considered a proprietorship rather than a partnership. This is the easiest form of business to establish. You only need to obtain whatever licenses you require and begin operation. For its simplicity, sole proprietorship is the most widespread form of small business organization and is especially popular with new auto repair services.

Advantages to sole proprietorship The first and most obvious advantage of a proprietorship is ease of formation. There is less formality and fewer legal restrictions associated with establishing a sole proprietorship. It needs little or no governmental approval and is usually less expensive to start than a partnership or a corporation.

Another advantage to a proprietorship is that it doesn't require that you share profits with anyone. Whatever is left over after you pay the bills (including the tax man) is yours to keep. You will report income, expenses, and profit to the IRS using Schedule C and your standard 1040 form, and make quarterly instead of annual estimated tax payments to the IRS so you don't get behind.

Control is important to the successful auto repair service. A proprietorship gives that control and decision-making power to a single person, you.

Proprietorships also give the owner flexibility that other forms of business do not. A partner must usually get agreement from other partners. In larger matters, a corporation must get agreement from other members of the board of directors or corporate officers. A proprietor simply makes up his or her mind and acts.

One more plus: the sole proprietor has *relative* freedom from government control and special taxation. Sure, the government has some say in how you operate and what taxes you will pay. But the government has *less* to say to the sole proprietor.

Disadvantages to sole proprietorship Yes, there's a downside to being the only boss. Most important is unlimited liability. That is, the individual proprietor is responsible for the full amount of business debts that might exceed the proprietor's total investment. With some exceptions, this liability extends to all the proprietor's assets, such as house and car. (Homestead laws exempt your home up to a specified value.) One way around this is for the proprietor to obtain sufficient insurance coverage to reduce the risk from physical loss and personal injury. But if your suppliers aren't getting paid, they can come after your assets.

When the business is a single individual, the serious illness or death of that person can end the business.

Individuals typically cannot get the credit and capital available to partnerships and corporations. Fortunately, most auto repair services don't require extensive capital. But when they do, they seriously consider the advantages of taking on a partner or becoming a corporation.

Finally, as a sole proprietor you have a relatively limited viewpoint and experience because you are only one person. You are more subject to "tunnel vision" or seeing things in a narrow way based on your experiences. You don't have someone with a commitment to your business who can give you a fresh viewpoint or new ideas.

Partnerships

The Uniform Partnership Act (UPA) adopted by many states defines a partnership as "an association of two or more persons to carry on as co-owners of a business for profit." How the partnership is structured, the powers and limitations of each partner, and their participation in the business are written into a document called the Articles of Partnership. The articles or descriptions can be written by the partners, found in a legal form from a stationery store, or written by an attorney. Obviously, using an attorney is the best option because it ensures that the document is binding and reduce disputes that typically come up once the business begins to grow.

Your firm's Articles of Partnership should include:

- The name, location, length, and purpose of the partnership.
- The type of partnership (covered in the next paragraph).
- A definition of the partners' individual contributions.
- Agreement on how business expenses will be handled.
- An outline of the authority of each partner.
- A summary of the accounting methods that will be used.
- Definition of how profits and losses will be distributed among the partners.
- The salaries and capital draws for each partner.
- An agreement of how the partnership can be modified or terminated. This includes dissolution of the partnership by death or disability of a member or by the decision of partners to disband.
- Description of how the members will arbitrate and settle disputes as well as change terms of the partnership agreement.

There are many types of partners within a partnership. An active partner is one who actively participates in the day-to-day operation of the business and is openly identified as a partner in the business. A secret partner is an active partner who is *not* openly identified as a partner for whatever reason. A dormant partner is one who is inactive and not known as a partner; he usually participates by furnishing money or advice. A silent partner is one who doesn't actively participate in the business, but might have his name on the partnership, such as a retired owner or figurehead. If the silent partner is only lending his name to the business he is not actually a true partner, he is a nominal partner. Finally, a limited or special partner is one who agrees to furnish financial assistance, but does not participate in the ongoing business decisions. Why would someone want to do that? Because a limited partner can only lose their investment in the business, creditors cannot go after other assets; his liability is limited.

Advantages to partnerships Partnerships are easier and less costly to form than corporations. All that's really needed is Articles of Partnership, as discussed above. In fact, that isn't always a legal requirement. If you want to form a partnership with a handshake, you can in many states.

A partner is naturally more motivated to apply his best abilities to the job than if the same person worked for an employer or a corporation. An active partner is more directly rewarded.

A partnership can typically raise capital more easily than a proprietorship. This is because there are more people whose assets can be combined as equity for the loan. Also, lenders will look at the credit ratings of each partner. So make sure that your business partners have good credit.

Partnerships are frequently more flexible in the decision-making process than a corporation, but less flexible than a proprietorship, as discussed earlier.

And, like proprietorships, partnerships offer relative freedom from government control and special taxation. A partnership doesn't pay income tax. Rather, all profits and losses flow through the partnership to the individual partners who pay income and other taxes as if they were sole proprietors.

Disadvantages to partnerships Of course, there are some minuses to partnerships. At least one partner will be a general partner and assume unlimited liability for the business. Obtain sufficient insurance coverage to reduce the risk of loss from physical loss or personal injury, but remember that the general partner is still liable.

A partnership is as stable or as unstable as its members. Elimination of any partner often means automatic dissolution of the partnership. However, the business can continue to operate if the agreement includes provisions for the right of survivorship and possible creation of a new partnership. Partnership insurance can help surviving partners purchase the equity of a deceased partner.

Though a partnership might have less difficulty getting financing than a sole proprietorship, the fragile nature of partnerships sometimes makes it difficult to get long-term financing. The best source, as discussed earlier, is using the combined equity of the partners from assets they own as individuals. In fact, many partnerships are started because an active partner needs equity or financing that he cannot get without a partner who has more assets or better credit.

Depending upon how the partnership agreement is drawn up, *any* partner may be able to bind all of the partners to financial obligations. Make sure your Articles of Partnership accurately reflect your intent regarding how partners can or cannot obligate the partnership.

A major drawback to partnerships is the difficulty faced when arranging for a partner to leave. Buying out the partner's interest might be difficult unless terms have been specifically worked out in the partnership agreement.

As you can see, there are numerous pluses and minuses to partnerships. Many of the disadvantages can be taken care of in your Articles of Partnership. This is why it is recommended that you use an attorney experienced in such agreements when you construct your partnership. The cost is usually less than the value.

Experienced auto repair shop owners agree. Few partnerships are lasting because of personal conflicts and disagreements. Choose your partner as carefully as a spouse.

Corporation

We've been moving from the simplest to the most complex forms of business: proprietorship, partnership, and now corporation. Businesses, as they grow, often become corporations, identified by an extension to their name: Corp., Inc., or, in Canada, Ltd.

So what is a corporation? Over 150 years ago, the United States Supreme Court defined a corporation as "an artificial being, invisible, intangible, and existing only in contemplation of the law." In other words, a corporation is a distinct legal entity, distinct from the individuals who own it. It is a legal being.

A corporation is usually formed by the authority of a state government. Corporations that do business in more than one state must comply with federal laws regarding interstate commerce as well as with individual state laws. To form a corporation, begin by writing incorporation papers and issuing capital stock. Approval of these actions then must be obtained from the Secretary of State in the state in which your corporation is being formed. Only then can the corporation act as a legal entity separate from those who own its stock.

Advantages to a corporation The primary advantage to a corporation is that it limits the stockholder's liability to their investment. If you buy $1000 of stock in a corporation and it fails, you can only lose up to the $1000 investment. The corporation's creditors cannot come back to you demanding more money. The exception is when you put up some of your own assets up as collateral for the corporation.

Ownership of a corporation is a transferable asset. In fact, the New York Stock Exchange and other exchanges make a big business out of transferring stock, or partial ownership in corporations, from one investor to another. If your auto repair business is a corporation you may sell partial ownership or stock in it within certain limits. In fact, this is how many corporations get money to grow. A corporation may also issue long-term bonds to obtain the cash required to purchase assets or build the business.

Your corporation has a separate and legal existence. Your corporation is not you or anybody else. It is itself. For example, in the event of illness, death, or other cause for loss of a corporate officer or owner, the corporation continues to exist and do business.

The corporation may also delegate authority to hired managers, although they are often one and the same. Thus you become an employee of the corporation.

And the corporation can draw on the expertise and skills of more than one individual.

Disadvantages to a corporation The corporation's state charter might limit the type of business it does to a specific industry or service. However, other states allow broad charters that permit corporations to operate in any legal enterprise.

Corporations face more governmental regulations on all levels: local, state, and federal. That means your business will spend more time and money fulfilling these requirements as a corporation than it would as a proprietorship or a partnership.

If your corporate manager is not also a stockholder, he will have less incentive to be efficient than he would if he had a share in your business.

As you can imagine, a corporation is more expensive to form than other types of businesses. Even if you don't use an attorney, there are forms and fees that will quickly add up. However, an attorney is a good investment if you incorporate your auto repair business.

Finally, federal and some state governments are able to tax corporate income twice: once on the corporate net income and again when it's received by the individual stockholders in the form of salary or dividends. A Subchapter S corporation is taxed the business as if it were a partnership (no income tax), which passes the tax liability on to the individual stockholders. Talk with your attorney about this option.

YOUR SUCCESS ACTION LIST

This chapter gives you more pieces to the business puzzle. We have looked at how to find customers and prospects, select a business name, determine the legal structure your business should take, open a business account, and decide where to locate your auto repair service. The next chapter tells you exactly where to get help when starting and running your money-making business. Here's how to put this chapter into action.

_____ Write down six reasons why potential customers would buy auto repair service from you.

_____ Answer the question: What factors do all of your potential customers have in common?

_____ Contact your local or state department of motor vehicles to learn if lists of auto registrations are available to the public, what information is available, and how much it costs.

_____ Start a file card or contact management software files to keep track of prospects and future customers.

_____ List four potential names for your auto repair service(s).

_____ Select your assumed business name and file it with the appropriate authorities.

_____ Talk with the local zoning office to determine the type of zone in which your auto repair business can be located.

_____ Start researching appropriate locations for your auto repair business. Talk with property owners and managers about rental and lease fees.

_____ Contact your state or local licensing office to determine what business and trade licenses you might need.

_____ Open your business checking account with a local bank that specializes in serving small businesses.

_____ Decide what legal form you will give your auto repair business: proprietorship, partnership, or corporation, and take action.

3
Planning for success

Building your successful auto repair business can be exciting and rewarding. Thousands of men and women have learned how to make it happen. So can you.

This chapter will show you how to gather the tools and knowledge you need to reduce the frustrations of building a business. In it you'll learn how and where to find a profitable auto repair or related franchise, how to get money and assistance from the government, and how to use technology to move ahead of your competition even before you open your shop. Each topic is developed with specific information that you can use today to successfully build your auto repair business.

AUTO REPAIR SERVICE FRANCHISES

Franchising is a form of licensing by which the owner (the franchiser) of a product or service distributes through affiliated dealers (the franchisees). The franchise license is typically given for a specific geographical area.

The product or service being marketed by a brand name (such as AAMCO Transmissions) and the franchiser control the way that it is marketed. The franchiser requires consistency among the franchisees: standardized products or services, trademarks, symbols, equipment, and storefronts. The franchiser typically offers assistance in organizing, training, merchandising, and management. In exchange, the franchiser receives initial franchise fees and an on-going fee based on sales levels.

Why consider a franchise for your auto repair business? Because a successful franchise can reduce your risks, increase initial sales through name recognition, and help you make more money. A franchise helps ensure your success and gets you off to a faster start. It ensures that you have ample capital to start your business—and keep some of it.

There are numerous opportunities available for people wanting to start their own auto repair service franchise. An excellent source of information is the *Franchise Opportunities Handbook* produced and published by the U.S. Department of Commerce and available through the Superintendent of Documents (U.S. Government Printing Office, Washington, DC 20402) or your regional federal bookstore. This handbook lists basic information on franchises available in 44 categories including Automotive Products/Services. Information includes the name and address of the franchiser, a description of the operation, number of franchises, how long the franchise has been in business, how much equity capital is needed, how much financial assistance is available, what training is provided, and what managerial assistance is available.

Another source of information on franchises is the International Franchise Association, located at 1350 New York Avenue N.W., Suite 900, Washington, DC 20005.

The IFA's *Franchise Opportunities Guide* is a comprehensive listing of franchisers by industry and business category. *Franchising Opportunities* is their bimonthly magazine. Their newsletter, *Franchising World*, includes information on developing trends in franchising. Other sources include *Entrepreneur, Income Opportunities*, and other magazines available on most newsstands.

POPULAR FRANCHISES

Here are a few of the numerous franchises available to those who wish to offer automotive services.

AAMCO Transmissions Inc.
1 President Blvd.
Bala Cynwyd, PA 19004
800-523-0402

ABT Service Centers
2750 E. 3300 South
Salt Lake City, UT 84109
801-487-0726

Acc-U-Tune and Brake
2510 Old Middlefield Way
Mountain View, CA 94043
415-968-8863

Brake Check Canada
10216 124th St., #306
Edmonton Alberta T5N 4N3 CANADA
403-488-8881

Der Wagen Haus
P.O. Box 18421
Greensboro, NC 27419
919-852-6938

Great Bear Automotive Centers, Inc.
445 Northern Blvd.
Great Neck, NY 11021
516-829-4013

Jiffy Lube International, Inc.
P.O. Box 2967
Houston, TX 77252
713-546-4100

King Bear Enterprises, Inc.
1390 Jerusalem Ave.
North Merrick, NY 11566
516-483-3500

MAACO Auto Painting and Bodyworks
381 Brooks Rd.
King of Prussia, PA 19406
215-265-6606

Mark I Auto Service Centers, Inc.
8426 Manchester Rd.
St. Louis, MO 63144
314-968-0718

Meineke Discount Muffler Shops, Inc.
128 S. Tryon St., Suite 900,
Charlotte, NC 28202
800-634-6353

Midas Muffler and Brake Shops
225 N. Michigan Ave.
Chicago, IL 60601
800-621-0144

Mighty Distribution System of America, Inc.
50 Atlanta St.
Norcross, GA 30092
404-448-3900

Mobile Auto Systems
11887 Dublin Blvd.
Suite 245
Dublin, CA 94658
415-828-2131

Precision Tune, Inc.
1319 Shepard Dr.
Sterling, VA 22170
800-231-0588

Speedy Muffler King
8430 W. Bryn Mawr
Suite 400
Chicago, IL 60631
800-736-6738

Truckaline Suspension Centers, Inc.
1420 Hillcrest Pkwy
Altoona, WI 54720
800-221-2836

Ziebart Car Improvement Specialists
1290 E. Maple Rd.
Troy, MI 48007
800-877-1312

How do you know if the franchise that you're considering is reputable? There are numerous laws regulating franchising. Trade regulations issued by the Federal Trade Commission offer you important legal rights. You have the right to receive a disclosure statement and standard franchise agreement at your first personal meeting with a franchiser. You must also receive documentation on how the franchiser arrived at any earnings claims. If you have questions about your rights or think that they have been violated by a franchiser you can contact the Franchise and Business Opportunities Program, located at Federal Trade Commission, Washington, DC 20580. In addition, your state might have a franchise monitoring office. The point is, once you've done your homework, purchasing a franchise license can be less risky than starting a business by yourself—and more expensive.

HELP FROM PROFESSIONAL ASSOCIATIONS

As the owner of an auto repair business, you are a professional. Fortunately, there are national and regional associations of professionals just like you who can help your business grow through knowledge. Obviously, they are not going to share their trade secrets, but most will help your business become more professional and more profitable.

Automotive Service Association
1901 Airport Freeway
Suite 100
Bedford, TX 76095
817-283-6205
ASA represents over 10,000 automotive service businesses including body, paint, and trim shops, engine rebuilders, radiator shops, brake and wheel alignment services, transmission shops, tune-up services, and air conditioning services. Maintains a 130-volume library of automotive repair videotapes.

Coalition for Auto Repair Choice
1667 K Street
Suite 605
Washington, DC 20037
202-223-6655

Convenient Automotive Services Institute
P.O. Box 34595
Bethesda, MD 20817
301-897-3191
CAS offers membership to owners and operators of quick oil change and lubrication service stores.

Gasoline and Automotive Service Dealers Association
6338 Avenue N
Brooklyn, NY 11234
718-241-1111
GASDA serves owners and operators of service stations or auto repair facilities.

National Association of Independent Lubes

12800 Hillcrest
Suite 214
Dallas, TX 75230
214-458-9468
NAIL represents owners and operators of independent oil change shops.

National Institute for Automotive Service Excellence

13505 Dulles Technology Drive
Herndon, VA 22071
703-742-3800
NIASE promotes the highest standards of automotive service in the public interest through training and testing programs.

Service Station Dealers of America

499 S. Capital St. SW
Washington, DC 20003
202-479-0196
SSDA represents service station operators who are members of affiliated state and local associations. They can direct you to affiliated associations in your area.

Society of Collision Repair Specialists

1612 Teller St.
Lakewood, CO 80215
714-838-3115
SCRS offers services and representation to owners and managers of auto collision repair shops and related trades.

GOVERNMENT ASSISTANCE

Federal and state governments can also help you succeed with your own auto repair business. The most widely known and used government resource is the Small Business Administration, or SBA. Founded more than 40 years ago, the SBA, located at 1441 L Street N.W., Washington, DC 20416, has offices in 100 cities across the United States with a charter to help small businesses start and grow. The SBA offers counseling, booklets on business topics, and administers a small business loan guarantee program. In addition, it sponsors the 13,000 Service Corps of Retired Executives (SCORE) volunteers, Active Corps of Executives (ACE) volunteers, Business Development Centers, and Technology Access Centers.

Publications

The SBA offers a number of valuable publications and videotapes for starting and managing small business. VHS videotapes on business plans, marketing, and promotions can be purchased from the SBA or borrowed through many public libraries. Publications are available on products/ideas/inventions, financial management, management and planning, marketing, crime prevention, personnel management, and other topics. The booklets can be purchased for one or two dollars each at SBA offices or from SBA Publications, P.O. Box 30, Denver, CO 80201. Ask first for SBA Form 115A, *The Small Business Directory*, that lists available publications and includes an order form.

In addition, the SBA offers low-cost videos on business plans, marketing, promotion, and home-based businesses through the Small Business Video Library. Your SBA office will have more information or you can write to SBA/Success Videos, P.O. Box 30, Denver, CO 80202-0030.

The SBA also funds small business "incubators" throughout the country. Incubators are facilities in which a number of new and growing businesses operate under one roof with affordable rents, share services and equipment, and have access to a variety of business services. For more information, contact your regional SBA office or the Office of Private Sector Initiatives, 1441 L St. NW, Room 317, Washington, DC 20416.

SBA loans

The volume of business loans guaranteed by the SBA has increased from $3 billion in 1989 to a projected $7.5 billion in 1993. According to the SBA, the average loan is for $250,626 over a term of 11.5 years. About one-fifth of these loans went to companies that were less than two years old. Here is a summary of current SBA loan opportunities:

SBA 7(a) guaranteed loans   These loans are made by private lenders and can be guaranteed up to 80 percent by the SBA. Most SBA loans are made under this guaranty program. The maximum guaranty of loans exceeding $155,000 is 85 percent. SBA has no minimum size loan amount and can guarantee up to $750,000 of a private sector loan. SBA provides special inducements to lenders providing guaranteed loans of $50,000 or less. The lender must be a financial institution who participates with the SBA. The small business submits a loan application to the lender who makes the initial review and, if the lender cannot provide the loan directly, the lender might request an SBA guaranty. The lender then forwards the application and their analysis to the local SBA office. If approved by the SBA, the lender closes the loan and disburses the funds.

SBA direct loans   Loans of up to $150,000 are available only to applicants unable to secure an SBA-guaranteed loan. Direct loan funds are available only to certain types of borrowers such as handicapped individuals, nonprofit sheltered workshops, Vietnam-era veterans, disabled veterans, businesses in high-unemployment areas that are owned by low-income individuals, or for businesses located in low-income neighborhoods. The applicant must first seek financing from at least two banks in their area.

Loan terms   Working capital loans generally have maturities of five to seven years unless they are used to finance a fixed asset such as the purchase or major renovation of business real estate. The SBA requires that available assets, such as your home, be pledged to adequately secure the loan. Personal guaranties are required from all principals owning 20 percent or more of the business and from the chief executive officer with any share in the business.

If you're interested in applying for an SBA guaranteed or direct loan, call your regional office of the SBA. Even better, ask for the name of an SBA-certified lender in your area. The SBA loan program, notorious for its paperwork requirements, can be expedited by a banker who knows how to work within the system. You'll get your loan faster. In fact, those bankers that have preferred-lender status can handle your SBA loan without the SBA even being involved.

SCORE

SCORE, located at 1441 L Street N.W./Room 100, Washington, DC 20416, is a national nonprofit association with the goal of helping small business owners. SCORE members include retired men and women as well as those who are still active in their own business (ACE). These individuals donate their time and experience to counsel individuals regarding small business. SCORE is sponsored by the SBA and the local office is usually in or near that of the local SBA office.

To take advantage of the counseling services of a SCORE counselor, complete a SCORE Request for Counseling Worksheet (FIG. 3-1) and return it to the local office in person or by mail. The interview will be in person at a mutually agreed time. The questionnaire will ask the type of business, whether you are starting, buying, or currently operating the business, how much experience you have in this business, how much knowledge you have of accounting, and ask you to categorize your questions into one or more of the following categories:

- accounting/taxes
- patents/copyrights
- construction
- insurance
- marketing
- distribution
- legalities
- manufacturing
- importing/exporting
- business plans
- home industries
- sales projections
- customer service
- other:_____

U.S. SMALL BUSINESS ADMINISTRATION

REQUEST FOR COUNSELING

A. NAME OF COMPANY	B. YOUR NAME (Last, First, Middle)	C. TELEPHONE (H) (B)

D. STREET	E. CITY	F. STATE	G. COUNTY	H. ZIP

I. TYPE OF BUSINESS (Check one)
1. ☐ Retail   4. ☐ Manufacturing
2. ☐ Service   5. ☐ Construction
3. ☐ Wholesale 6. ☐ Not in Business

J. BUS. OWNSHP./GENDER
1. ☐ Male
2. ☐ Female
3. ☐ Male/Female

K. VETERAN STATUS
1. ☐ Veteran
2. ☐ Vietnam-Era Veteran
3. ☐ Disabled Veteran

L.
- INDICATE PREFERRED DATE AND TIME FOR APPOINTMENT
  DATE _____ TIME _____
- ARE YOU CURRENTLY IN BUSINESS?   YES_____ NO_____
- IF YES, HOW LONG? _____
- TYPE OF BUSINESS (USE THREE TO FIVE WORDS)
  _____

M. ETHNIC BACKGROUND

a. *Race:*
1. ☐ American Indian or Alaskan Native
2. ☐ Asian or Pacific Islander
3. ☐ Black
4. ☐ White

b. *Ethnicity:*
1. ☐ Hispanic Origin
2. ☐ Not of Hispanic Origin

N. INDICATE, BRIEFLY, THE NATURE OF SERVICE AND/OR COUNSELING YOUR ARE SEEKING

_____

_____

O.
- IT HAS BEEN EXPLAINED TO ME THAT I MAY USE FURTHER SERVICES SPONSORED BY THE U.S. SMALL BUSINESS ADMINISTRATION   YES_____ NO_____
- I HAVE ATTENDED A SMALL BUSINESS WORKSHOP   YES _____ NO _____
- CONDUCTED BY_____

P. HOW DID YOU LEARN OF THESE COUNSELING SERVICES?
1. ☐ Yellow Pages   3. ☐ Radio   5. ☐ Bank   7. ☐ Word-of-Mouth
2. ☐ Television   4. ☐ Newspapers   6. ☐ Chamber of Commerce   8. ☐ Other _____

Q. SBA CLIENT (To Be Filled Out By Counselor)
1. ☐ Borrower   2. ☐ Applicant   3. ☐ 8(a) Client   4. ☐ COC   5. ☐ Surety Bond

R. AREA OF COUNSELING PROVIDED (To Be Filled Out By Counselor)
1. Bus. Start-Up/Acquisition   5. Accounting & Records   9. Personnel
2. Source of Capital   6. Finan. Analysis/Cost Control   10. Computer Systems
3. Marketing/Sales   7. Inventory Control   11. Internat'l Trade
4. Government Procurement   8. Engineering R&D   12. Business Liq./Sale

I request business management counseling from the Small Business Administration. I agree to cooperate should I be selected to participate in surveys designed to evaluate SBA assistance services. I authorize SBA to furnish relevant information to the assigned management counselor(s) although I expect that information to be held in strict confidence by him/her.

I further understand that any counselor has agreed not to: (1) recommend goods or services from sources in which he/she has an interest and (2) accept fees or commissions developing from this counseling relationship. In consideration of SBA's furnishing management or technical assistance, I waive all claims against SBA personnel, SCORE, SBDC and its host organizations, SBI, and other SBA Resource Counselors arising from this assistance.

SIGNATURE AND TITLE OF REQUESTER	DATE

FOR USE OF THE SMALL BUSINESS ADMINISTRATION

RESOURCE	DISTRICT	REGION

SBA FORM 641 (7-91) PREVIOUS EDITION IS OBSOLETE

3-1   SBA Request for Counseling form.

SCORE counselors are typically highly experienced businesspeople, some might have direct experience in the auto repair business. There is no charge for their time and assistance, nor are you required to follow their advice. But the more counselors you have, the greater your opportunity for success in the auto repair service.

Business Development Centers

Business Development Centers (BDCs) are regional centers funded by the SBA and managed in conjunction with regional colleges. A BDC offers free and confidential counseling for small business owners and managers, new businesses, home-based businesses, and people with ideas including retail, service, wholesale, manufacturing, and farm businesses. They sponsor seminars on various business topics, assist in developing business and marketing plans, inform entrepreneurs of employer requirements, and teach cash flow budgeting and management. BDCs also gather information sources, assist in locating business resources, and make referrals.

Call your local SBA office or college campus to determine if there is a BDC near you and, if so, what services they can provide you as you build your auto repair business.

Technology Access Centers

Here's a new and little-known service provided by the SBA and the National Institute of Standards and Technology (NIST), a division of the U.S. Department of Commerce. In fact, there are now just six Technology Access Centers (TACs) in the United States. Your local SBA office can tell you if there is one near you and how to contact it.

TACs use the power of the computer to access information from large computer libraries called databases. You pick the topic and the TAC will search these computerized libraries for information about the topic. In fact, some of the information for this book was located through a regional TAC.

As an example, you can ask for articles and data on auto repair, information on your competitors, information about codes and regulations in your region, and related topics. Depending on which databases they can access, TACs can find data that will help you make your business or marketing plan better identify profitable opportunities for your specialty.

The process is simple. A TAC representative will interview you to determine what information you need. He or she will then write it in terms that can be searched in computer databases. If the search is successful, you will get a printed report of the results mailed to you. There is often a charge, but it is only a fraction of the cost charged by the database firm. The TAC sponsors pay the rest to encourage small business development.

Innovation Assessment Centers

Let's say you've invented a new product, process, or service, such as a new repair tool. How can you determine it's commercial potential? Innovation Assessment Centers (IACs), funded by the SBA through some regional BDCs, can help you evaluate your invention. For a small fee, the evaluator studies the legality, safety, environmental impact, potential market, product life cycle, feasibility, investment costs, need, price, payback period, and numerous other factors in relation to your invention. If you're interested in this service, contact your regional BDC or the SBA.

Other government resources

One more valuable federal resource is the United States Department of Commerce, Washington, DC 20230. It's Office of Business Liaison is the initial contact point for questions about the department's business assistance. The Bureau of the Census is part of the Commerce Department and it has detailed statistics on people and businesses in the United States compiled from many sources. There's even a contact for automotive services to help you determine the size of your local market.

Some of the publications available through the Department of Commerce include *Census of Business: Retail-Area Statistics—United States Summary, County Business Patterns, County and City Data Book, Directory of Federal Statistics for Local Areas: A Guide to Sources,* and *Standard Metropolitan Statistical Areas.* These publications are available from the Department of Commerce, Government Printing Office, Superintendent of Documents, Washington, DC 20402-9328, or at federal GPO bookstores in most major cities.

The Commerce Department's Economic Development Administration located at Room 7800B, Washington, DC 20230 provides financial and technical assistance to businesses who are willing to locate in economically distressed areas of the nation.

The Commerce Department's Minority Business Development Agency located at Room 5053, Washington, DC 20230 encourages the development of minority-owned businesses. It provides management, marketing, financial, and technical assistance through BDCs (see preceding), minority business trade organizations, and MBDA field offices.

The U.S. Treasury Department's Internal Revenue Service offers numerous Small Business Tax Education Program Videos through their regional offices. Topics include depreciation, business use of your home, employment taxes, excise taxes, starting a business, sole proprietorships, partnerships, self-employed retirement plans, S-corporations, and federal tax deposits.

States, too, want to encourage small businesses. Check with your state corporation division, your state legislator, or similar sources to find out what resources are available to you. After all, government is a partner in your business. In fact, they will take their profit (taxes) before you get yours.

PROFESSIONAL TOOL REQUIREMENTS

I will not presume to tell you all of the tools that you should have in your toolbox. First, your experience will probably have built up a supply of functional tools. Second, your specialty might require very specialized tools that will be found in few auto repair toolboxes.

The December 1992 issue of *Motor Service* magazine, located at Hunter Publishing, 950 Lee St., Des Plaines, IL 60016 includes a comprehensive listing of companies that manufacture tools and equipment for the automotive service industry. Other trade publications are also an excellent resource for information and advertisements about tools you will need for your auto repair service.

The term *tools* includes any product or service that will help you perform your service more efficiently and more profitably. This includes books and manuals, trade magazines, and periodicals.

BOOKS AND MANUALS

No auto mechanic can know all there is about repairing all cars ever made. Smart auto repair firms begin building a library of books that make the mechanic's job easier and help management efficiently estimate job requirements. You might also need annual shop manuals from the various automakers. Here are some popular books and manuals.

Auto Repair Manual
Motor Publications
555 W. 57th St.
New York, NY 10019
published annually.

Automotive Suspension, Steering: Theory and Service
   by Ellinger and Hathaway
Prentice-Hall
Route 9W
Englewood Cliffs, NJ 07632

Chilton's Auto Service Manuals and *Chilton's Service Bay Handbook*
Chilton Co.
Chilton Way, Radnor, PA 19089

Mitchell Manuals for Automotive Professionals
Mitchell International Inc.
P.O. Box 26260
San Diego, CA 92126

Import Parts Guide and Cross Reference Directory
Meyers Publishing
6211 Van Nuys Blvd.
Suite 200
Van Nuys, CA 91401

MAGAZINES AND PERIODICALS

To keep up with the on-going changes in your industry, consider subscribing to independent trade publications in addition to those that come with association membership. Some of the most popular are:

Auto Service Today
2315 Broadway
New York, NY 10024

Automotive Body Repair News
5 Revere Drive
Suite 202
Northbrook, IL 60062

Automotive Rebuilder
11 S. Forge St.
Akron, OH 44304

Automotive Service Market
53 Hamilton Place
Tenafly, NJ 07670

BodyShop Business
11 S. Forge St.
Akron, OH 44304

Brake and Front End
11 S. Forge St.
Akron, OH 44304

Exhaust News
P.O. Box 778
Azle, TX 76020

Import Car and Truck
11 S. Forge St.
Akron, OH 44304

Motor Age
Chilton Way
Radnor, PA 19089

Motor Magazine
645 Stewart Ave.
Garden City, NY 11530

Motor Service
950 Lee St.
Des Plaines, IL 60016

Super Automotive Service
7300 N. Cicero Ave.
Lincolnwood, IL 60646

Tire Review
11 S. Forge St.
Akron, OH 44304

Transmission Digest
3057 E. Cairo
Springfield, MO 65801

Truck Parts and Service
707 Lake Cook Road
Suite 300
Deerfield, IL 60015

FURNISHING YOUR BUSINESS OFFICE

Assuming you've selected the shop most appropriate to your needs and budget, you'll need to start gathering the tools and equipment for your office to manage your business efficiently.

Office equipment

Depending on your auto repair specialty and the initial size of your business, there are many pieces of office equipment you should consider. Stick with the basics until your business is profitable.

Desks All offices require some type of desk or flat surface on which you can place your telephone, records, and other business tools. It can be as simple as a hollow-core door laid horizontally across two file cabinets. It's practical, inexpensive, and can withstand abuse. It's just not very pretty. A 30-inch door fits well over standard two-drawer file cabinets. If you're budget won't allow two cabinets, buy one and add a couple of legs to the other side.

Depending on how much time you spend in your office, you could graduate to a desk from a business supply store for $250 and up. How large? If you plan to keep a phone, a fax machine, a computer, files, and trays all on top of your desk, you'll want a large unit. If your partner, secretary, or office assistant will share some of the duties, you should consider two small desks.

Many small businesspeople place their desk facing a wall or in a corner so they can attach shelves or mount notes that can be easily read while on the phone.

Chairs Most office workers soon learn the value of a good quality chair, especially if they sit in it more than a couple of hours a day. If you're out of the office and in the shop most of the time, you can buy an inexpensive chair. Even a folding chair might serve you until your business is built up. Once your business is successful and you are spending more time in the office, invest in a good quality chair that will keep you comfortable all day and reduce stress.

Shelves Depending on your specialty, you might want shelves on or near your desk so you can refer to flat rate books, shop manuals, large phone books, directories, and other materials that you want handy.

If cost is a greater concern than attractiveness, consider setting bricks or building blocks a couple feet apart on the floor, then laying a 1-by across the top, followed by more blocks and 1-bys. However, don't build your block shelves higher than 32 inches unless they are securely anchored.

If you have clients coming to your office and feel that they need to be impressed, consider renting office equipment that will show better than what's described here. This is especially important if you are working with larger repair jobs where clients aren't familiar with the typical look of an auto repair service's office, dislocated clutter.

Office supplies

You will also need a variety of office supplies to help you gather, record, correspond, and track your business. These supplies include paper clips, a stapler, pens and pencils, a pencil sharpener, file folders and labels, rubber bands, typing paper, calculator tape, stationery (letterhead and envelopes), and postage.

If your office won't include a computer, you should have a typewriter. Look for a good used electric typewriter and make sure that ribbons are readily available.

Telephones

The most important tool for your auto repair service's office is the telephone. With it you can talk directly to dozens of prospects or clients each day without leaving your office. Without a telephone you must wait and hope that customers see your signs and drive in. Later, I'll show you how to use your telephone to profitably market your services, even if you don't like talking on the telephone. For now, let's consider how to select your first business phone.

Depending on local phone company requirements, even if your office is in your home you will probably need to order a separate business telephone line for your auto repair business. If you will answer with a business name rather than a personal name, you need a business phone line. If your name is Bob Jones and your firm is Bob Jones Auto Repair Service, you can answer Bob Jones and not confuse your prospects and clients. But if you're ABC Auto Repair Service and you answer Bob Jones, some callers might think that they have the wrong number.

The cost of a business line has decreased over the last few years because of the competition among telephone companies. But this competition can also make the selection of the *best* telephone service more difficult. Not so for the small, fledgling auto repair business. Your phone bills will not be so large that the typical discount structure will make much difference. Go with your favorite until you've built up your business and better know what your telephone service needs will be. Then you can review the small business packages offered by the competing phone companies to see which will save you the most money. Now a word or two about telephone equipment.

Standard telephones Discount stores, drug stores, and many other retail outlets offer standard telephones that can support basic services offered by many telephone companies, such as call forwarding, call waiting, redial, speed dial, etc. The cost is typically under $50 per phone. You don't want something fancy, you want something sturdy with standard features. Again, go with brands you know and buy from someone who will take it back within a reasonable time if it doesn't work.

Cordless telephones The price goes up for cordless phones, but so does the convenience. Today you can buy a good quality cordless telephone for $100 or less. Full featured models are a little more. The greatest advantage to the cordless phone is its portability. You can carry it throughout your shop, wherever you're working, to avoid the quick dash to your desk to catch it before the third ring.

With every plus there's a minus or two. In the case of cordless telephones, the minus is that it runs on batteries that need to be recharged. If you keep it with the main unit, it will charge. But then it won't be handy. So look for a cordless telephone that can run the longest time away from the main set. Many can operate up to a week off the base unit. Another minus can be overcome. You might forget where you put the gadget. However, many new cordless phones have a paging button that can be pressed on the main set and will beep at the hand set (if the battery isn't dead!) to tell you where it is.

Another drawback of cordless and cellular phones is that you can't be certain of privacy. Some people buy scanners to listen to phone conversations. Maybe your competitors?

As with other tools, buy the best quality phone that you can reasonably afford and purchase it from someone who knows the product. Their product might cost a couple of dollars more than the discount house, but you will get added value because you bought the most appropriate tool for your budget.

Cellular telephones Mobile or cellular phones offer the ultimate portability. You can take them in your tow or service truck, in a briefcase, to your home, and still answer calls from your prospects and clients.

How do they work? Cellular phones are battery operated and require long-life batteries. Your vehicle battery can support a cellular phone. Or you can carry a rechargeable battery pack with you. The signal is carried by wire or satellite link to a transmitter or repeater that covers a wide area. So your conversation is being broadcast much like the signal of an FM radio station. The difference is that anyone with a radio can listen to the FM station. Only you (hopefully) can hear your cellular phone conversation. I say hopefully because, with the right equipment, a competitor can listen in on your conversation unless you have special scrambling equipment.

Rather than get into the specifics of cellular phone technology, which changes almost daily, call a local cellular phone service and find out what's new. Prices, too, are changing. To get more customers, cellular services are offering telephones at low initial costs, but you must sign up for at least six months of their service. Because of air-time charges, it's more expensive to use a cellular phone than standard-line phone service, but it might be a bargain if you're a one-person office who performs most services on the road, such as a tow truck service.

And, if you're brave, ask for a demonstration of a portable cellular workstation. Housed in a briefcase, it's a cellular telephone, laptop computer, modem, fax board, and other goodies. The complete set weighs as much as a bowling ball, about 16 pounds. But it's a whole office for those on the go.

Pagers

A pager is one of the most valuable, and most annoying, tools an auto repair service can have. A pager allows other people (office employees, customers, suppliers, field employees) to contact you wherever you are.

Which type of pager should you select? That depends on your budget and how you will use your pager. A tone pager simply alerts you to call a pre-agreed telephone number, usually that of your office. A voice pager delivers directly a message recorded on your office phone regardless of wherever you are. A digital display pager will page you and write out the telephone number you should call. An alphanumeric display pager can give you a written message.

Many mobile auto repair services start by renting a tone pager, then, as business requires, moving up to a voice or display pager. Check your local telephone book's yellow pages under Paging & Signaling Equipment & Systems or similar headings for local suppliers.

Answering machines

Not long ago, an answering machine was an annoying and misused tape recorder that attempted to drive off the people that called you. Today's answering machine is more accepted, especially in business. It's also easier to use and to buy.

Tape answering machines will use either mini- or standard-sized audio tapes to record an outgoing and any incoming message. The good ones have a separate tape for each. The better ones don't have time limits for incoming messages. The best ones have features that allow you to hear your messages from any other telephone, can let you know if you have any messages at all, and will allow you to easily change your messages from a remote location.

Digital answering machines uses computer chips to record outgoing messages and, in some cases, incoming calls. The sound quality is often better, but the length of the message might be limited. However, advances in digital sound technology will make next year's models even more useful. Be certain that the system you purchase announces the date and time of the call on the incoming message so you know when they tried to call you.

Unfortunately, many businesses misuse their answering system by putting cryptic announcements and background music on the system. These can confuse or intimidate callers. An effective message should be something like this.

Hello, this is ABC Auto Repair Service's answering system. Your call is important to us. Please leave your name and telephone number after the beep and someone will get back to you as soon as possible. Or, if you'd prefer, please call again later. Thank you.

Actually, once you and your clients get comfortable with using an answering machine, you'll find them even more effective than taking live calls. You call a client or supplier and leave a list of questions on their machine, then make some other calls. They call your answering machine and leave the answers while your regular phone is busy. Telephone tag becomes obsolete. And, if necessary, you can review the recorded conversation to ensure that you have the information accurate. You can even leave important or confidential messages in private mailboxes on your system that can only be accessed with a code by your shop manager, your best client, or other important person. It's how business will be conducted in the future.

Fax machines

The digital facsimile (fax) machine is actually over 100 years old in concept. But it wasn't practical until about a decade ago. Today, there are over 25 million fax machines in the world, with most of them installed in businesses.

The concept of the fax machine is simple. It reads a sheet of paper for light and dark spots much like a copy machine. It then converts these spots into a code that is sent across a telephone line at a speed of nearly 10,000 bits of information per second. Based on some international standards, the fax machine on the other end knows how to read these signals and convert them into light and dark spots that conform to the image that was sent. This image is printed on a piece of paper and you have a fax.

The auto repair service can now send quotes, parts orders, sales letters, literature, copies of invoices, and other printed material to suppliers, clients, and others in just seconds. A typical one page fax (FIG. 3-2) takes less than 30 seconds to transmit on a Group 3 fax machine. It, too, is dramatically changing the way that businesses conduct business.

Facsimile machines look like a small printer with a tray to hold outgoing paper and a telephone set either attached or nearby. You call the fax number, your fax machine sends out a tone that tells the other fax machine it would like to transmit a facsimile. The receiving machine sends your machine a high-pitched tone, you manually press your machine's start button and hang up the phone. The information is being transmitted. Some machines automate the process. You simply put the document into the machine and press a button that calls a specific telephone in memory and sends the information without any help. Smart fellers.

ABC
Auto Repair
Service

123 Main Street, Yourtown

FAX COVER

To: Frank Simpson

Company Name: Yourtown Auto Parts

Fax Number: 234-8888

From: Bill Smith

Description:

Attached is our parts order for this week.

Also, the clutch plate you just sent over doesn't include the bearings. Have Bert drop them by (Part # 98765-4321) on his way out for lunch. Thanks.

Golf Saturday?

Number of pages (including cover): 3

Date sent: June 30, 19xx   Time sent: 11:20 am

If there are any problems receiving this transmission please call:
234-6754

3-2 Faxes can make communication easier and more accurate.

There are dozens of things to know about buying a fax machine for your business. However, many are frills. Most important is that your fax machine is Group 3 compatible. Beyond that, explain to the salesman what you need your fax machine for and let him or her show you the newest features and whistles. You can get a basic fax machine for $300 to $400, a better one for $400 to $800, and your heart's desire for a $1000 or more. Or you can lease a fax machine. This is an especially good idea with products like faxes that quickly become obsolete.

Some fax machines you look at will combine other functions. They might have a standard telephone handset that you can use for your primary or secondary business line. Some also include a tape or digital answering machine. In some ways, this makes sense because you have the business phone line feeding into one machine that can serve three purposes, you can answer a call, take messages, or send and receive faxes. But, like any machine that combines functions, if one goes out or becomes obsolete, they might all go. Compare the cost of a combined unit against the cost of individual units. If there is little difference, go for the separate components.

There's one other option you should consider. In a moment, I'll cover the small computer, one of the greatest tools to reach small business in a century. If you decide to purchase a computer for your auto repair business, consider PC fax boards. They are printed circuit boards that are installed inside your computer, even small ones, and allow you to plug in a phone and use it as a fax. There are even models that will serve as your answering machine. Fax boards are typically purchased through computer stores.

SELECTING A COMPUTER

Many people are still intimidated by computers, perhaps it's because they haven't discovered how friendly and helpful computers can be. A computer can assist you in dozens of ways. You can write letters, keep track of your income and outgo, manage your accounts receivables and make collections easier, keep track of your customers and their vehicles, and your prospects, schedule jobs, order parts, learn about your competitors, and much more.

People are often frightened by computers because of all the new terminology that they must decipher: CPUs, bits, bytes, bauds, networks, boards, hard disks, RAM, monitor interlacing, and on and on. Don't worry about it. You'll quickly pick up what the terms mean. Here's a simplified introduction to computers, or it might be a review. As most business computers are IBM-compatible, that's what we'll discuss. Apple's MacIntosh computers use a different operating system, but the basics are the same.

CPUs   A CPU is a central processing unit. The name gives it away. It is an electronic machine built around a small chip called the microprocessor that processes information for you. It obviously does different work, but you could loosely compare it to the engine in a car.

The CPU is typically called by the same name as the microprocessor chip that is its brain. As an example, early personal computers (PCs) used a microprocessor chip called the 8088. So they were called 88s or by the IBM brand name for the model, the XT. The next generation microprocessor and CPU was the 80286, referred to as the 286 or by the IBM brand model, the AT. Then came the 386, the 486, and, just recently, the 586 or Intel Pentium microprocessor and CPU. These could be relatively compared to the two-cylinder, four-cylinder, six-cylinder, V8, fuel-injected V8, and other engines. Each CPU is at least five times faster than the previous model.

In-between chips like the 386 and 486 are incremental steps identified by letters like SX (a half step) and DX (a full step). Don't worry about them for now.

The next number to remember in looking at CPUs is the clock speed. In our simplified automotive comparison, the clock speed would be like the transmission in that it makes the engine (chip and CPU) go faster. XT chips had a clock speed of about 5 MHz (mega—or million—hertz). Today's 486 and newer microprocessors have clock speeds of 50 MHz and more! What's so amazing to me is that a 486 chip does all that hocus-pocus magic stuff in a chip that's about the size of your thumbnail.

So all you really need to know about buying a PC is that a 486 is faster and more powerful than a 286 or 386, and a clock speed of 66 MHz is faster than one that is 33 MHz. You'll want the newest and fastest CPU that you can afford, especially if you're going to do some drafting or have pictures (graphics) in your system. Fortunately, there's not more than a few hundred dollars difference between darn good and great.

Hard disks So where do you keep all this information? Believe it or not, the hard disk drives in your PC can hold thousands of pages of information on stacked disks, which look like miniature LP records stacked on a record player. It knows where to look for any information you've put into it, and it can give you the information in a fraction of a second.

A hard disk is measured by the number of bytes or computer (not English) words that it can store. Actually, capacity is normally measured in megabytes (Mb). Older PCs were equipped with hard disks of 10, 20, or 40 Mb. Newer PCs can store 80, 120, 200 Mb, or even a gigabyte (Gb) or more. That's *one billion* bytes. To put that in terms that are more real, a 1 Gb hard disk can theoretically store about a half-million typed pages, quite a large library!

Why so much? Because graphics or picture files often require a lot of storage space on the hard disk. Some need a megabyte or more per picture. For your auto repair service, a hard drive of 100 to 500 Mb is generally sufficient.

RAM A hard disk is a storage area, much like a library, where millions of pieces of information can be kept. But a computer also needs a work area, like library tables, where books can be open and used. This place is called the random access memory or RAM.

Depending on the size of the programs you'll use, your PC's RAM should be at least 2 Mb. Older PCs offered between ½ and 1 Mb of RAM, but today's PCs typically come with 4 to 16 Mb. The larger this work area is, the more work that can be done simultaneously. Some programs like Microsoft Windows and Novell Netware require at least 2 Mb and really work better if you have 8 Mb of RAM or more. And RAM doesn't cost much to upgrade, especially if you do so when you buy your PC.

Diskette drives So how does all this information get into your PC in the first place? It usually enters on small, portable diskettes that are slipped into your PC's diskette drive and copied to your computer's hard disk. These diskettes, sometimes called floppies, can store from ⅓ Mb to up to nearly 3 Mb of information. Then, once you've written your letter or drawn your plans, you can remove the data by instructing the PC to copy it to a diskette.

In the past 10 years, since PCs have become popular, a number of diskette formats have evolved. A format is what tells the diskette how much information it can store on its surface. Earlier diskettes were 5¼ inches square, and were made of a thin, round plastic disk placed in a bendable (hence floppy) sleeve and sealed. As programmers learned more about storing information on diskettes, they were able to get more information on each diskette. It started with 360 Kb (kilo— thousand—bytes), and quickly multiplied to 1200 Kb or 1.2 Mb. Many PCs still use this format.

Another format soon emerged, the 3½ inch diskette with a thin, round plastic diskette housed in a hard plastic case. The first popular format stored 720 Kb or twice that of the larger 5¼ diskette of the time. But soon, technology doubled storage on the same size diskette to 1.44 Mb. And the newest format can store up to 2.88 Mb of information—more than 1400 single-page letters—on a diskette that will fit into a shirt pocket. Amazing!

As you consider and shop for a PC for your auto repair business, you will also want to know about ports where you can plug in printers and other equipment. Most PCs today have sufficient ports for most applications. Just let your PC store know what you want to do and they will help you select the appropriate PC and peripherals or related equipment.

Finally, you'll need a monitor. A monochrome (black-and-white) monitor is the least expensive. Color monitors are easier to read and more attractive, but also more expensive. Rather than get into a boring description of interlacing and pixels, look for a quality monitor that is easy to read. If you can't see the difference between a $300 monitor and one that costs $1000, don't buy the expensive one.

Later in this chapter, I'll show you how to use computer programs to bring years of business experience to your auto repair business.

SELECTING A PRINTER

Computers are great, but you want a printed copy of your information to share with others: work orders, invoices, business letters, work schedules, income statements. That's where the printer comes in. You can attach a printer to one of your PC's ports and transfer computer data into a readable form.

There are many types of printers to select from. But we only need to cover the basics of them here so you'll know which ones to look for as you go shopping.

Dot matrix The dot matrix printer forms letters from a bunch of dots. A 9-pin printer uses nine tiny pins, three rows of three, to form each letter. The 24-pin printer does the same job but uses 24 pins, four rows of six. So the letters formed by a 24-pin printer are easier to read than that of a 9-pin printer. Today, most dot matrix printers use 24 pins. Some will even run over each line twice, once offset, to make the letters easier to read.

Laser A laser is simply a beam of light that is focused by a mirror. A small laser in your printer actually writes the characters on a piece of paper, then some black dust called toner is passed over it and it sticks to the places the laser light touched, then the sheet travels through a heater that fuses the black toner to the paper. Magic! Your words are printed. Some so-called laser printers use LEDs or light-emitting diodes instead of laser beams. Same results.

Bubble jet   Similar to the laser, the bubble jet printer sprays special ink on to the page in patterns cut by heat. Bubble jet printers are typically less expensive than laser printers.

Which type of printer should you buy? That depends on the type of work you do on your computer. More important, review your needs, and your budget, with your local computer shop. They can help you make a good choice.

SELECTING A COPY MACHINE

Copy machines can be very useful to your auto repair business, especially if you don't have a PC and printer. You will want to conveniently copy outgoing correspondence, quotes, parts lists, agreements, diagrams, procedures, and other business documents. A good copier can be purchased for under $500. If you are producing a client newsletter, your own brochures, direct mail pieces, or other marketing documents, your copy machine might be more cost-effective than running down to the copy shop or printer for a few copies every day.

Features you want to look for in a copier include enlargement and reduction capabilities, paper trays, collating of multiple copies, and reproduction of photos. You won't need a copier the first day you open your doors so wait until you have a genuine need before you buy. By then you'll know what features you require.

If you purchase a medium-to-large copier, you consider a service contract, especially if routine maintenance calls are included at a nominal charge. In your busy office you might forget to perform such maintenance and it can eventually add up to a major repair. But be careful of costs. Some maintenance programs are more profitable for the copy machine representative than for the machine owner.

SELECTING COMPUTER SOFTWARE

Now that you understand the basics of computers, you can better see how computer programs work for you. And, even though computer hardware has been discussed first, you should probably select the computer programs or software before you choose the computer or hardware to run it on. Again, the majority of business computers are IBM-compatible, but a growing number of businesses use MacIntosh computers (or Macs) if they find preferred software in that format.

A computer program is a set of instructions written in a language that your computer understands. The program can be as simple as putting your words on to paper or as complex as drafting a job plan.

Types of software

Computer software can be grouped by their application: horizontal or vertical. Horizontal software is generic programs that can be used for nearly all businesses. Vertical software is programs designed to help a specific type of business or industry such as auto repair services.

Word processors Word processors simply process words. They let you type words into the computer, move them around, insert words, take some out, and make any changes you want before you print them on paper. You can use word processors to write letters or other documents to suppliers, clients, prospects, employees, regulatory boards, or anyone else. I've been using word processors for 10 years and would never go back to manual or even electric typewriters. Word processors let you change your mind.

You don't need a fancy word processing program. If one comes with your computer, use it. If not, you can buy a good one for less than $200 and a great one for less than $500. You only need a great one if you're publishing what you write into brochures or other sales documents. Many of the budget word processors also include a built-in function that can help you check spelling. Your high school English teacher will never know!

Spreadsheets A spreadsheet is to numbers what a word processor is to words. It puts them into readable form. Spreadsheets are named after the wide multi-columnar sheets that accountants use to make journal entries. You can find many ways to use a spreadsheet software program.

As an example, you can purchase a basic spreadsheet program for about $100 that will let you enter horizontal rows or lines of job expense names (Labor, Materials, etc.) and vertical columns of numbers ($428.52, etc.). Most important, you can then tell the program to total any or all of the columns or rows and it will do so in less than a second. If you update a number, it automatically recalculates the total for you.

Fancier and more costly spreadsheets can follow instructions, called macros, you write, to automatically do special calculations. A macro is simply a collection of repeated keystrokes. You might want to write a macro that will select all of the invoices over 60 days old and total them up. Better spreadsheets also do fancy graphs and pie charts that impress bankers and other financial types.

Databases A database software program is much like an index-card file box. You can write thousands or even millions of pieces of information and store it. But a database program is even better than a file box because it finds information in the files in a fraction of a second.

The most common application of a database program for auto repair services is a client vehicle file. If you only have a few clients, this might not be necessary. But as you add clients, prospects, and other business contacts, you might soon need at least a simple database program to keep track of them.

Your prospect/client database can keep information about their name, address, city, state, zip code, phone and fax numbers, contact names, annual budget information, list of projects you've completed for them, information about their vehicles, business, even their hobbies. Then, if you want to find out how many of your clients are located in a specific area of your city and did more than $1000 in business with you last year, you simply tell your database program to search its files for you. It's that easy.

One note on selecting a database program: there are so-called relational databases and flat-file databases. Unless you are going to catalog all of your inventory, raw materials, and every bit of information in your business, you probably don't need to spend the extra money for a relational database. Buy a flat file version at a lower price.

Integrated programs Speaking of relational databases, you can purchase integrated software programs that combine the three primary programs: word processor, spreadsheet, and database. Ask your local computer store to recommend a good integrated program. Some also include other related programs such as communications software that lets your PC talk to other PCs over the phone using modems. A modem (*mo*dulate-*dem*odulate) translates information into a format that can be sent over telephone lines. The cost of a good quality integrated system is usually much less than the total price for the individual components.

Here's another plus to integrated programs: they talk to each other. That is, your word processor can include financial figures from your spreadsheet in your correspondence, and send it by modem to someone listed in your database. Just as important, an integrated group of programs developed by a single software firm will have similar commands in each program. You won't have to learn three separate programs, you'll learn one larger program.

Integrated programs are especially recommended for those who don't want to spend a lot of time selecting and learning numerous software programs.

Other helpful programs Once you're hooked on computers, you'll buy a PC magazine or two, get on someone's mailing list and soon be saturated with information about new software programs. The following might help you sort it out.

DOS stands for disk operating system. DOS translates English commands like "copy" into a language that your PC understands.

A shell program makes your PC easier to use and it performs a number of important maintenance functions. It's called a shell because it wraps around the less-friendly DOS program and makes it easier to copy, delete, and manage files. Some shell programs also include utilities or special programs that help you keep your data organized and safe.

Windows is a program developed by Microsoft that lets you open a number of overlapping boxes or windows on your computer screen, each with different programs. You can be writing a letter when a client calls and then quickly switch to a window with information about the client and your current project.

CAD is an acronym for computer-aided design. It's a drafting system for your PC that helps you to draw plans quickly and easily. Auto repair services typically don't use CAD programs.

Back-up programs let you copy the information on your hard disk to diskettes and make a back-up of your data. It ensures that if something happens to your hard disk and you lose your data, you will have a replacement copy. Of course, this means you must back up your hard disk regularly. The process takes only a few minutes every day and is well worth the time.

Vertical software

As noted, the above programs are called horizontal software programs because they can be used by most businesses, not just auto repair services. So vertical software is programs written specifically for your trade. Some will be advertised in auto repair service trade journals. Others can be found by talking with noncompeting auto repair services or local association members. Vertical software is typically available in the IBM-compatible format, but some also have MacIntosh versions.

Here are some of the features you can expect to find in computer software programs written for auto repair services and related businesses.

- Point-of-sale manages financial interaction with the customer.
- Customer history keeps records of prior services performed for customers as well as data on customers' vehicles.
- Inventory control keeps track of all parts and tools you have in stock or have ordered.
- Shop management helps you schedule employees, and keeps track of jobs and work orders.

Some vertical program packages include their own word processor, spreadsheet, or database programs. Others allow you to integrate their data into your favorite programs. A few do both. Here is a list of vertical software programs written for auto repair and service stations.

Auto Exec
Auto Data Systems
1207 10th St.
Ballinger TX, 76821
800-854-9889

Auto Repair Shop Controller
MicroBiz Corp.
500 Airport Executive Park
Spring Valley, NY 10977
800-637-8268

Auto Repair-Pro Helper
Dietrich-Nichols Associates
10 Industrial Park Road
Hingham, MA 02043
617-749-0067

Bay-Writer
Applied Computer Resources
1201 Route 37 East, #10
Toms River, NJ 08753
800-922-2378

C.S.S.
Compatible Software Systems
119 Townsend St.
Pepperell, MA 01463
508-433-2489

CARS-Computer Assisted Repair System
Softlab, Ltd.
2441 Peppertree Court
Lisle, IL 60532
708-369-5188

COSST
Matador Company
1208 County Line Road
Rosemont, PA 19010
215-525-7548

Fingertips Automotive Software
Advanced Tools
543 Oakshade Road
Indian Mills, NJ 08088
800-232-6565

GarageKeeper
Interstate Business Computers
97 Winsor St.
Ludlow, MA 01056
413-589-1391

Gas-Pro
Creative Logic Inc.
564 Columbian St.
Weymouth, MA 02190
617-337-0234

HITS Plus for Tire and Auto Service
Andreoli & Associates Inc.
9943 Gilead Rd.
Huntersville, NC 28078
800-438-4487

Lube, Oil and Filter
Softlab, Ltd.
2441 Peppertree Court
Lisle, IL 60532
708-369-5188

The Manager's Bookkeeping Assistant
Precision Data Systems
4711 Midlothian Turnpike
Suite 15
Crestwood, IL 60445
708-371-6555

Tracker IV-Service & Repair
Byte Designs
816 Peace Portal Drive
Blaine, WA 98230
604-534-0722

YOUR SUCCESS ACTION LIST

As an auto repair service owner, you have a world of tools and resources available to you. Some are expensive and some are free. All offer valuable help in adding to your knowledge of how to build a successful auto repair business. You might or might not use all of the tools that technology offers, but knowing what they are and what they can do for you can help you keep ahead of the pack. You'll be successful longer. Chapter 4 can help you find and make money. Here's how to put this chapter into action.

_____ Call or write at least six of the auto repair service franchises listed in this chapter or in other reference books.

_____ Call or write all of the associations listed in this chapter that serve your selected auto repair service.

_____ Contact your regional SBA office and ask them what services are available to you as you start your new business, including incubators.

_____ Call or visit your regional SCORE office to set up an interview with a SCORE volunteer who might have experience with auto repair businesses.

_____ Write for a copy of _The Small Business Directory._

_____ Contact your regional Business Development Center (address supplied by the SBA) to find out what resources and services they offer local businesses.

_____ If there is a Technology Access Center in your area, call them to learn what resources they can offer you and how much they cost.

_____ Contact the Department of Commerce for information on your industry and for census records of your trade area.

_____ Begin gathering books and reference works you will need for your new auto repair service.

_____ Write to appropriate trade publications listed in this chapter and ask for a sample copy and subscription information.

_____ Decide what basic office furniture you need.

_____ Call vertical software manufacturers for information on their systems to determine if they can help you build your business.

_____ Decide whether if you will purchase a computer for your auto repair service and, if so, begin selecting specific hardware and software.

4
Start-up money

Money is the root of all . . . business! Money certainly isn't everything, but it is an excellent way to keep score. Increased sales say that you are satisfying your customer's needs. Increased profits say that you are working efficiently.

Of course, it takes money to make money. And that's what this chapter is about: finding money to start your new business. In the coming pages you'll learn how to estimate start-up costs, how to get a low-cost loan, and how to set reasonable and profitable fees for your services. Take out your business notebook and let's get started.

HOW MUCH MONEY WILL YOU NEED?

You've decided to start your own auto repair business, but you're not sure how much money you'll need. Let's develop a Capital Requirements Worksheet on which you can figure start-up and operating costs.

Estimating start-up costs

The first step toward estimating capital requirements is to determine how much it will cost to start your business. Answer the following questions.

- How much will it cost to prepare your selected business site to be an auto repair service office?
- How much will it cost to purchase or lease the tools and equipment you need to start your business?
- How much will it cost to equip your office with desks, chairs, shelves, and other office equipment?
- How much will it cost to purchase initial office supplies?
- How much will it cost to purchase a start-up inventory of parts and supplies?
- How much will it cost to equip your office with a telephone, answering machine, fax, computer, printer, and software?
- How much will it cost to make the necessary utility deposits?
- How much will it cost to obtain the required licenses, permits, and certifications?
- How much will it cost to purchase initial insurance coverage and surety bonds?
- How much will it cost to hire legal and financial professionals to help you organize your business?

- How much will it cost to purchase initial signs?
- How much will it cost to advertise the opening of your business?
- How much will it cost to cover unanticipated expenses?
- What is the total of the above start-up costs?

Estimating operating costs

Once your auto repair business is operating and you cover initial start-up costs, you will be in business. You will have income and expenses. Your next step is to determine your average monthly expenses. Answer the following questions. How much money do you need each month to:

- Live comfortably without a significant change in your current lifestyle?
- Pay the employees you plan to hire?
- Pay the rent on your garage, shop, or other location?
- Pay your office utilities (including telephone service)?
- Maintain a minimum amount of advertising (yellow pages contracts, service directory listings, etc.)?
- Continue insurance premiums for your business?
- Replace office supplies used each month?
- Replace materials and inventory used each month?
- Pay required local, state, and federal taxes?
- Maintain your business equipment and vehicles?

What is the total of your estimating operating expenses for an average month? Complete FIG. 4-1 to estimate income and expenses for the first three years of operation.

Estimating total capital requirements

A large number of small businesses fail each year. Some of which were established by otherwise qualified professionals. There are a number of reasons for these failures, but one of the main reasons is insufficient funds. Too many entrepreneurs try to start up and operate a business without sufficient capital.

So how much is enough? Obviously, the more the better. But a reasonable amount is enough to cover your start-up expenses and operating expenses for three months. So add the total amount of start-up expenses you've calculated to the total of three months estimated operating expenses. That's the minimum amount of capital or money you should have before you start your auto repair business. If you have the resources, a six-month reserve of estimated operating expenses is much better.

Now let's consider some exceptions to this guideline. If you have a working spouse whose income is sufficient to cover household expenses while your business gets on its feet, your capital requirements will be much less than that of a sole breadwinner with eight kids. In addition, if you have a number of regular clients who have already made firm commitments to you for work, you won't need as much operating reserves. However, keep in mind that even if you start work for these clients tomorrow you might not get paid for 60 or even 90 days.

	Year:	19___	19___	19___
Gross Receipts		$ ___	$ ___	$ ___
Merchandise Cost		___	___	___
Gross Profit . . (Receipts less merch. cost)		___	___	___
Expenses				
Officer's Salaries. . . (if corporation)		___	___	___
Employee		___	___	___
Accounting & Legal Fees		___	___	___
Advertising		___	___	___
Rent		___	___	___
Depreciation		___	___	___
Supplies		___	___	___
Electricity		___	___	___
Telephone		___	___	___
Interest		___	___	___
Repairs		___	___	___
Taxes		___	___	___
Insurance		___	___	___
Bad Debts		___	___	___
**Miscellaneous (Postage, etc.)		___	___	___
Total Expenses		___	___	___
Net Proft . . (Gross profit less total expenses)		___	___	___
Less Income Taxes . . (if corporation)		___	___	___
Net Profit After Taxes		___	___	___
Less Withdrawals (i.e., loan payments,				
Proprietorship/Partnership)		___	___	___
Net Profit		___	___	___

**If sum is large, please itemize.

4-1 Worksheet for recording estimated income and expenses for the first three years of operation.

The best advice from those who have been there is "build up your reserves before you start and keep your operating expenses at a bare minimum until your business is established."

FINDING START-UP CAPITAL

Few people know their true financial net worth. That is, how much they own minus how much they owe. Before you decide to start your auto repair business you must determine your financial net worth.

Your assets

Assets are simply what you own. Maybe you have more financial assets than you know. First, there are two types of assets: short-term and long-term. A short-term asset is one that can be liquidated or turned quickly into cash. If someone owes you $1000 and promises to pay you next week, that is a short-term asset. If they won't pay you for another five years, that's a long-term asset. A short-term asset is usually defined as one that can be turned into cash within one year. So an asset is important, but also important is its liquidity.

- How much cash do you have in your checking accounts, savings accounts, in a safe deposit box, or other resources?
- How much money do you have in certificates of deposit, savings certificates, stocks, bonds, securities, and other easily-sold short-term assets?
- How much money is owed to you (accounts receivable)?
- What is the market value of real estate that you own (how much could you sell it for)?
- What is the book value of automobiles and other vehicles that you own, even if you have a loan against them?
- What is the cash value of insurance policies in your name?
- What is the value of other assets you own (furniture, jewelry, tools, equipment, etc.)?
- What is the total value of all short-term assets (those you could turn into cash within one year)?
- What is the total value of all long-term assets (those that require more than one year to turn into cash)?
- What is the total value of all short-term and long-term assets?

Your liabilities

Your liabilities are the money that you owe to others. Some are secured by assets; others are secured by your signature or personal pledge to pay. As with assets, there are short-term liabilities and long-term liabilities. A short-term liability is one that will be paid off within a year, such as a credit card. A long-term liability is one that will take more than a year to pay off, such as a car loan.

- How much do you owe on credit cards?
- How much do you owe on installment payments for furniture, appliances, or other household items?
- How much do you owe on your vehicles?
- How much do you owe on local, state, and federal taxes?
- How much do you owe on educational loans?
- How much do you owe on a mortgage or note against your home or other real estate?
- Do you have second mortgages on any real estate?
- How much do you owe on other liabilities?

- What is the total value of all short-term liabilities (those that must be paid off within one year)?
- What is the total value of all long-term liabilities (those that won't be paid off within the next year)?
- What is the total value of all short and long-term liabilities?

Estimating total net worth

The purpose of this exercise is to discover your total financial net worth. That's your assets minus your liabilities. In other words, if you sold everything you owned and paid off everything you owed, how much would you have left?

Don't be discouraged by the results of this exercise. There are a number of things that you can do to improve your financial net worth. In fact, once your business becomes successful your total net worth will grow. You'll own more and more assets while owing less and less people. Even if the total is in negative numbers—you actually owe more than you own—this worksheet can help you learn what to do about it.

FINANCIAL RESOURCES

Okay. You now know how much you need and how much you have to start your auto repair business. Maybe you've determined that you don't have enough assets to start your business. Or maybe you're determined to put a reserve equal to six months operating expense in the bank before you start. Here are some sources for additional funds.

Who you know By now, you've probably met hundreds of people in your lifetime; maybe thousands. Each is a potential source of funding. You're not begging from them. You're simply asking them if they wish to invest money in a potentially profitable enterprise and reap some reward for their investment. You might ask: relatives, friends, current employers, past employers, your banker, your accountant, your attorney, your doctor, your prospective clients, your suppliers, friends of friends of friends, or members of associations, clubs, and churches to which you belong.

Some of these contacts will not be interested, others might want to participate in the investment, but don't want to put in more than $1000 dollars. Still others will become your primary resources. Why would they do so? Because they expect a return on their investment. So develop a business plan that can help investors understand what you're doing, how much it will cost, what you need, and what they will get for risking their money. This tells them that you mean business. In nearly every case you won't be looking for general partners to advise you on how to run your business. In fact, you don't want that. You probably want investors or limited partners who will invest money but stay out of the day-to-day management.

Commercial bankers A banker is much like you. He has a product that he receives from others—money—and sells it at a profit to someone who needs it. This, too, is not charity. It is good business. But bankers are notoriously not risk-takers. The caricature that bankers carry umbrellas year-round is not true, but is based on truth. They are stewardly.

So your approach to bankers must be conservative. If you want to borrow from them you will need a complete written description of what you want to do, how you plan to do it, how much it will cost, and the profit you expect to make. Most important: how will you pay off the loan?

Venture capitalists   There are people who look for small business opportunities in which to invest—at a significant rate of return. They're called venture capitalists. You can find them through your banker, financial institutions, your accountant, venture capital directories, investment brokers, and ads in metropolitan newspapers.

The Small Business Administration   One of the most noteworthy services offered by the Small Business Administration (SBA) is to guarantee loans made by bankers who would not otherwise loan money to new businesses. Take time to review the SBA's loan guarantee program and then talk with an SBA office in your region.

SBICs   The Small Business Investment Act allows the SBA to license small business investment companies or SBICs. The SBICs supply equity capital to companies unable to raise funds from other sources. They are privately owned, operate for profit, and are chartered under state law. Your regional SBA office can help you find SBICs in your area that might be able to help you find additional assets.

Proprietorships and partnerships can receive long-term loans from an SBIC as long as it is secured by real estate or other collateral. Corporations can receive funds from long-term loans or equity financing. Equity financing can be in the form of stock purchased in your company by the SBIC, or loans with stock as equity, or other collateral.

Stock   If you incorporate your business, you can sell shares or portions of it to investors. The type of investment they make, the risk involved, how they receive their profits or dividends, and how dividends to them are taxed depend on the type of stock you issue and they purchase. Talk with your attorney or accountant about how to issue stock in your state in order to develop additional capital for your business.

GETTING A LOAN

The ability to get a loan when you need it is as necessary to the operation of your business as is the right equipment. Before a bank or any other lending agency will lend you money, the loan officer must feel satisfied with the answers to these five questions:

What sort of person are you?   In most cases, the character of the borrower comes first. Next is your ability to manage your business.

What are you going to do with the money?   The answer to this question determines the type of loan and the duration. Money to be used for the purchase of job materials requires quicker repayment than money used to buy fixed assets.

When and how do you plan to pay back the loan?   Your banker's judgment of your business ability and the type of loan will be a deciding factor in the answer to this question.

Is the cushion in the loan large enough?   In other words, does the amount requested make suitable allowance for unexpected developments? The banker decides this question on the basis of your financial statement, which sets forth the condition of your business and on the collateral pledged.

What is the outlook for business in general and for your business in particular? Adequate financial data is a must. The banker wants to make loans to businesses that are solvent, profitable, and growing. The two basic financial statements used to determine those conditions are the balance sheet and the income statement. The balance sheet is the major yardstick for solvency and the income statement. A continuous series of these two statements over a period of time is the principal device for measuring financial stability and growth potential.

When interviewing loan applicants and studying their records, the banker is especially interested in the following facts and figures.

General information Are your books and records up-to-date and in good condition? What is the condition of the accounts payable? Of notes payable? What are the salaries of the owner-manager and other company officers? Are all taxes paid currently? What is the order backlog? What is the number of employees? What is the insurance coverage?

Accounts receivable Are there indications that some of the accounts receivable have already been pledged to another creditor? What is the accounts receivable turnover? Is the accounts receivable total weakened because many customers are far behind in their payments? Has a large enough reserve been set up to cover questionable accounts? How much do the largest accounts owe and what percentage of your total accounts does this amount represent?

Fixed assets What is the type, age, and condition of the equipment? What are the depreciation policies? What are the details of mortgages or conditional sales contracts? What are the future acquisition plans?

For many people, the additional capital needed to start a business comes from a loan from a banker, a venture capitalist, a supplier, or other sources. What types of loans are available? And how can you get a loan at the lowest rates? Let's consider these significant questions.

TYPES OF LOANS

When you set out to borrow money for your firm, it is important to know the type of money you need: short term, long term, or equity capital.

Keep in mind that the purpose the funds are to be used for is an important factor when deciding the type of money you need. But even so, deciding what type of money to use is not always easy. It is sometimes complicated by the fact that you might be using some of the various types of money at the same time and for identical purposes.

The important distinction among the types of money is the source of repayment. Generally, short-term loans are repaid from the liquidation of current assets that they have financed. Long-term loans are usually repaid from earnings. Equity capital usually is not repaid because it is gained from selling an interest in your business.

Short-term bank loans You can use short-term bank loans for purposes to finance accounts receivable for 30 to 60 days. Or you can use them for purposes that take longer to pay off, such as the purchase of needed equipment. Usually, lenders expect short-term loans to be repaid after their purposes have been served. For example, accounts receivable loans should be paid off when the outstanding accounts have been paid.

Banks loan such money either on your general credit reputation with an unsecured loan or on a secured loan. The unsecured loan is the most frequently used form of bank credit for short-term purposes. You don't have to put up collateral because the bank relies on your credit reputation. The secured loan involves a pledge of some or all of your business assets. The bank requires security to protect its depositors against the risks that are involved, even in business situations where the chances of success are good.

Term borrowing Term borrowing provides money that is to be paid back over a fairly long period. Some people break it down into two forms: intermediate (1 to 5 years) and long-term (over 5 years). However, for your purpose of matching the type of money to the needs of your company, think of term borrowing as money that you probably will pay back in periodic installments from earnings.

Equity capital Some people confuse term borrowing and equity (or investment) capital. Yet there is a big difference. Equity capital is money you get by selling interest in your business in the form of stock or partnerships. You take people into your company who are willing to risk their money in it. They are interested in potential income rather than an immediate return on their investment.

Let's discuss loans and other types of credit. There are numerous types of loans available, each with their own unique name. Even so, they fall into one of the following categories:

Signature loan A signature loan involves no collateral except your promise to pay the lender back on terms upon which you both agree. If your money needs are small, you only need the money for a short time, your credit rating is excellent, and you're willing to pay a premium interest rate because you are not using physical collateral, a signature or character loan is an easy way to borrow money in a hurry.

Term loan A term loan is one that requires good credit and typically some type of collateral, either equipment or real estate. The length of a short-term loan is 1 year or less. A long-term loan might be paid off over a period longer than a year. Payments can be set up to be monthly, quarterly, annually, or seasonally, depending on security and your business cash flow.

Collateral loan A collateral loan is one in which some type of asset is put up as collateral; if you don't make payments you lose the asset. Because the lender wants to make sure that the asset is worth more than the value of the loan, a bank usually loans only 50 to 75 percent of the asset's value. A new auto repair service often does not have sufficient collateral—real estate, equipment, inventory—to secure a collateral loan unless an owner uses personal assets such as a home.

Personal credit cards Many a small business has found at least some of its funding in the owner's personal credit card. Tools, equipment, materials, fees, office supplies, office expenses, and other costs can be covered with your personal credit card. However, interest rates on credit cards are extremely high, sometimes double what you might pay on a collateral loan. But they can also get you quick cash when you need it. If this is an option for you, talk to your credit card representative about raising your credit limit. It will be much easier to do so while you are employed by someone else instead of self-employed.

Line of credit A line of credit is similar to a loan except that you don't borrow it all at once. You get a credit limit, say $20,000, that you can tap anytime you need money for business purposes. The most common is the revolving line of credit that you can draw from when business is off and pay back when business is good, providing that you don't exceed your limit. A line of credit is an excellent way for an auto repair service to work through the ups and downs of seasonal business. With some restrictions, a line of credit can be established using a portion of your home equity as collateral. Using a secured equity earns you a lower interest rate.

Cosigner loan This type of loan should be one of the most popular loans for small businesses, but many businesspeople never consider it. Simply, you find a cosigner or a co-maker with good credit or assets that guarantees the loan with you. If you have a potential investor who believes in your business, but doesn't want to put up the cash you need, ask him to cosign for a loan with you. Your chances of receiving the loan are much better. Some cosigners require that you pay them a fee of 1 to 4 percent of the balance, or a flat fee; others will do it for your friendship, or the hope of future business from you. In any case, this as an excellent source of capital for your new auto repair business.

Equipment loan If you're purchasing an auto repair vehicle, special equipment, or other assets for your business, the supplier might loan or lease the equipment to you. This often requires about 25 percent down so be ready to come up with some cash of your own.

Factoring Once you've completed some jobs and billed your clients, you don't have to wait for them to send you the money. You can sell your accounts receivable—at a discount, of course. This is called factoring. Or you can use your best accounts receivable as collateral for a loan. There are certainly some pluses and minuses to this method of raising capital, but it is a commonly used option. Talk to your accountant, banker, financial adviser, or another auto repair business owner about finding a reputable factoring broker.

Trade credit Depending on your suppliers, you can build working capital for your business by developing trade credit. Once approved, your supplier will give you additional time in which to pay your bill to them. You might start off with 60 days credit, then earn 90 days, and even 120 days before you must pay their bill. There will typically be a finance charge on any balance more than 30 days old, but some suppliers give you low- or no-interest "loans" of materials for this period. Compare prices versus credit terms as you shop for primary and secondary suppliers.

Seasonal line of credit The SBA offers a short-term loan guaranty program for businesses that need a seasonal line of credit. For more information, contact your regional SBA office.

A recent survey of small businesses indicates that 23 percent had lines of credit, 7 percent had financial leases, 14 percent had mortgage loans, 12 percent had equipment loans, and 25 percent had vehicle loans. For larger firms, the percentages about double in each category.

COLLATERAL

Sometimes your signature is the only security the bank needs to make a loan. At other times, the bank requires additional assurance that the money will be repaid. The type and amount of security depends on the bank and on the borrower's situation. Of course, a banker will attempt to get as much security as possible, sometimes even more than is required.

If the required loan can't be justified by the borrower's financial statements alone, a pledge of security might bridge the gap.

Endorsers, co-makers, and guarantors As noted earlier, borrowers often get other people to sign a note in order to bolster their own credit. These endorsers are contingently liable for the note they sign. If the borrower fails to pay up, the bank expects the endorser to make the note good. Sometimes the endorser might be asked to pledge assets or securities, too. A co-maker is one who creates an obligation jointly with the borrower. In such cases, the bank can collect directly from either the maker or the co-maker. A guarantor is one who guarantees the payment of a note by signing a guaranty commitment. Both private and government lenders often require guarantees from officers of a corporation in order to assure continuity of effective management. Sometimes a manufacturer or supplier will act as guarantor for customers.

Assignment of leases The assigned lease as security is similar to the guarantee. It is used, for example, in some franchise situations. The bank lends the money on a building and takes a mortgage. Then the lease, which the dealer and the parent franchise company work out, is assigned so that the bank automatically receives the rent payments. In this manner, the bank is guaranteed repayment of the loan.

Chattel mortgages If you buy equipment such as a tow truck, you might want to get a chattel mortgage loan. You give the bank a lien on the equipment you are buying. The bank also evaluates the present and future market value of the equipment being used to secure the loan. How rapidly will it depreciate? Does the borrower have the necessary fire, theft, property damage, and public liability insurance on the equipment. The banker has to be sure that the borrower protects the equipment used as chattel.

Real estate Real estate is another form of collateral for long-term loans. Before making a real estate mortgage, the bank finds out the location of the real estate, its physical condition, its foreclosure value, and the amount of insurance carried on the property. Many auto repair service owners use their home as collateral for a real estate loan to begin their business.

Accounts receivable Banks often lend money on accounts receivable. In effect, you are counting on your customers to pay your note. The bank might take accounts receivable on a notification or a non-notification plan. Under the notification plan, the purchaser of the goods is informed by the bank that his or her account has been assigned to it and must make account payments directly to the bank. Under the non-notification plan, your customer continues to pay you the sum due on his or her accounts and you pay the bank. Unfortunately, under a notification plan your customers might assume that your business is financially unsound and reduce future business with you.

Savings account Sometimes you can get a loan by assigning a savings account to the bank. In such cases the bank gets an assignment from you and keeps your passbook. If you assign an account in another bank as collateral, the lending bank asks the other bank to mark its records to show that the account is held as collateral.

Life insurance Another kind of collateral is life insurance. Banks will lend up to the cash value of a life insurance policy. You have to assign the policy to the bank. If the policy is on the life of an executive of a small corporation, corporate resolutions must be made to authorize the assignment. Most insurance companies allow you to sign the policy back to the original beneficiary when the assignment to the bank ends. Some people like to use life insurance as collateral rather than borrow directly from insurance companies. One reason is that a bank loan is often more convenient to obtain and might be obtained at a lower interest rate.

Stocks and bonds If you use stocks and bonds as collateral, they must be marketable. As a protection against market declines and possible expenses of liquidation, banks usually lend no more than 75 percent of the market value of high grade stock. On federal government or municipal bonds, they might be willing to lend 90 percent or more of their market value. The bank might ask the borrower for additional security or payment whenever the market value of the stocks or bonds drops below the bank's required margin.

For more information on business credit, write to the Federal Trade Commission, Washington, DC 20580; Attn: Public Reference. Ask for their booklet on *Getting Business Credit*. It's free.

OTHER FINANCIAL RESOURCES

Auto repair services never seem to have enough money. Bankers and suppliers play an important role in financing small business growth through loans and credit, but an equally important source of long-term growth capital is the venture-capital firm.

One way of explaining the different ways in which banks and venture-capital firms evaluate a small business seeking funds is that banks look at their immediate future, but are most heavily influenced by thier past. Venture capitalists look to their long-term future.

Of course, venture-capital firms are interested in many of the same factors that influence bankers in their analysis of loan applications. All financial people want to know the results and ratios of past operations, the amount and intended use of the needed funds, and the earnings and financial condition of future projects. But venture capitalists look more closely at the features of the service and the size of the market than do commercial banks.

Banks are creditors. They're interested in the market position of your company. They look for assurance that your service business can provide steady sales and generate sufficient cash flow to repay the loan. They look at projections to be certain that the owner has done his homework.

Venture-capital firms are owners. They hold stock in your company, adding their invested capital to its equity base. Therefore, they examine with extreme care existing or planned services and their potential markets. They invest only in firms they believe can rapidly increase sales and generate substantial profits.

Why? Because venture-capital firms invest for long-term capital, not for interest income. A common estimate is that they look for a return of three to five times their investment in five to seven years.

Of course, venture capitalists don't realize capital gains on all their investments. Certainly, they don't make capital gains of 300 to 500 percent except on a very limited portion of their total investments. But their intent is to find venture projects with this appreciation potential to make up for investments that aren't successful.

As you can imagine, venture capital is a risky business because it's difficult to judge the worth of companies in their infancy. Because their investments are unprotected in the event of failure, many firms set rigorous policies to reduce risks, including venture proposal size, maturity of your company, requirements, and evaluation procedures.

There is quite a variety of types of venture-capital firms.

- Traditional partnerships that are often established by wealthy families to aggressively manage a portion of their funds by investing in small companies.

- Professionally managed pools that are made of institutional money and that operate like the traditional partnerships.

- Investment banking firms that usually trade in more established securities, but occasionally form investor syndicates for venture proposals.

- Insurance companies that often require a portion of equity as a condition of their loans to smaller companies as protection against inflation.

- Manufacturing companies that sometimes look upon investing in smaller companies as a means of supplementing their research and development programs.

- Small Business Investment Corporations (SBICs) that are licensed by the SBA and that might provide management assistance as well as venture capital. Contact your regional SBA office for information on SBICs that work in your region or trade.

In addition to these venture-capital firms there are individual private investors and finders. Finders, which can be firms or individuals, often know the capital industry and might be able to help the small company seeking capital to locate it.

THE VENTURE PROPOSAL

Most venture-capital firms are interested in investment projects that require an investment of $250,000 to $1,500,000. Projects requiring less than $250,000 are of limited interest because of the high cost of investigation and administration. However, some venture firms will consider smaller proposals if the investment is intriguing enough.

The typical venture-capital firm receives over 1000 proposals a year. About 90 percent of these will be rejected because they don't fit the established geographical, technical, or market area policies of the firm, or because they have been poorly prepared.

The remaining 10 percent are investigated with care. These investigations are expensive, costing the venture firm $2000 to $3000 per company investigated. Of these, 10 or 15 proposals per year earn a second investigation. Finally, the venture firm selects one or two in which to invest.

Most investment capital firms' investment interest is limited to projects proposed by companies with some operating history, even though they might not yet have shown a profit. Companies that can expand into a new product line or a new market with additional funds are particularly interesting. The venture-capital firm can provide funds to enable such companies to grow in a spurt rather than gradually as they would on retained earnings.

Most venture-capital firms concentrate primarily on the competence and character of the proposing firm's management. They feel that even mediocre products or services can be successfully developed, promoted, and distributed by an experienced, energetic management group.

Finally, most venture-capital firms seek a distinctive element in the strategy, market, or process of the firm. This distinctive element might be a new feature, a particular skill, or technical competence. They're looking for something that will provide a competitive advantage for the firm in which they invest.

Writing the venture proposal

A successful venture proposal must satisfy the venture capitalists that it is worthwhile for them to invest. Here are the components of a typical venture proposal.

Purpose and objectives   This is a summary of the what and why of the project.

Proposed financing   Explain the amount of money you'll need from the beginning to the maturity of the project proposed, how the proceeds will be used, how you plan to structure the financing, and why the amount designated is required.

Marketing   Provide a description of the market segment you've got or plan to get, the competition, the characteristics of the market, and your plans (with costs) for getting or holding the market segment you desire.

History of the firm   Give a summary of significant financial and organizational milestones, a description of employees and employee relations, an explanations of banking relationships, and a recounting of major services or products your firm has offered during its existence.

Description of the product or service   Write a detailed description of the product (process) or service offered by your firm and the costs associated with it.

Financial statements   Provide these statements for the past few years and pro forma projections (balance sheets, income statements, and cash flows) for the next three to five years, showing the effect anticipated if the project is undertaken and if the financing is secured. This should include an analysis of key variables that might affect financial performance, showing what could happen if the projected level of revenue is not attained.

Capitalization   This is a list of shareholders, how much is invested to date, and in what form (equity or debt).

Biographical sketches Give the work histories and qualifications of key owners and employees.

Principal customers and suppliers Provide a list and description of your current clients and suppliers, as well as those you will have if funding is approved for your project.

Problems anticipated and other pertinent information This is a candid discussion of any contingent liabilities, pending litigation, tax or patent difficulties, and any other contingencies that might affect the project you're proposing.

Advantages Write a discussion of what's special about your service, product, marketing plans, or channels that gives your project unique leverage.

How venture capitalists participate

What happens when, after the exhaustive investigation and analysis, the venture-capital firm decides to invest in your company? Most venture firms prepare an equity financing proposal that details the amount of money they will provide, the percentage of common stock that must be surrendered in exchange for these funds, the interim financing method that will be used, and the protective covenants that are to be included.

Venture-capital financing is not inexpensive for the owners of a small business. The partners of the venture firm buy a portion of the business equity in exchange for their investment. They become part of the ownership.

This percentage of equity varies, of course, and depends upon the amount of money provided, the success and worth of the business, and the anticipated investment return. It can range from a 10-percent interest in an established and profitable business to as much as 80 or 90 percent for new or financially-troubled firms.

Most venture firms, at least initially, don't want a position of more than 30 to 40 percent because they want the owners to have the incentive to keep building the business. If additional financing is required to support business growth, the outsiders' stake might exceed 50 percent, but investors realize that small business owners/managers can lose their entrepreneurial zeal under these circumstances. The venture firm wants to leave control in the hands of the company's managers because it is really investing in that management team more than in the business.

Control is a much simpler issue to resolve. Unlike the division of equity over which the parties are bound to disagree, control is an issue in which they have a common, though perhaps unapparent, interest. While it's understandable that the management of a small company will have some anxiety in this area, the partners of a venture firm typically have little interest in assuming control of the business. They have neither the technical expertise nor the managerial personnel to run a number of small companies in diverse industries. They much prefer to leave operating control to the existing management.

The venture-capital firm does, however, want to participate in any strategic decision that might change the basic product/market character of the company and in any major investment decisions that might divert or deplete the financial resources of the company. They will, therefore, generally ask that at least one partner be made a director of your company.

The investment of the venture-capital firm might be in the final form of direct stock ownership, which does not impose fixed charges. Financings also might be straight loans with options or warrants that can be converted to a future equity position at pre-established charges.

Venture-capital firms generally intend to realize capital gains on their investments by providing for a stock buy-back by the small firm, by arranging a public offering of stock of the company in which they have invested, or by providing for a merger with a larger firm that has publicly traded stock. They usually hope to do this within five to seven years of their initial investment.

Venture capital might be the funding source you require to successfully grow your auto repair business.

HOW MUCH YOU SHOULD BORROW

The amount of money you need to borrow depends on the reason you need funds. Figuring the amount of money required for business expansion is relatively easy. However, determining the money you'll need for business startup is more difficult.

While rule-of-thumb ratios might be helpful as a starting point, a detailed projection of sources and uses of funds over some future period of time, usually 12 months, is a better approach. In this way, the characteristics of the particular situation can be taken into account. Such a projection is developed through the combination of a predicted budget and a cash forecast.

The budget is based on recent operating experience plus your best judgment of performance during the coming period. The cash forecast is your estimates of cash receipts and disbursements during the budget period. Thus, the budget and the cash forecast together represent your plan for meeting your working capital requirements.

To plan your working capital requirements, it is important to know the cash flow that your business will generate. This involves simply a consideration of all elements of cash receipts and disbursements at the time they occur. These elements are listed on the income statement that has been adapted to show cash flow. They should be projected for each month.

REDUCING COSTS

Money is a commodity, bought and sold by lenders. Just like other products, you can save money by shopping around. Here are some points to consider as you shop for money.

First, are there any loan fees or other charges required to set up or service the loan? Some lenders require that a loan fee (points) of 1 or 2 percent, or more, be paid in advance. Others will roll the loan fee into the loan, so you actually pay interest upon interest. Others will deduct a monthly service fee from each payment as it is made. This arrangement is not necessarily bad. After all, the lender must get his profit from you in some manner. Just make sure that you understand what the actual cost of the loan is before you agree to it. You also need to know actual interest rates as you compare rates between lenders.

Second, consider whether your best option is fixed rate or variable rate interest. Fixed rate interest means that the interest rate charged by the lender is the same throughout the life of the loan. Variable rate interest can vary during the term of the loan based on some outside factor. This factor is usually the cost of the money to the lender. The difference between the lender's cost and what he charges you is called the spread. From that spread comes the lender's sales costs, office overhead, salaries, and profit. It's also based on the amount of risk the lender is taking when loaning the money to you. Higher risk means a higher spread. There are numerous indexes used to establish the cost of money. Review all of the options with your lender, ask which one makes the most sense for your needs, then get a second opinion.

Keep in mind that variable rate interest reduces the amount of risk the lender is taking, especially on long-term loans. He is virtually assured that, unless the money market goes crazy and exceeds the cap, he will get his margin of profit from every dollar you send him. Lower risk means lower rates. The point is that you shouldn't disqualify variable rate loans from consideration. In many cases, they cost less than fixed rate loans and many lenders are more willing to make them.

To make sure that you pay the best interest rate available, don't jump into the arms of the first loan offer that comes to you. Shop around and compare. You might eventually decide to take that first offer, but only because you've found nothing better.

But don't worry about getting the absolute lowest interest rate available. You might want to accept your regular banker's loan terms, even though it's a quarter of a percentage point higher, in order to maintain a mutually profitable relationship. That quarter point might only mean a few dollars to you, but will reinforce your business relationship with your banker.

While we're on the subject, let's talk about credit. Credit is simply someone else's faith that you will keep your promise to them. You buy computerized diagnostics equipment on credit and the lender believes that you will pay him what you've borrowed, or have assets that he can sell to cover what you've borrowed. So how do you build credit? Easy. You borrow small amounts, pay it back on time, borrow larger amounts, pay it back, and so on. It also helps to have some assets, like stocks or land, that are already paid off, or in which you have some equity.

A good way to start building your business credit is to use personal assets, signature, real estate equity, as collateral for your business. One enterprising auto repair businessperson simply applied for a credit card in his business name from the same company that sponsored his long-standing personal credit card. He asked for a small credit limit, used it and paid it off, then asked for an increased credit limit. Meantime, he used the credit card as a reference for a new account with a supplier. Other new businesspeople use equity in their homes or investment land as collateral for credit with banks and suppliers, as discussed earlier.

SETTING YOUR RATES

You might think that this question is one of the most important questions in the book. It really isn't. Many other questions will be just as important to the success of your business. However, this question is often the first one that new auto repair services ask. So let's get it answered. Let's consider the three C's of pricing: cost, competition, and customer.

How much does my service cost me to furnish?

Once you've established your start-up costs and your monthly operating costs, you'll have a pretty good idea of how much your service will cost you to furnish to your customers. But there's another important factor that you need to include: your amount of available time.

A month with 20 work days offers you approximately 160 hours of time that you can sell to customers. You might wind up working many more, but 160 is probably all you'll be able to bill to clients. In fact, depending on the size and structure of your auto repair business, you might not be able to bill that many. One-person businesses require about a quarter of their time to market their services and to manage the business. So they're down to 120 billable hours per month, unless they do all marketing and management after normal working hours. If the operating or overhead costs calculated earlier total $6000 a month, that amount is divided by 120 billable hours to come up with an hourly fee of $50. With monthly operating expenses of $4000 and 160 billable hours in a month, the hourly shop rate becomes $25.

How much do my competitors charge?

A few telephone calls should get you the shop rates charged by your competitors. Of course, you must make sure that you're comparing apples with apples. Your competitor might not have your level of skill, or he might have more. Or your competitor might be including costs for some specialized tools and equipment that you don't have yet.

Why should you care what your competitors charge? Because your clients will probably get bids from them as well as you. You don't necessarily have to match or beat their bids, but you do need to know what their rates are so that you can help the client make a fair comparison.

How much does the customer expect to pay?

This is a toughie. The question isn't how much will the customer pay, it's how much does he *expect* to pay? The difference is expectations. You might get some customers for your service to pay an excessive fee for awhile, but they'll soon move to other sources. What you want to find out is what they think your service is actually worth to them. Most understand that if they pay you too little, you will soon be out of business and won't be able to help them in the future. They might not admit it, but they know it.

How can you know how much the consumer expects to pay for your skills? Ask a few of them. They might tell you what they're used to paying, what they think is a fair charge, or maybe what they expected to pay for the job. Take them all into consideration. Ask the question of them and let them take a few minutes to explain why they think so. You'll get some valuable insight into what customers expect from you, as well as what you should expect from them.

As before, make sure that you're comparing similar skills and similar fees. A customer might expect more skills than you can offer, or maybe fewer.

Establishing your hourly service rate is a simple process of adding overhead and expected profit to the cost of labor. That is, if an employee is paid $16 per hour and has a payroll tax/benefits package worth $4 per hour, add to this your overhead, say $9 an hour, and your expected profit, such as 10 percent of the labor/benefits cost or $2. You come up with a total of $31 per hour. If you pay your employees for pickup and delivery time, but the customer doesn't, then you need to add a charge for travel. If it's typically 10 percent of the workday, then add that percent of the labor/benefits package, or $2 in this example, to your hourly service rate. It's now up to $33 per hour.

Rich Day, a retired auto repair shop owner, says his sharp-eyed bookkeeper found an expense that was as great as the shop's profit: NPN or no part number materials. This included shop towels, spray lubricants, parts cleaners, etc. Rich simply added an additional 5 percent of the labor charge to cover these necessary materials. No one ever complained, and some of his competitors began doing the same.

Once you've established your charge per hour, you can apply it to estimates from your industry's flat-rate manual to estimate job time and determine what you will charge for a specific service. Then establish your price list (FIG. 4-2).

Some states require that written estimates or quotes for all service be signed by the customer before the service is performed.

PRICE vs. VALUE

Now you know what your time costs you, what your competitors charge for their time and skills, as well as what customers expect to pay for your time and skills. So which figure is right? All and none. Theoretically, what you want is a charge that will drive away about 10 percent of your prospects as too high, and another 10 percent as too low.

Here's a technique that can make your business more profitable, put your business above your competitors, and keep your customers happy: sell *value* not price. How can a fancy restaurant charge five times as much as the diner next door for the same ingredients? They sell value. Call it ambiance or image or snobbery or whatever; it's value. The fancy restaurant makes the client's purchase an event rather than just a transaction. The fancy restaurant treats the client like a person rather than a number, gives extra service, uses finer dinnerware, and decorates the food to make it more appetizing.

You'll see the same technique, selling value rather than price, in any competitive business where one firm wants to stand out from the others. Chevys are sold on price; Cadillacs are sold on value; both are built by General Motors. Value says that whether the price is large or small you will get your money's worth.

So how does an auto repair service sell value? By treating customers like valued friends. By offering services that other auto repair services do not. By maintaining a clean and orderly image with well-maintained trucks and signage. Or by simply turning questions of price into explanations of value.

Extra service There are many extra services that a value-oriented auto repair service can perform for its clients that don't cost much to implement, yet add value to the service. Depending on the type of work done, some auto repair services hire a part-time shop helper, usually a high school or vocational college student at minimum wage, who goes for parts, cleans car interiors, washes customers' cars, and performs other helpful jobs. The cost to the auto repair business is minimal, and is factored into the shop's hourly rate. The extra-mile service, however, is a courtesy that few auto repair services offer.

Value-priced auto repair services can step ahead of their competition by eliminating problems for the client such as picking up and delivering the car rather than making the customer find a way to do so. This service gives you another chance to

123 Main Street, Yourtown USA 12345

Date: June 30, 19xx

Code	Description	Unit Cost
OC	Oil Change	$16.95
OFC	Oil Change with Filter Change	$21.95
OFCL	Oil/Filter Change with Lubrication	$26.95
TUP	Tune-up: pre-1986 passenger car or pick-up	$79.95
TUN	Tune-up: 1987-newer passenger car or pick-up	$99.95
TUC	Tune-up: commercial truck (2-ton+)	$129.95
AR	Automotive Repair (per hour plus parts)	$45.00

4-2 A written price list can help you standardize your pricing and ensure profit.

sell the value of your service to a client or prospect. Just cleaning the windshield makes a car seem to run better.

The rule: treat your customers as you would like your suppliers to treat you. Maybe even better. What extra services can you offer in your specialty that will set you apart from your competitors and help you sell value rather than price?

Professional image Imagine seeing a can of tomato sauce on the grocer's shelf that was discolored, dented, and had a torn label. You'd probably pass it by for one that looked neat, fresh, and undamaged. Yet the contents of each can might be of exactly the same quality. Appearance does make a difference, even in the auto repair business. For just a few dollars more, your auto repair business can maintain a clean, professional appearance that tells prospects and customers that you offer quality.

First, make sure that all service vehicles are all well-painted and reasonably clean. This is vital if they have your business name written on them. One auto repair service owner purchased a spray can of paint that matched his older truck's paint and made sure that any job-site scrapes were quickly and easily covered. Another auto repair service owner paid his children a few dollars every Sunday afternoon to wash the truck.

Signage is important. Go to your local library and check the yellow pages in out-of-state phone books for auto repair service ads. Is there a design or insignia that appeals to you? Modify it to fit your own business and make it your design. Ask local sign shops to quote you a price for designing and making signs for you. You'll want signs on your vehicles, your shop, and your office. The only exception is a home office in a neighborhood that doesn't allow business signs.

A clean, well-painted service truck with an attractive business sign will typically stand out among the shabby and dirty vehicles parked there. It will tell your client and passersby that you own and manage a quality auto repair service that cares about its image.

Satisfaction guaranteed   Offering to refund all or a specific portion of a customer's bill if they are not satisfied with your work can be costly. It can also be a profitable investment when you are developing good customer relations. Of course, your customer supports this investment by paying slightly higher hourly rates, but most are willing to pay the difference for the assurance that the job will be done to their satisfaction. To reduce losses, simply don't take on any jobs that you can't guarantee.

Talk value   The question of charges always comes up with a client or prospect. Many auto repair service business owners dread it and would rather avoid the discussion. A successful business owner encourages the question of charges because he wants to talk about value. He wants the client to know why the client should pay as much or more for his services.

Price or charges is the *cost* of something. Value is the *worth* of something. Why is your service worth something? You are knowledgeable; you know about auto repair and how to manage difficult jobs. You are efficient; you know how to work smart to get the job done in less time. You are honest; you will not knowingly mislead your client or charge for services not performed. You are helpful; you want to solve the client's problem not just perform a job. You are fair; you charge a reasonable fee for an important service. You are accessible; you respond to questions, you answer telephone calls, you follow up with clients.

Successful auto repair services don't shun the question of charges or apologize for high rates. They look forward to the question so that they can explain why their service is worth more than that of other auto repair services. They sell—and give—value.

ESTIMATING A JOB

An estimate is a calculation of your value stated in dollars. Clients of your auto repair service, if not government agencies, will require written estimates. You must learn how to write job estimates that are accurate, fair, and profitable for both you and the client. There are forms that can help you estimate costs and value. There are also computer programs, discussed in Chapter 3, that automate the estimating process and print out auto repair estimates.

An estimate is simply a written offer to perform a job at a specified charge. An estimate might also be called a quote, a charge quotation, or a proposal. In each case, once the document is accepted and signed it is a legally binding document.

If you specialize in a segment of auto repair that doesn't have preprinted forms, you can modify available forms or develop one that can serve your specific requirements. You might want to incorporate the wording of your estimates into a computer word processing program so that you can develop and submit an estimate in the shortest time.

An estimate record is simply a written record of estimates prepared and submitted. It gives you the opportunity to track your success as an estimater, and to determine whether there are specific competitors that are taking too much business from you.

Types of estimates

Auto repair services different types of estimates, depending on the requirements of the customer and the marketplace. Here are the most common.

Time and material Labor is billed at hourly service rates established for each worker. Material is billed at the shop rate for that service. Overhead costs are built into the labor rates. Profit comes from the hourly service rates, as well as from the sale of parts (FIG. 4-3). Most repairs are charged this way.

Fixed price The total charge includes the cost of materials, labor, direct job expenses, prorated overhead costs, and profit. This method is used for jobs done frequently such as brake relining. Extra services needed are added to the fixed price.

Unit price The total charge is broken down into components: labor, job expenses, overhead, profit on units of material. This method is used to estimate jobs like wheel balancing.

Cost plus percentage The costs of materials, labor, and job expenses are reimbursed at actual cost, plus a percentage to cover overhead and profit. A cost-plus arrangement might be worked out with a fleet owner for full service on all vehicles.

Guaranteed maximum The total lump-sum charge with the assurance that, if final costs are under the limit, the savings will be split. A special arrangement could be made for a guaranteed maximum on an especially large repair job.

Labor only The auto repair service furnishes labor, tools, and equipment, and the customer furnishes parts. The labor charge includes the cost of labor, taxes/benefits, overhead, and profit. A very special customer might get this favored treatment (FIG. 4-4).

Most auto repair services use time and materials or unit price estimates for retail customers and cost plus percentage for fleet accounts. Labor only is sometimes used by rebuilding services.

After an estimate is accepted and signed by the customer, write a work order (FIG. 4-5) and have it signed by the customer.

123 Main Street, Yourtown USA

Date: June 30, 19xx

Quote # 4321

Client: Jake Jefferson

345 Valley Road

Yourtown USA 12345

234-7323

Materials

Quantity	Description	Cost Per Unit	Total
1	Muffler for 1984 Honda Accord	$64.00	$64.00
1	Tailpipe for 1984 Honda Accord	$48.00	$48.00
2	Muffler/Tailpipe Mounting Brackets for 1984 Honda Accord	$6.88	$13.76
		Total Cost:	$125.76

Labor

	Hours	Description	Cost Per Hour	Total
REGULAR	1.2	Install New Muffler and Tailpipe for 1984 Honda Accord	45	$54.00
OVERTIME				
			Total Cost:	$54.00

GRAND TOTAL $179.76

Authorized Signature   Date

4-3 Estimates or quotes include both estimated parts and labor charges.

123 Main Street, Yourtown

NUMBER
1234

DATE
June 30, 19xx

Proposal Submitted to:

NAME
Morgan Racing

ADDRESS
876 Main St.

CITY
Yourtown

STATE
USA

ZIP CODE
12345

Job Site Information:

JOB NAME
Formula 3 car

JOB LOCATION
ABC Auto Repair Service

JOB PHONE
234-6666

We hereby submit specifications and estimates for:

ABC Auto Repair Service shall store and maintain Morgan Racing's Formula 3 race car at 123 Main Street, Yourtown, and perform weekly high-performance tune-ups in preparation for Saturday afternoon racing at Broadway Motor Raceway. All work shall be done at the rate of $35 per hour plus parts. In addition, Morgan Racing shall include lettering on said car and other resources indicating that "ABC Auto Repair Service, Yourtown, 234-6666" is a co-sponsor of the car.

We hereby propose to furnish material and labor - complete in accordance with the above specifications for

_____ dollars $ _____

Payment to be made as follows:

Billed monthly; paid within 15 days of invoice.

All matter is guaranteed to be as specified. All work to be completed in a workmanlike manner according to standard practices. Any alternation or deviation from above specifications involving extra costs will be executed only upon written orders, and will become an extra charge over and above the estimate. All agreements contingent upon strikes, accidents, or delays beyond Our Company. Owner is to carry necessary insurance. Our Company workers are fully covered by Workman's Compensation Insurance.

Authorized Signature

X _____

Note: This proposal may be withdrawn
by us if not accepted within _____ days

Acceptance of Proposal. The above prices and specifications are satisfactory and hereby accepted. You are authorized to do the work as specified. Payment will be made as outlined above.

X _____
Signature

X _____
Signature

_____
Date of Acceptance

4-4 Larger service projects, such as fleet service, should be developed on a proposal.

123 Main Street, Yourtown USA 12345

CUSTOMER ORDER NUMBER
23456

NAME	LOCATION
Mary Cooper	Pick up at house; repair at shop; return to house
ADDRESS	TELEPHONE NUMBER
778 Canyon Road	234-4352
CITY / STATE / ZIP	DATE OF ORDER
Yourtown USA 12345	June 30, 19xx

JOB NUMBER	JOB NAME	JOB LOCATION
462	Transmission Service	Bay 4

DATE STARTED	TERMS	ORDER TAKEN BY
June 30, 19xx	Full payment on invoice	Bob

PARTS AND

Quantity	Description	Price	Amount
1	Transmission Filter	$28.45	$28.45
3	Transmission Fluid	$3.25	$9.75
1	Transmission Plate	$15.66	$15.66
		TOTAL MATERIALS	**$53.86**

SUBLET REPAIRS

Quantity	Sublet Repairs	Price	Amount
		TOTAL SUBLET	

LABOR

Hours	Labor	Rate	Amount
2	Transmission Service	$45.00	$90.00
		TOTAL LABOR	**$90.00**

Description of work done.
Service automatic transmission, adjust, and replace damaged plate

SUB TOTAL	$143.86
TAX %	
TOTAL	$143.86

WORK ORDER BY

I hereby acknowledge the satisfactory completion of work done.

4-5 Many states require a written work order to be signed by the customer before you perform the work.

Terms

How will you get paid for your job? That depends upon the terms that you offer in the estimate or upon the requirements of the estimater. Here are some common payment schedules: 100 percent due on completion of the work is most common and good for the shop; 50 percent at midpoint in the job and 50 percent on completion is better yet for the shop; 20 percent down with scheduled progress payments throughout the job (20 percent due when one quarter of the job is done, then at one half, three quarters, and completion) is best for major work. Billing the first of every month for work completed during the previous month is a good method for fleet accounts.

Rich Day, an experienced auto repair shop owner, advises not to give credit to anyone. His successful policy has been that the customer must pay in full when the repaired vehicle is picked up. If a vehicle is not picked up within 24 hours of when the vehicle is ready, he charges a storage fee. To make payment easier for the customer, be prepared to accept payment with Visa, MasterCard, Discover, American Express, and other credit cards. Insist on check-guarantee cards for any checks you receive. Once that car is out the door, says Rich, it's gone, and so is your money.

How many estimates will it take to get a job? This depends on many factors: your local market, economic conditions, your charges, the perceived value of your estimate, and the presentation of your estimate. Typically, one out of five estimates will probably come to a job. Based on this 20 percent factor, if you want sales of $200,000 in the coming year, you'd better write good estimates for about $1 million. Your factor might be higher or lower, but it's a good rule of thumb.

You can improve your percentage through good customer relations. The idea is to get customers to want *you* to do the job, with the cost, and even timing, of secondary importance.

YOUR SUCCESS ACTION LIST

In this chapter you've learned how and where to find the money you need to start your own successful auto repair service. You've also learned how to establish fair charges, and how to sell your services on value rather than price.

In Chapter 5, you'll learn how to keep track of the money you make. First, here's how to put this chapter into action. Complete the estimated start-up cost worksheet:

Estimated Operating Cost Worksheet

_____ Complete the estimated operating cost worksheet.

_____ Determine the total capital requirements of your new auto repair service business.

_____ List your assets and liabilities to determine your personal net worth.

_____ Make a list of financial resources that you might be able to use to develop start-up capital for your venture.

_____ Write out your responses to the five questions you'll need to answer to get a loan.

_____ Decide which of the numerous types of loan is most appropriate for your financial status.

_____ List any collateral you have for a loan.

_____ Contact your regional SBIC to determine whether they or other venture capitalists would be interested in participating in the funding of your auto repair service.

_____ Decide how much your auto repair service should charge for specific services or processes.

_____ List the ways you can sell value rather than price.

_____ Establish your quote system and the terms you will offer customers.

5
Keeping track
of your money

One of the problems faced by many otherwise successful auto repair business owners is how to keep track of the money they make. They're not sure if their business is profitable or not, or where their money is coming from or going to. You can solve this problem before you start by using the sample forms in this book and by considering a computer-based accounting system discussed earlier. An accurate and easy to maintain recordkeeping system can take away unnecessary frustration and give you time to do what you enjoy.

In this chapter, you'll discover the basics of setting up a good recordkeeping system, from entries through reports. You'll learn which reports can help you manage better and where to find them. Most important, you'll learn how to give your financial records a checkup by comparing them to standard ratios.

HOW TO KEEP TRACK OF YOUR MONEY

Why keep records? For many reasons. For the individual just starting an auto repair business, an adequate recordkeeping system helps increase the chance of survival and reduces the probability of early failure. In addition, established auto repair services can enhance their chances of staying in business and of earning increased profits with a good recordkeeping system.

How do good accounting records decrease the chances of failure and increase the likelihood of remaining in business and making a profit? Here are some of the things that good business records can tell you.

- How much business am I doing?
- How much credit am I extending?
- How much is tied up in receivables?
- How many of my receivables are more than 60, 90, or 120 days overdue?
- How are my collections?
- What are my losses from credit sales?
- Who owes me money?
- Should I continue extending credit to delinquent accounts?
- When can I anticipate realizing a return on my accounts receivable?

- How much cash do I have on hand?
- How much cash do I have in the bank?
- Does this amount agree with what records tell me I should have, or is there a shortage?
- What is my investment in materials?
- How often do I turn over my inventory?
- Have I allowed my inventory to become obsolete?
- How much do I owe my suppliers and other creditors?
- Have I received credit for returned materials?
- How much gross profit or margin did I earn?
- What were my expenses, including those not requiring cash outlays?
- What is my weekly payroll?
- Do I have adequate payroll records to meet the requirements of workers' compensation insurance, wage and hour laws, social security insurance, unemployment compensation insurance, and withholding taxes?
- How much net profit did I earn?
- How much income taxes do I owe?
- What is my capital?
- Are my sales, expenses, profits, and capital showing improvements or did I do better than this last year?
- How do I stand as compared with two periods ago?
- Is my business position about the same, improving, or deteriorating?
- On what services am I making a profit, breaking even, or losing money?
- Am I taking full advantage of cash discounts for prompt payments?
- How do my discounts taken compare with my discounts given?
- How do the financial facts of my auto repair business compare with those of similar businesses?

Get the point? Your business requires a good recordkeeping system to help you work smarter rather than harder.

Keeping accurate and up-to-date business records is, for many people, the most difficult and uninteresting aspect of operating a business. If this area of business management is one that you believe might be hard for you, plan now to handle this task. Don't wait until tax time or until you're totally confused. Take a course at a local community college, ask a volunteer SCORE representative, or hire an accountant to advise you about how to set up and maintaining you record-keeping system.

Your records will be used to prepare tax returns, make business decisions, and apply for loans. Set aside a special time each day to update your records. It will pay off in the long run with more deductions and fewer headaches.

What business expenses are deductible? There's a long list. The best answer is found in a free publication offered by the Internal Revenue Service, *Business Expenses*. Ask for Publication 535.

WHAT RECORDS YOU NEED TO KEEP

So what do you need for a good recordkeeping or accounting system. A good recordkeeping system should be simple to use, easy to understand, reliable, accurate, consistent, and timely.

There are several published systems and software systems that provide simplified records, usually in a single record book. These systems cover the primary records required for all businesses; some are modified specifically for the auto repair business. Check your local office supply store, your auto repair association, or advertisements in auto repair trade journals for more information on specialized record books.

A good recordkeeping system can identify the sources of your receipts, keep track of deductible expenses, figure depreciation allowances, record details of assets, determine earnings for self-employment tax purposes, and support items reported on tax returns.

Simply, your records should tell you these three facts and more: 1) how much cash you owe; 2) how much cash is owed to you; and 3) how much cash you have on hand. To keep track of everything, you should have five basic journals:

Check register or cash disbursements This record shows each check disbursed, the date of the disbursement, the number of the check, to whom it was made out (payee), the amount of money disbursed, and for what purpose (FIG. 5-1).

ABC Auto Repair Service
123 Main Street, Yourtown USA 12345

Cash Disbursements Register
PERIOD ENDING: June 30, 19xx

Date	Check Number	Account Number	Amount	Name
June 4	3456	6666	$221.34	Jones Auto Parts--May Parts
June 7	3457	9942	$1,721.43	Mack McLean--Payroll
June 13	3458	2123	$891.21	Internal Revenue Service--Estimated Taxes
June 19	3459	9827	$76.14	Petty Cash--Replenish Petty Cash Fund
June 25	3460	3260	$389.19	Bigtown Insurance Agency--Business Insurance
June 29	3461	1975	$192.20	Tools R Us--Equipment Lease
June 30	3462	1111	$2,156.60	Capital Draw--Owner's Salary

5-1 Cash Disbursements Register records cash outlays.

Cash receipts This journal shows the amount of money received, from whom, and for what (FIGS. 5-2 and 5-3).

General journal This record is for noncash transactions and those involving the owner's equity in the business.

Sales journal This journal shows each business transaction, the date, for whom it was performed, the amount of the invoice, what was charged for labor and what for materials, and any applicable sales tax.

Voucher register This journal records bills, money owed, the date of the bill, to whom it is owed, the amount, and the service performed.

In addition, here are other records you will need to keep for your business:

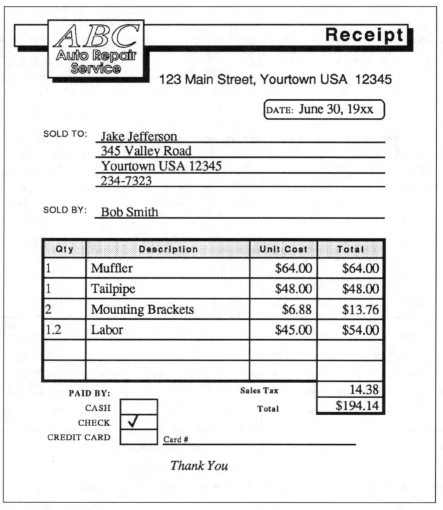

5-2 Receipt for work done.

ABC Auto Repair Service

123 Main Street, Yourtown USA 12345

PERIOD ENDING: June 30, 19xx

Date	Check Number	Account Number	Amount	Name
June 27	4432	9876	$129.43	Bob Franklin--Tune-up, Lube
June 27	Cash	3229	$45.11	Margie Smith--Lube, Oil Change
June 27	502	9832	$437.55	Jim Varney--Replace Clutch
June 28	1123	3104	$128.98	Bigtown Motors--On Account
June 28	421	9834	$764.19	Monte Johnson--Short Block Replacement
June 28	876	2410	$45.00	Bill Jackson--Diagnostics
June 29	Cash	2109	$232.10	Nancy Jones--Towing and Repair
June 29	1145	1899	$39.15	Bev Smith--Lube, Oil Change
June 29	565	9754	$200.00	Al's Transmissions--On Account
June 30	887	3264	$598.00	Coast Trucking--Valve Job
June 30	Cash	4309	$189.00	Mark Unger--Towing and Repair

5-3 Cash Receipts Register records cash payments.

Accounts receivable This is the record of accounts on which you will receive money because you have sold your customers something for which they haven't paid.

Accounts payable This is the record of accounts on which you have to pay money because you have purchased a product or service for which you haven't paid.

Inventory This is a record of your firm's investment in parts or materials that you intend to resell (FIG. 5-4).

Equipment This is a record of your firm's investment in equipment that you will use to provide your service and will not normally resell.

Payroll This is a record of the wages paid employees and the deductions taken for income, FICA, and other taxes, as well as other payroll deductions.

Some businesses combine all of these journals into a single journal. In fact, there are many good "one write" systems available that allow you to make a single entry for each transaction. We'll cover them in a moment.

SINGLE-ENTRY VS. DOUBLE-ENTRY RECORDING

Two ways to record business transactions are single entry or double entry. The primary advantage to single-entry recordkeeping is that it is easy. As the name implies,

123 Main Street, Yourtown USA

Date	June 30, 19xx
Page 4	of 4

Department : Service

Location : Shop

Item#	Qty	Description	Price	Total
89345	120	Penzoil 10-40	$1.25	$150.00
89333	84	Penzoil 20-50	$1.30	$109.20
88444	12	AC Oil Filters #22-8765	$2.45	$29.40
88555	8	AC Oil Filters, #23-9876	$2.60	$20.80
87666	3	AC Fuel Filters, #44-1234	$3.10	$9.30
			TOTAL	1848.96

Priced By: Bob Smith	Called By: Ed Jones
Checked By:	Entered By:

5-4 Inventory Sheet records inventory assets.

you make a single entry that records the source of each income or the destination of each expense. Each entry is either a plus or a minus to the amount of cash that you have. Receipt of a check on an outstanding account is a plus. Payment of a parts order is a minus. As long as you have a limited number of transactions, single-entry accounting is adequate.

But as your business grows in complexity, you will want a check-and-balance system that ensures that records are accurate. Double-entry accounting requires that you make two offsetting entries that balance each other. A check received on an outstanding account is a debit to Cash and a credit to Accounts Receivable. Payment for a parts order is a debit to Parts Expense and a credit to Cash.

Every account has two sides: a left or debit side and a right or credit side. The posted debits must always equal the posted credits. Some types of accounts are called debit accounts because their balance is typically a debit. Asset accounts (cash, accounts receivable) are debit accounts. Liability accounts (accounts payable, notes payable) usually carry a credit balance. Income carries a credit balance while expenses carry a debit balance. Everything else within double-entry bookkeeping is based on the above rules. Here are some examples of common double entries:

- cash income = debit cash and credit income
- accrued income = debit accounts receivable and credit income
- cash expense = debit the expense account and credit cash
- accrued expense = debit the expense account and credit accounts payable
- prepaid expense = debit prepaid expenses and credit cash.

If, at the end of the month, the debits don't equal the credits, check for debits erroneously posted as credits, credits erroneously posted as debits, transposition of numbers (123 to 132), and incorrect math.

A double-entry accounting system on a computer, such as AccPac or DacEasy, will do this automatically for you. Single-entry systems such as *Quicken* and *Manage your Money* work well, too. Bookkeeping becomes almost fun.

ASSETS, LIABILITIES, AND NET WORTH

Assets include not only cash, inventory, land, building, equipment, machinery, furniture, and the like, but also money due from individuals or other businesses (known as accounts or notes receivable).

Liabilities are funds acquired for a business through loans or the purchase of property or services by the business on credit. Creditors do not acquire ownership in your business, but promissory notes to be paid at a designated future date (known as accounts or notes payable).

Net worth (or shareholders' equity or capital) is money put into a business by its owners or left in it as retained earnings for use by the business to acquire assets. The formula for this structure is:

$$\text{assets} = \text{liabilities} + \text{net worth}$$

That is, the total funds invested in assets of the business is equal to the funds supplied to the business by its creditors plus the funds supplied to the business by its owners, plus retained earnings. If a business owes more money to creditors than it possesses in value of assets owned and retained earnings, the net worth or owner's equity of the business will be a negative number. This is not a desirable situation. This accounting formula can also be expressed as:

$$\text{assets} - \text{liabilities} = \text{net worth}$$

BANK ACCOUNTS

As noted earlier, establish a separate bank account for your business before your first sale. Then you will have a complete and distinct record of your income and expenditures for tax purposes, and you won't have to remember which expenses were business and which were personal. In no case should business and personal funds be mingled.

CASH OR ACCRUAL METHOD

Many small businesses operate primarily on a cash basis. The customer buys products with cash, the merchant buys inventory with cash or short-term credit. As businesses become larger and more complicated, many keep records on the accrual basis. The dividing line between cash basis and accrual basis might depend on whether or not credit is given to customers as well as the amount of inventory required.

Accrual basis is "a method of recording income and expenses in which each item is reported as earned or incurred, without regard to when actual payments are received or made." Charge sales are credited at once to sales and charged to accounts receivable. When the bills are collected, the credit is to accounts receivable. Accruals should also be made for larger expense items payable in the future, such as annual or semi-annual interest on loans.

If you're comfortable with accounting, accrual can be the most accurate basis for records. But the cash basis is easiest to understand. As long as you don't prepay many of your expenses and are not incorporated, a cash basis is fine for your new auto repair business.

KEEPING A JOURNAL

All businesses that do not use computer accounting systems need some form of journal or book where all business transactions can be recorded. Information for each transaction or journal entry is derived from original source documents: check stubs, invoices, statements, credit vouchers, purchase orders, expense records and receipts, etc.

A general ledger is kept to record transactions and balances of individual accounts: assets, liabilities, capital, income, and expenses.

At the end of each fiscal year or accounting period, accounts are balanced and closed. Income and expense account balances are transferred to the Summary of Revenue and Expenses and are used to make the Income Statement. The remaining asset, liability, and capital accounts provide figures that are included on the Balance Sheet.

How many accounts should your business have? Not so many as to make analysis confusing. Break down sales into enough categories to show a clear picture of the sources of your business income. Use different expense accounts to cover frequent or substantial expenditures, but avoid minor distinctions that will tend to confuse rather than qualify. Use miscellaneous expense for small unrelated items.

ACCOUNTS RECEIVABLE

Income not paid to you is called accounts receivable. If you do not insist on payment in cash from customers, here are a few rules that can help you keep your accounts receivable current. First, be sure bills are prepared immediately after the service is performed. And make sure that a statement is mailed to the correct person and address with sufficient information on the statement to fully identify the source and purpose of the charge. Note that some businesses simply set aside any bills that they question.

At the end of each month, "age" your accounts receivable. That is, list accounts and enter the amounts that are current, unpaid for 30 days, and those 60 days and older. In fact, most accounts receivable computer programs can produce reports on aged receivables. Then call each account in the 60+ days column and find out why the bill is unpaid. Keep an especially close watch on larger accounts.

To ensure that you get paid promptly, pay close attention to customers' complaints about bills. If a complaint is justified, offer an adjustment and reach an agreement with the customer. Then get a date from the customer as to when you can expect to receive the payment.

If you do give credit, ask each new customer who asks for credit to complete a simple form listing name, address, telephone number, employment, bank and credit references. Such credit application forms (FIG. 5-5) are available at many office supply and stationery stores. A sample is produced in the appendix. Make sure the customer is worthy of credit before you grant it.

One more tip. If you will advertise to sell your services on credit ("No money down with no interest for 6 months.") order *How to Advertise Consumer Credit*— (018-000-00334-1) from the Superintendent of Documents, United States Government Printing Office, Washington, DC 20402; cost: $2.

MANAGING PAYROLL RECORDS

Quarterly and yearly reports of individual payroll payments must be made to federal and state governments. Each individual employee must receive a W-2 form after the end of the calendar year that shows total withholding payments made for the employee during the previous year.

A payroll summary should be made each payday for each employee that shows the name, employee number, rate of pay, hours worked, overtime hours, total pay, and amount of deductions for FICA (social security insurance), medicare insurance, state and federal withholding taxes, deductions for insurance, pension, savings, and child support, as required. In addition, if your business employs union members, you might have additional deductions for union dues, pensions, and other fees.

To ensure that you maintain adequate records for this task, keep an employee card for each of your employees. The employee card or computer file should show the employee's full legal name, social security number, insurance number, address, telephone number, name of next of kin and their address, marital status, number of exemptions claimed, and current rate of pay. Attach the federal W-4 form completed and signed by the employee to the employee card or record.

Also maintain a running total of earnings, pay and deductions for each individual employee. To begin your payroll system, contact the Internal Revenue Service, Washington, DC 20224 and request the *Employer's Tax Guide (Circular E)*. Also apply for a nine-digit Employer Identification Number (EIN). The IRS will send you deposit slips (Form 8109) with your new EIN number printed on them. Use these deposit slips each time you pay payroll taxes. Payroll taxes are paid within a month of the end of a quarter. Quarters end January 31, April 30, July 31, and October 31. As your business grows, you might be required to pay payroll taxes more frequently. Ask your accountant to help you determine your needs and the process.

ABC
Auto Repair
Service

123 Main Street, Yourtown USA

DATE: June 30, 19xx

BUSINESS INFORMATION		DESCRIPTION OF BUSINESS		
NAME OF BUSINESS Tom's Car Sales		NO. OF EMPLOYEES 2	CREDIT REQUESTED 2000.00	TYPE OF BUSINESS Auto Sales

LEGAL (IF DIFFERENT)

IN BUSINESS SINCE 1987

ADDRESS 345 Main Street

BUSINESS STRUCTURE
- ☐ CORPORATION ☐ PARTNERSHIP ☑ PROPRIETORSHIP
- ☐ DIVISION/SUBSIDIARY
  NAME OF PARENT
  COMPANY _____
  HOW LONG IN BUSINESS _____

CITY Yourtown

STATE USA **ZIP** 12345 **PHONE** 234-5678

COMPANY PRINCIPALS RESPONSIBLE FOR BUSINESS TRANSACTIONS

NAME :	TITLE:	ADDRESS:	PHONE:
Tom Franklin	Owner	999 9th St., Yourtown	234-8765
NAME:	TITLE:	ADDRESS:	PHONE:
NAME:	TITLE:	ADDRESS:	PHONE:

BANK REFERENCES

NAME OF BANK Bank of Yourtown	NAME TO CONTACT Betty Johnson
BRANCH Uptown	ADDRESS 456 Main Street, Yourtown
CHECKING ACCOUNT NO. 3456-7890	TELEPHONE NUMBER 234-4321

TRADE REFERENCES

FIRM NAME	CONTACT NAME	TELEPHONE NUMBER	ACCOUNT OPEN SINCE
Mack's Auto Parts	Mack Smith	234-9876	1989
State Wholesale Cars	Mary Rivers	992-7654	1990
Yourtown Stationery	Joe Johnson	234-7654	1992

CONFIRMATION OF INFORMATION ACCURACY AND RELEASE OF AUTHORITY TO VERIFY

I hereby certify that the information in this credit application is correct. The information included in this credit application is for use by he above firm in determining the amount and conditions of credit to be extended. I understand that this firm may also utilize the other sources of credit which it considers necessary in making this determination. Further I hereby authorize the bank and trade references listed in this credit application to release the information necessary to assist this firm in establishing a line of credit.

X_____
SIGNATURE

_____
TITLE

June 30, 19xx
DATE

POLICY STATEMENT: INITIAL ORDER FROM NEW ACCOUNTS WILL NOT BE PROCESSED UNLESS ACCOMPANIED BY THE ABOVE REQUESTED INFORMATION.
TERMS: NET 30 DAYS FROM DATE OF INVOICE UNLESS OTHERWISE STATED.

5-5 A Credit Application lets you qualify your customers.

Rather than handle your payroll, you can turn it over to a payroll service. For a fee, the service saves you time and ensures that all government regulations and deadlines are met. Remember, though, that you are ultimately responsible for your payroll records, not the payroll service.

PETTY CASH FUND

Most auto repair business expenses are paid by business check, credit card, or placed on account with the seller. However, there might be some small expenses that will be paid by an employee or with cash that requires reimbursement. Because the amount is typically small, the fund from which the reimbursement comes is usually known as petty cash.

Set up a revolving petty cash fund to be used for payments of small charges that are not covered by invoices. Draw a check for, say, $100. Cash the check and place the money in a box or drawer. When you make small cash payments for items such as postage, freight, or bus fares, list the items on an invoice or receipt and take out the money. When the fund is nearly exhausted, summarize the items and draw a check to cover the exact amount spent. Cash the check and replenish the fund. At all times, the cash in the drawer plus the listed expenditures should equal the established amount of the petty cash fund. A sample petty cash register is included in this book's appendix.

EQUIPMENT RECORDS

Keep an accurate and up-to-date list of the permanent equipment you use in your auto repair business. It is especially important that you keep track of equipment used for a year or longer and of appreciable value. Equipment records should show the purchase date, the name of the supplier, a description of the item, the check number, the number of payment(s), and the amount of the purchase including tax. If you own a number of items, keep a separate list for vehicles, tools and related work equipment, and office furniture and fixtures. From these records you can develop depreciation and provide supporting information for fixed asset accounts.

A note about depreciation: a charge to expenses should be made to cover depreciation of fixed assets other than land. Fixed assets are any item you purchase to use in your business for a year or longer. Examples are buildings, vehicles, tools, equipment, furniture, and office fixtures. Smaller businesses usually charge depreciation at the end of their fiscal year, but if your business grows and you have major fixed assets, you or your accountant might decide to calculate depreciation monthly.

As clarification, a calendar year is 12 consecutive months beginning January 1 and ending December 31. A fiscal year is 12 consecutive months ending on the last day of any month other than December. A short tax year is less than 12 months because your firm was not in business a full year or you have changed your tax year.

INSURANCE RECORDS

Insurance helps safeguard your business against losses from fire, illness, injury, liability, and other hazards. You cannot operate without it. Your auto repair business must have several types of insurance. Keep a list of each policy. Include the type of insurance coverage (automotive, fire, theft, bonding, etc.), the name of the insurance company, the expiration date, the premiums (monthly and annual) and the agent's name, address, and phone number. Keep all of your insurance policies in one file, or in separate files according to the type of policy. In addition to fire, theft, and hazard insurance, some of the most common types of business insurance are listed below.

- Liability coverage protects you in case a service you perform leads to an injury of the user or damage to a customer's vehicle.
- Auto liability insurance covers any vehicle that you use in your business in any way.
- Medical payment insurance pays if someone is injured while at your place of business.
- Workers' compensation insurance covers people who work for you in case of an on-the-job injury.
- Business interruption insurance covers you in case your business is damaged by fire, flood, or some other hazard that requires that you totally or partially suspend operation.
- Disability income protection is a form of health insurance that covers you if you become disabled.
- Business life insurance provides funds for transition if you die.

Be sure to keep all of your insurance records and policies in a safe place, either with your accountant or in a safe deposit box at your bank. If you keep them in your office for convenience, give your policy numbers and insurance company names to your accountant or attorney or put them in your safe deposit box.

OUTSIDE ACCOUNTING SERVICES

Many new auto repair services have the right skills to ply their trade, yet fail because of poor financial management. Sometimes the best decision is to hire the services of a public accounting firm. An accountant can design records, set up ways to maintain them, draw off vital information, and help relate that information to a profitable operation.

Daily bits of information will flow into your auto repair business. As customers are served, pieces of information are generated about sales, cash, equipment, purchase expenses, payroll, accounts payable, and, if credit is offered to customers, accounts receivable.

To capture these facts and figures, a system is necessary. If you don't feel comfortable setting up and managing such a system, don't be shy about hiring an accounting service. An accountant can help design a system to record the information that you need to control finances and make profitable decisions.

Once a system of records is set up, the question is: Who should keep the books? The accounting service who has set up the books might keep them. However, if you have a general understanding of recordkeeping you can do them yourself and save some money. Ask your accountant to check and analyze your records. After your business grows, you might consider hiring someone to keep your records and perform other office functions. Or maybe your spouse can assist you.

In addition to recordkeeping, an accountant can advise you on financial management. He or she can provide you with cash flow requirements, budget forecasts, borrowing, business organization, and tax information.

Using a cash flow forecast, as shown in Chapter 7, an accountant can help you work out the amount of cash you will need to operate your firm for a specific period, for example, 3 months, 6 months, the next year. He or she considers how much cash you will need to carry customer accounts receivable, to buy equipment and parts, to pay current bills, and to repay loans. In addition, an accountant can determine how much cash will come from the collection of accounts receivable and how much will have to be borrowed or pulled from an existing line of credit. While working out the cash requirements, your accountant might notice and call your attention to danger spots such as accounts that are past due.

When you borrow, your accountant can assemble financial information such as a profit-and-loss (or income) statement and a balance sheet (FIG. 5-6). The purpose of such data is to show the lender the financial position of your business and its ability to repay the loan. Using this information, your accountant can advise you on whether you need a short-term or long-term loan. The financial data that your accountant compiles might include: assets you will offer for collateral, your current

Balance Sheet

Cash	$ 1,896	Notes payable, bank	$	2,000
Accounts receivable	1,456	Accounts payable		2,240
Inventory	6,822	Accruals		940
Total current assets	$ 10,174	Total current liabilities	$	5,180
Equipment and fixtures	1,168	Total liabilities	$	5,180
Prepaid expenses	1,278	Net worth		7,440
Total assets	$ 12,620	Total liabilities and		
		net worth	$	12,620

Income Statement

	Dollars	Percent
Net sales	$ 68,116	100.0
Cost of services	47,696	70.0
Gross profit on sales	$ 20,420	30.0
Expenses		
Wages	$ 6,948	10.2
Shop expense	954	1.4
Bad debts allowance	409	0.6
Communications	204	0.3
Depreciation allowance	409	0.6
Insurance	613	0.9
Taxes	1,021	1.5
Advertising	1,566	2.3
Interest	409	0.6
Other charges	749	1.1
Total expenses	13,282	19.5
Net profit	$ 7,138	10.5
Other income	886	1.3
Total net income	$ 8,024	11.8

5-6 These are a typical Balance Sheet and Income Statement.

debt obligations, a summary of how you will use the money you borrow, and a schedule of how you intend to repay the money borrowed.

If you have never borrowed before, your accountant might help you by introducing you to a banker who knows and respects the accountant's reputation. This, alone, might be worth the cost of hiring an accountant to advise and help you.

Taxes are another area in which an accountant can contribute advice and assistance. Normally, a recordkeeping system that provides the information you need to make profitable decisions will suffice for tax purposes. However, if you purchase a lot of equipment that requires special depreciation, have employees that handle cash or require payroll taxes, and have extensive bad debts, a good accountant can help you identify the problems, suggest a method for keeping good records, and help you minimize your tax obligation by "writing off" bad debts as a business expense.

FINANCIAL REPORTS

As the owner of an auto repair firm, you need accurate information on a regular basis to ensure that your business runs smoothly. As a single-person firm you might have all the information you need in your head. But as your firm grows you might need some information daily, other information weekly, and still other data on a monthly basis. Let's take a look at what you might need and when.

Daily reports

In order to manage your auto repair firm, you will want the following information on a daily basis: cash on hand, bank balance, daily summary of sales and cash receipts, daily summary of monies paid out by cash or check, and corrections of any errors from previous reports.

You can either prepare this information yourself, have your office employee prepare it for you, or rely on your accountant. While daily records will not show you trends, they can help you get a feel for the level of business that you're doing. And you'll be able to spot problems before they become serious.

Weekly reports

Once a week, you or someone in your employ should prepare a weekly report on your firm. While still not sufficient for long-term planning, weekly figures can help you make small corrections in the course your business is taking. These are the reports you'll want each week.

- An Accounts Receivable report that lists accounts that require a call because they are more than 60 days overdue.
- An Accounts Payable report that lists what your business owes, to whom, and if a discount is offered for early payment.
- A Payroll report that includes information on each employee, the number of hours each worked during the week, rate of pay, total wages, deductions, net pay, and related information.

- A Tax report that must be sent to city, state, and federal governments.

Your weekly reports should be prepared by the end of business Friday so you can review them over the weekend or early Monday morning.

Monthly reports

Once a month you will want to review a number of pieces of information that were too small to analyze by the day or week. Information about cash flow, accounts receivable, and other parts of your business make more sense, and can be more easily acted upon, with figures accumulated over a month's time. Below are some of the reports and information you will want to see every month.

- A general ledger that includes all journal entries.
- An income statement that shows income for the prior month, expenses incurred to obtain the income, overhead, and the profit or loss received.
- A balance sheet that shows the assets, liabilities, and capital or current worth of the business.
- A reconciled bank statement that shows what checks were deposited, which were applied by payees against your business checking account, and verifies that the cash balance is accurate.
- A petty cash fund report to ensure that paid-out slips plus cash equals the beginning petty cash balance.
- A tax payment report that shows that all federal tax deposits, withheld income, FICA taxes, state and other taxes have been paid.
- An aged receivables report that shows the age and balance of each account (30, 60, 90 days, past due, etc.).

RECORDKEEPING SYSTEMS

There are numerous commercial recordkeeping systems available through local office suppliers, stationers, and auto repair supply firms. Below are a few systems designed specifically for auto repair services:

Columbia Bookkeeping System for Garages
2 Central Square
Gafton, MA 01519

Dome Simplified Records
Dome Building
Providence, RI 02903

Marcoin Business Services for Garage and Auto Repair
1924 Cliff Valley Way NE
Atlanta, GA 30329

McBee Systems for Garage and Auto Repair
151 Cortlandt St.
Belleville, NJ 07109

Safeguard Business Systems for Garage or Auto Repair
470 Maryland Dr.
Fort Washington, PA 19034

Shaw/Walker for Garage or Auto Repair
57 E. Willow St.
Millburn, NJ 07041

Simplified Master Systems: Garage or Auto Repair
233 E. Lancaster Ave.
Ardmore, PA 19003

YOUR BALANCE SHEET

Your balance sheet is a summary of the status of your business—its assets, liabilities, and net worth—at an instant in time. By reviewing your balance sheet along with your income statement and your cash flow statement, you will be able to make informed financial and business planning decisions.

The balance sheet is drawn up using the totals from individual accounts kept in your general ledger. It shows what you have left when you pay all your creditors. Remember assets less liabilities equal capital or net worth. The assets and liabilities sections must balance, hence the name balance sheet. This report can be produced quarterly, semi-annually, or at the end of each calendar or fiscal year. If your record-keeping system is manual you will be less likely to update frequently your balance sheet. Many accounting software programs can give you a current balance sheet in just a couple of minutes.

While your accountant can draw up your balance sheet, you must understand it. Current assets are anything of value you own such as cash, inventory, or property that the business owner can convert into cash within a year. Fixed assets are things such as vehicles, equipment, and real estate. Liabilities are debts the business must pay. They might be current, such as amounts owed to suppliers or your accountant, or they might be long-term, such as a note owed to the bank. Capital, also called equity or net worth, is the amount of assets and retained earnings you have after you subtract your liabilities.

YOUR INCOME STATEMENT

The income statement is a detailed, month-by-month tally of your income from sales and the expenses incurred to generate those sales. It is a good assessment tool because it shows the effect of your decisions on profits. It is a good planning tool because you can estimate the impact of decisions on profit before you make them. Your income statement includes four kinds of information.

- Sales information lists the total revenues generated by the sale of your service to clients.
- Direct expenses include the cost of labor and materials to perform your service.
- Indirect expenses are the costs you have even if you have no customers, including salaries, rent, utilities, insurance, depreciation, office supplies, taxes, and professional fees.

- Profit is shown as pre-tax income (important to the IRS) and after-tax or net income (important to you and your loan officer).

YOUR CASH-FLOW STATEMENT

Your business must have a healthy cash flow to survive. Cash flow is the amount of money available to your business at any given time. To keep tabs on cash flow, forecast the funds you expect to disburse and receive over a specific time. Then you can predict deficient or surplus cash and decide how best to respond.

A cash-flow projection serves another useful purpose in addition to planning. As the actual information becomes available to you, compare it to the monthly cash-flow estimates you previously made to see how accurately you are at estimating. This can help you make more accurate estimates and plans for the coming months. As your ability to estimate improves, your financial control of your business will increase.

PROFITABLY MANAGING CASH

If your auto repair business is a "one-man band," you'll have no problem with one of the greatest enemies of business: employee theft. However, as your business grows and you hire others to handle some of your tasks, you will need to manage them to ensure that employee theft doesn't become a major problem. The following are some ideas for handling cash and checks within your business.

- The person who handles your cash receipts shouldn't be the person who makes bank deposits. Cash is misappropriated too easily. Don't tempt an employee by letting him or her handle both of these duties.
- Deposit your daily cash receipts in the bank each day.
- Set up and use a petty cash fund and voucher system for small cash outlays.
- For the same reason, the person who writes the checks should not also sign them or have the authority to sign them. Whenever checks are signed, the signer should view the bill being paid and then write the check number on the bill.
- Use only numbered checks and maintain records of all canceled or voided checks.
- The monthly bank reconciliation should be done by the owner or an outside accountant.

Remember that human error is more common than dishonesty, but that both can damage your business. Employee theft can be minimized by setting your business up to eliminate the opportunity and temptation.

WHAT TAXES YOU HAVE TO PAY

Like it or not, the government is your business partner. And, as your partner, they receive a portion of your profits, even before you do. However, government can also help you make a profit through the Small Business Administration (SBA), Department of Commerce, state corporate divisions, and numerous other business services.

The owner-manager of a small business plays two roles when managing taxes. In one role, you are a debtor. In the other, an agent or tax collector.

As a debtor you are liable for various taxes and you pay them as part of your business obligations. For example, each year you owe federal income taxes that you pay out of your business earnings. Other tax debts include state income taxes and real estate taxes.

As an agent you collect various taxes and pass the funds on to the appropriate government agency. If you have employees, you deduct federal income, social security insurance or FICA taxes, and in some states you collect state income taxes from the wages of your employees. If your state requires sales tax on parts sold by your auto repair business, you can collect it from your customers.

If you are a proprietor, you pay your income tax as any other individual citizen. Your income, expenses, and profit or loss are calculated on IRS Schedule C that is filed with your annual Form 1040. A partnership files its own tax forms and passes the profits on to the partners for filing on their personal income tax forms. A corporation files IRS Form 1120 or 1120A (short form).

Individual proprietors and partners are required by law to put the federal income tax and self-employment tax liability on a pay-as-you-go basis. That is, you file a *Declaration of Estimated Tax* (Form 1040 ES) on or before April 15, then make payments on April 15, June 15, September 15, and January 15.

Corporate income tax returns are due on the 15th of the third month following the end of its taxable year, which might or might not coincide with the calendar year. To find out more about your tax obligations, contact your regional IRS office or call 1-800-829-3676 for the following publications:

- *Tax Guide for Small Business* (Publication 334)
- *Guide to Free Tax Services* (Publication 910)
- *Your Federal Income Tax* (Publication 17)
- *Employer's Tax Guide* (Circular E)
- *Taxpayers Starting a Business* (Publication 583)
- *Self-Employment Tax* (Publication 533)
- *Retirement Plans for the Self-Employed* (Publication 560)
- *Tax Withholding and Estimated Tax* (Publication 505)
- *Business Use of Your Home* (Publication 587)

In addition, there are a number of federal forms you'll need for good record-keeping and accurate taxation:

- *Application for Employer Identification Number* (Form SS-4) if you have employees
- *Tax Calendars* (Publication 509)
- *Employer's Annual Unemployment Tax Return* (Form 940)
- *Employer's Quarterly Federal Tax Return* (Form 941)
- *Employee's Withholding Allowance Certificate* (W-4) for each employee
- *Employer's Wage and Tax Statement* (W-2) for each employee
- *Reconciliation/Transmittal of Income and Tax Statements* (W-3)
- *Instructions for Forms 1120* and *1120-A* for corporate taxes.

KEEPING YOUR BUSINESS ON BUDGET

Managing your auto repair business requires that you manage your business budget so you can continue to provide service, support, and employment to others as well as a profit to yourself. When you first start your business, you establish a preliminary budget. After your business is operating, you must establish an operating budget.

A budget is a forecast of all cash sources and cash expenditures. It is organized in the same format as a financial statement, and most commonly covers a 12-month period. At the end of the year, the anticipated income and expenses projected in the budget are compared to the actual performance of the business as recorded in the financial statement.

A budget greatly enhances your chance of success by helping you estimate future needs and plan profits, spending, and overall cash flow. A budget allows you to detect problems before they occur and to alter your plans to prevent those problems.

In business, budgets help you determine how much money you have and how you will use it, as well as help you decide whether you have enough money to achieve your financial goals. As part of your business plan, a budget helps convince a loan officer that you know your business and have anticipated its needs.

A budget indicates the cash required for necessary labor and materials, day-to-day operating costs, revenue needed to support business operations, and expected profit. If your budget indicates that you need more revenue than you can earn, you can adjust your plans by:

- reducing expenditures (hire fewer employees, purchase less expensive furniture, eliminate a telephone line);
- expanding sales (offer additional services, conduct an aggressive marketing campaign, hire a salesperson); or
- lowering profit expectations (not my first choice!).

A budget has three main elements: sales revenue, total costs, and profit.

Sales revenue Sales are the cornerstone of a budget. It is crucial that you estimate anticipated sales as accurately as possible. Base your estimates on actual past sales figures. Once you target sales, calculate the related expenses necessary to achieve your goals.

Total costs Total costs include fixed and variable costs. Estimating costs is complicated because you must identify which costs might change, and by how much, and which costs will remain unchanged as sales increase. You must also consider inflation and rising prices as appropriate.

Variable costs are those that vary directly with sales. The price of parts is an example of a variable cost for your auto repair business. Fixed costs are those that don't change regardless of sales volume. Rent is considered a fixed cost, as is an equipment lease. Semi-variable costs, such as office salaries, labor wages, and telephone expenses, have both variable and fixed components. For example, telephone line charges are listed as fixed expenses and long distance telephone charges are listed as variable expenses.

Profit Your profit should be large enough to make a return on your cash investment and a return on your work. Your investment is the money you put into the firm when you started it and the profit from prior years that you have left in the firm (retained earnings). If you can receive 10 percent interest on $25,000 by investing outside of your business, then you should expect a similar return when you invest $25,000 in equipment and other assets in your business. When you target profits, make sure you receive a fair return on your labor. Your weekly paycheck should reflect what you could be earning elsewhere as an employee.

ESTABLISHING AN OPERATING BUDGET

When you develop your budget, work with the basic budget equation:

$$sales = total\ costs + profit$$

This equation shows that every sales dollar you receive is partly of a recovery of your costs and partly of profit. Another way to express the basic budgeting equation is:

$$sales - total\ costs = profit$$

This equation shows that, after reimbursing yourself for the cost of producing your service, the remaining part of the sales dollar is profit. For example, if you expect $1000 for a specific job and you know that it will cost $900 to market and perform this service, your profit will be $100.

When you calculate your operating budget, make estimates based on past sales and cost figures. Adjust these figures to reflect price increases, inflation, and other factors. For example, for the past three years, an auto repair service spent an average of $3500 on advertising. For the coming year, the owner expects a price increase of 3 percent (0.03). To calculate the cost of next year's advertising, the owner multiplies the average annual advertising cost by the percentage price increase ($3500 × 0.03 = $105) and adds that amount to the original annual cost ($3500 + $105 = $3605). A shortcut method is to multiply the original advertising cost by one plus the rate of increase ($3500 × 1.03 = $3605).

If your auto repair business is a new venture and has no past financial records, rely on your own experience and knowledge of the industry to estimate demand for and costs of your service. Your accountant or trade association might be able to help you develop realistic estimates.

THE BUDGETING PROCESS

Before you create an operating budget, answer these three questions.

- How much net profit do you realistically want your business to generate during the calendar year?
- How much will it cost to produce that profit?
- How much sales revenue is necessary to support both profit and cost requirements?

To answer these questions, consider expected sales and all costs, either direct or indirect, that are associated with your auto repair service. To make safe estimates, most companies prefer to overestimate expenses and underestimate sales revenue.

Start constructing your budget with either a forecast of sales or a forecast of profits. For practical purposes, most small businesses start with a forecast of profits. In other words, decide what profit you realistically want to make and then list the expenses you will incur to make that profit.

The steps to creating an operating budget are: target desired profit, determine operating expenses, calculate gross profit margin, estimate sales revenues, and adjust figures.

A sample operating budget for ABC Auto Repair Service (TABLES 5-1 through 5-3) illustrates the main steps to budget preparation. As you follow the steps, calculate all the figures yourself. Once you have calculated projected sales, expenses, and profits, organize the figures in a readable format.

Table 5-1   Business budget for a three-year period.

	Year 1	Year 2	Year 3	Total	Average	Average percent of sales
Sales	$490,000	$508,333	$513,233	$1,511,566	$503,855	100
Cost of goods sold	$343,000	$355,833	$359,263	$1,058,096	$352,698	70
Gross profit margin	$147,000	$152,500	$153,970	$453,470	$151,157	30
Operating expenses:						
Advertising	$3,200	$3,700	$3,600	$10,500	$3,500	0.7
Depreciation	$4,000	$4,000	$4,000	$12,000	$4,000	0.8
Insurance	$1,700	$1,700	$1,700	$5,100	$1,700	0.3
Legal and accounting expenses	$3,400	$3,605	$3,800	$10,805	$3,602	0.7
Office expenses	$2,200	$2,400	$2,650	$7,250	$2,417	0.5
Rent	$24,000	$24,000	$24,000	$72,000	$24,000	4.8
Repair and maintenance	$300	$550	$420	$1,270	$424	0.1
Salaries	$33,000	$33,000	$33,000	$99,000	$33,000	6.6
Telephone and utilities	$6,000	$6,350	$6,200	$18,550	$6,183	1.2
Miscellaneous	$9,200	$8,195	$10,300	$27,695	$9,231	1.8
Total operating expenses	$87,000	$87,500	$89,670	$264,170	$88,057	17.5
Net profit	$60,000	$65,000	$64,300	$199,330	$63,100	12.5

Table 5-2   Establishing a year's budget.

	Amount ($)	Percent of sales
Sales	533,730	100
Cost of services	373,611	70
Gross profit margin	160,119	30
Operating expenses:		
Advertising	3,605	0.7
Depreciation	4,000	0.8
Insurance	4,100	0.8
Legal and accounting expenses	4,142	0.8

Table 5-2 Continued

	Amount ($)	Percent of sales
Office expenses	2,995	0.6
Rent	24,000	4.5
Repair and maintenance	437	0.1
Salaries	34,650	6.5
Telephone and utilities	7,683	1.4
Miscellaneous	9,507	1.8
Total operating expenses	95,119	17.8
Net profit	65,000	12.2

Table 5-3 Annual operating budget.

	Amount ($)	Percent of sales
Sales	523,063	100
Cost of services	366,144	70
Gross profit margin	156,919	30
Operating expenses:		
Advertising	3,605	0.7
Depreciation	4,000	0.8
Insurance	2,900	0.6
Legal and accounting expenses	4,142	0.8
Office expenses	2,995	0.6
Rent	24,000	4.6
Repair and maintenance	437	0.1
Salaries	34,650	6.6
Telephone and utilities	6,683	1.3
Miscellaneous	8,507	1.6
Total operating expenses	91,919	17.6
Net profit	65,000	12.4

Step 1: Target desired profit   During the three-year period, ABC Auto Repair Service averaged an annual net profit of $63,100. During Year 2, the company had its highest net profit of $65,000. In Year 3, sales were up, but net profit declined. For the coming year, Year 4, the company is targeting a net profit of $65,000.

Step 2: Determine operating expenses   ABC Auto Repair Service estimates that it will have many additional expenditures in Year 4. It will award a 5 percent wage increase to its two employees and purchase a more comprehensive medical insurance package for them at an additional annual cost of $2400. The company also plans to install additional telephone services at a cost of $1500.

In addition, ABC Auto Repair Service's accountant has advised it to plan on a 3 percent overall inflation rate next year. Taking these factors into consideration, ABC

Auto Repair Service figures its expenses as shown in the preliminary budget. Under fixed costs, the company estimates that:

- rent will remain unchanged at $24,000 per year;
- depreciation will remain unchanged at $4000 per year; and
- salaries will be raised by 5 percent (0.05).

The annual insurance expense of $1700 will be increased by $2400 to provide for additional medical coverage, so will now be budgeted at $4100. The company calculates variable costs as follows.

- Telephone and utilities expenses will be budgeted at $7683 (average annual cost plus the $1500 expected increase).
- Advertising, repair, maintenance, and miscellaneous expenses will increase by the 3 percent inflation factor.
- Due to company growth, office expenses increased 10 percent each year plus the 3 percent inflation factor.
- Legal and accounting expenses increased by 6 percent each year to which the 3 percent inflation factor should be added.

Step 3: Calculate gross profit margin Gross profit margin is the sum of net profit and total operating expenses, computed by working the preliminary budget backwards. ABC Auto Repair Service's gross profit margin is obtained by adding the estimated net profit of $65,000 to operating expenses of $95,119, equaling $160,119.

Step 4: Estimate sales revenue To target sales, analyze the gross profit margin. Income statements show that ABC Auto Repair Service experienced a gross profit margin equal to 30 percent of sales for three consecutive years. Since a gross profit margin of $160,119 is expected to equal 30 percent of net sales, then targeted sales should equal $533,730.

Step 5: Adjust figures If the preliminary figure for targeted net sales seems realistic, the budget is complete. If you question whether you will be able to generate the amount of targeted net sales, review and adjust the preliminary budget. In our example, the management of ABC Auto Repair Service is uncomfortable with the preliminary results. They don't believe the firm can generate sales of more than $525,000. To derive a more realistic operating budget, the owner decides to do the following.

- Delay installing additional telephone services to reduce telephone expenses by $1000.
- Carefully monitor expenses to reduce miscellaneous expenses by $1000.
- Choose a similar but less expensive employee benefit package with a higher employee deductible for medical insurance to reduce benefit expenses by $1200.

After making the preceding adjustments, ABC Auto Repair Service's new gross profit margin is $156,919 ($65,000 + $91,919). To compute the targeted sales, the company divides the gross margin by 30 percent for a targeted sales of $523,063. This figure is within the company's limit of $525,000.

The annual operating budget might need to be altered during the year to reflect changing circumstances. There might be a sharp rise or drop in one or more variable expenses or in revenues. Often, annual operating budgets are divided into smaller monthly or quarterly operating budgets. Monthly budgets are used to measure actual results against budgeted goals.

For large auto repair firms with several departments or work functions, expand the annual operating budget into a master budget. A master operating budget consists of a group of separate but interconnected operating budgets. These budgets will depend on and contribute to the company's overall plans.

An operating budget is an indispensable tool for converting plans into successful reality. A budget helps focus your efforts in the direction in which you are headed. It indicates how much cash you have to spend, your expenses, and how much you need to earn. By planning on paper first, you minimize some of the risks of owning and operating an auto repair firm. A good operating budget can also build morale by helping you organize, communicate, and motivate employees to do their part to achieve the company's financial goals.

PLAN FOR THE FUTURE

One simple reason why you should understand and explore financial planning in your business is to avoid failure. Many new businesses fail because of a lack of good financial planning. Financial planning affects how and on what terms you will be able to attract the funding you need to establish, maintain, and expand your business. Financial planning determines the human and physical resources you will be able to acquire to operate your business. It will be a major factor in whether or not you will be able to make your hard work profitable.

The balance sheet and the income statement are essential to your business, but they are only the starting point for successful financial management. The next step is called ratio analysis. Ratio analysis enables you to spot trends in a business and to compare its performance and condition with the average performance of similar businesses in the same industry. To do this, compare your ratios with the average of other auto repair services as well as with your own ratios over several years. Ratio analysis can be the most important early warning indicator for spotting business problems while they are still manageable.

One note before we get into ratios: members of trade associations will often share their balance sheet, income statement, and management ratios with other members through studies and reports published by the association. It's just one more good reason to join one of the local or national auto repair trade associations. The percentages can help you determine whether your auto repair business is operated as efficiently as other firms in your industry.

Balance sheet ratios

Balance sheet ratios measure liquidity (a business' ability to pay its bills as they come due) and leverage (a business' dependency on creditors for funding). Liquidity ratios indicate the ease with which a business can turn assets into cash. They include the current ratio, quick ratio, and working capital.

Current ratio The current ratio is one of the best known measurements of financial strength. It is figured like this:

$$\text{current ratio} = \frac{\text{total current assets}}{\text{total current liabilities}}$$

This ratio answers whether your business has enough current assets to meet the payment schedule of its current debts with a margin of safety? A generally acceptable current ratio among businesses is 2 to 1. That is, twice as many current assets as current liabilities. An ideal current ratio for auto repair services is 1.5:1. Let's say that you, or your lender, decide that your current ratio is too low. What can you do about it?

- Pay some debts.
- Combine some of your short-term debts into a long-term debt.
- Convert fixed assets into current assets.
- Leave in earnings or put profits back into the business.
- Increase your current assets with new equity (bring some more cash into the business).

Quick ratio The quick ratio is sometimes called the *acid test* ratio and is one of the best measurements of liquidity. It is figured like this:

$$\text{quick ratio} = \frac{\text{cash + securities + receivables}}{\text{total current liabilities}}$$

The quick ratio is a more exacting measure than the current ratio. By excluding inventories (typically small in auto repair businesses), it concentrates on the truly liquid assets that have a fairly certain value. This ratio helps answer the question of if all sales revenues should disappear, could my business meet its current obligations with the readily convertible "quick" funds in hand?

A ratio of 1:1 is considered satisfactory for auto repair services unless the majority of your quick assets are in accounts receivable, and the pattern of collection lags behind the schedule for paying current liabilities.

Working capital Working capital is more a measure of cash flow than a ratio. Bankers look at net working capital over time to determine a company's ability to weather financial crises. Bank loans are often tied to minimum working capital requirements. As a related indicator, the ideal ratio of gross revenue to working capital is 20:1 for smaller auto repair shops and 12:1 for larger shops. The result of the following calculation must be a positive number:

$$\text{working capital} = \text{total current assets} - \text{total current liabilities}$$

A general rule about these three liquidity ratios is that the higher they are the better, especially if your business is relying heavily on creditor money or financed assets.

Leverage ratio The leverage or debt/worth ratio indicates a business' reliance on debt financing (loans) rather than owner's equity. Here's how to figure it:

$$\text{leverage ratio} = \frac{\text{total liabilities}}{\text{net worth}}$$

Generally, the higher the ratio the greater the risk. The ideal ratio is 1:1.

Income statement ratios

Two commonly used ratios derived from your income statement or similar report are gross margin ratio and net profit margin ratio.

Gross margin ratio This ratio is valuable to auto repair services that stock and resell inventory rather than just sell services. The ratio is the percentage of sales dollars left after the cost of goods sold is subtracted from net sales. It measures the percentage of sales dollars remaining to pay the company's overhead. Comparing your business' ratio to those of other auto repair services can reveal the relative strengths or weaknesses in your business. Here's how to calculate the ratio:

$$\text{gross margin} = \frac{\text{gross profit}}{\text{net saes}}$$

Note that gross profit is calculated by deducting the cost of goods sold from net sales.

Net profit margin ratio This ratio shows the percentage of sales dollars left after subtracting the cost of goods sold and all expenses, except income taxes. It is a good way to compare your company's "return on sales" with the performance of other companies in the industry. It is calculated before income tax because tax rates and tax liabilities vary from company to company for a variety of reasons. The net profit margin ratio is calculated like this:

$$\text{net profit margin ratio} = \frac{\text{net profit before tax}}{\text{net sales}}$$

According to one source, the net profit for a typical auto repair business ranges from 3.5 percent of sales for firms doing over $6 million in annual sales to about 4.5 percent for firms with sales of under $1 million.

Management ratios

Other important ratios, often referred to as *management ratios*, are taken from information on the balance sheet and the income statement. They help you manage your business better.

Inventory turnover ratio If your auto repair business requires the resale of inventory, this ratio reveals how well your inventory is being managed. It is important because the more times inventory can be turned over in a given period, the greater the profit. A typical inventory turnover ratio for auto repair shops is 3 to 4 times per year. Here's how to calculate it:

$$\text{inventory turnover ratio} = \frac{\text{net sales}}{\text{average inventory at cost}}$$

Accounts receivable turnover ratio This ratio shows how well accounts receivable are being collected. If receivables are not collected reliably and on time, reconsider your credit policies. If receivables are too slow to convert to cash, your business might not be adequately "liquid." The ratio is figured like this:

$$\frac{\text{net credit sales}}{\text{year}} = \frac{\text{daily credit sales } 365 \text{ days}}{\text{year}}$$

then,

$$\text{accounts receivable turnover (in days)} = \frac{\text{accounts receivable}}{\text{daily credit}}$$

Return on investment ratio The ROI is perhaps the most important ratio of all. It is a percentage of return on money invested in the business by you, it's owner. In short, this ratio tells you whether or not all the effort you put into the business has been worthwhile. If the ROI is less than the rate of return on a risk-free investment (certificate of deposit or a bank savings account), you should consider selling the business and putting the money in a savings account. Here's how to calculate ROI:

$$\text{return on investment} = \frac{\text{net profit before taxes}}{\text{net worth}}$$

A goal for many successful businesses is a 25 percent ROI, depending on equity, market position, and risk. Larger auto repair services might get a 15 percent ROI, while smaller firms require 35 percent or more.

Sources of ratios As mentioned earlier, auto repair trade associations often supply members with typical current, quick, working capital, leverage, gross margin, net profit margin, inventory turnover, accounts receivable, and return on investment ratios. Your accountant or tax preparer might also be able to furnish you with these ratios in your specialty. Or, you might check your local or regional library for the following books on ratios:

- *Key Business Ratios,* Dun & Bradstreet, Inc.
- *Almanac of Business and Industrial Financial Ratios* by Leo Troy (Prentice Hall).
- *Annual Statement Studies* by Robert Morris Associates.

YOUR SUCCESS ACTION LIST

Chapter 5 is about keeping track of your business' money. We discussed how to set up an efficient recordkeeping system, use reports to manage your business better, and apply ratios to your financial data. In Chapter 6, you'll learn what you need to know about customers.

A number of things that you can do right now to ensure success for your auto repair service and put this chapter into action include:

_____ If you haven't already done so, select a paper or computerized accounting system for your auto repair service.

_____ Set up your cash receipts and disbursements, sales, and voucher records, or have them set up by your accountant.

_____ If you will have employees, contact the IRS for the *Employer's Tax Guide* (Circular E) and a nine-digit Employer Identification Number.

_____ Contact your state sales tax department for tax collection information.

_____ Set up a petty cash fund.

_____ Start your equipment and insurance records.

_____ Decide which daily, weekly, and monthly reports you need for your auto repair service and how you will get them.

_____ Establish your own procedures for ensuring that money doesn't fall through the cracks in your business.

_____ Call the toll-free IRS publications number (1-800-829-3676) and order _Tax Guide for Small Business_—(Publication 334), _Guide to Free Tax Services_—(Publication 910), _Your Federal Income Tax_—(Publication 17), and other booklets you need.

_____ Establish an operating budget for your auto repair business.

_____ Ask your trade association for current financial ratios for your specialized business.

6

Finding your customers

Your business' greatest asset is your customers. Without them you don't have a business. Unfortunately, many auto repair businesses don't know how to find and keep good customers. To do so, you must learn to think like a customer, and learn how to get customers to think like you do.

This is an important chapter. In it is information you'll need to find customers when you most need them, to develop prospects, to advertise, to keep customers happy and coming back, and, most important, to get your customers to bring you new customers.

WHAT YOU NEED TO KNOW ABOUT CUSTOMERS

Understanding your customers is so important that large corporations spend millions of dollars annually on market research. Although some formal research is important, a small firm usually can avoid this expense. Typically, the owner or manager of a small auto repair business knows his customers personally. From this foundation, a description of your customers can be built through systematic effort.

Figure 6-1 illustrates steps in the buying process. A seller characterizes what customers are buying as goods and services, toothpaste, drills, video games, or cars. But to understand buyers, you must realize that they purchase benefits as well as products. Consumers don't select toothpaste. Instead, some will pay for a decay preventive. Some seek pleasant taste. Others want bright teeth. For some, any toothpaste at a bargain price will do.

Similarly, industrial purchasing agents are not interested in drills. They want holes. They insist on appropriate quality, reliable delivery, safe operation, and reasonable prices.

You must find out, from your customers' point of view, what they are buying and why. Understanding your customers enables you to profit by providing what buyers seek: satisfaction.

Customers of an auto repair service don't really want repairs. They want to pick up their car or truck and know that it will run smoothly and relatively trouble-free for a price that they feel is less than the value. They want to feel safe when they drive their car. They don't want their windshield replaced, they want to be able to see clearly and know that it won't fall onto their lap. Customers don't want auto parts. They don't want to consider the actual part at all. They don't want a new

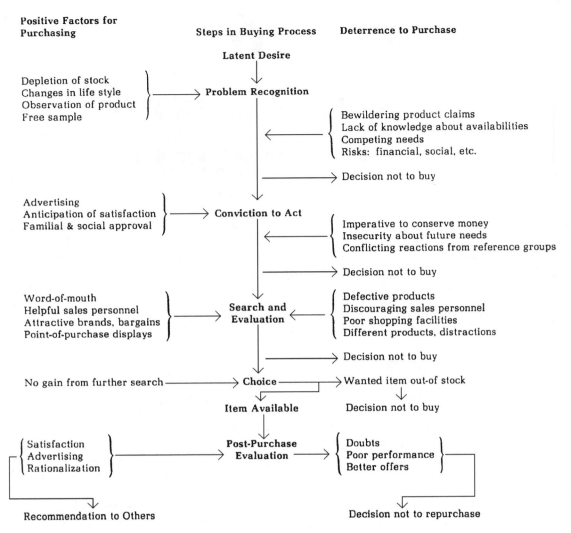

Positive Factors for Purchasing	Steps in Buying Process	Deterrence to Purchase

Latent Desire

Depletion of stock
Changes in life style
Observation of product
Free sample
→ **Problem Recognition**

Bewildering product claims
Lack of knowledge about availabilities
Competing needs
Risks: financial, social, etc.

→ Decision not to buy

Advertising
Anticipation of satisfaction
Familial & social approval
→ **Conviction to Act**

Imperative to conserve money
Insecurity about future needs
Conflicting reactions from reference groups

→ Decision not to buy

Word-of-mouth
Helpful sales personnel
Attractive brands, bargains
Point-of-purchase displays
→ **Search and Evaluation**

Defective products
Discouraging sales personnel
Poor shopping facilities
Different products, distractions

→ Decision not to buy

No gain from further search ——→ **Choice** ——→ Wanted item out-of-stock

Item Available   Decision not to buy

Satisfaction
Advertising
Rationalization
→ **Post-Purchase Evaluation** →

Doubts
Poor performance
Better offers

Recommendation to Others   Decision not to repurchase

6-1 Steps in the buying process for most consumer products and services.

brake job; they want safety and reliability. They can get a brake job anywhere. If you sell them peace of mind because your firm uses only quality parts installed by knowledgeable technicians at fair prices, they'll be back, and so will their friends.

There are three reasons why people buy automotive aftermarket products and services: to repair a problem, to avoid potential repairs, and to improve appearance or performance. And they only buy because they feel there is a need greater than the cost. A blown radiator hose is a problem with an immediate need. A tune-up is a current need that might avoid a future problem. A new sunroof is a perceived need that enhances the functionality of the car as well as the pride of the owner.

The point here is that you want to make your customers aware of their needs and how you can help them solve those needs with your service. A car that pulls into your shop with a flat tire has a need. You might be able to help the owner determine the extent of the need by pointing out that at least two other tires are nearly worn through and should be replaced soon to avoid the same problem.

Here's where a few auto repair services get into trouble. They abuse their position of trust by telling customers about needs that don't exist. They replace radiators when only a hose is required. They rebuild engines that only need a tune-up. They are dishonest. And they make it more difficult for customers to trust the honest and qualified auto repair services like yours.

Commit yourself to the rule that you will treat your customers as you wish to be treated by others. It can sometimes be a hard rule to follow if you know that payroll funds are low or that the shop rent might be a week late this month. But treating customers fairly can help you build a reputation of honesty, which will keep you in business to stay.

The key is to help your customers see and understand their true needs, then show them how to fulfill those needs at a price fair to both of you.

WHO YOUR CUSTOMERS ARE

Your market is the group of prospects who would most benefit from your services. The first step to defining your market is to define who you are to them. In an earlier chapter, you broadly defined your market in terms such as: "I am an auto repair service owner who specializes in one-man jobs that can be performed with minimal tools." Now let's get more specific.

Because there are dozens of types of auto repair services—and hundreds of potential markets—we will use broad examples. You'll quickly get the idea and be able to apply it to your specialty.

As a one-person auto repair service with minimal tools, your customers will be those with jobs that don't require a large labor force or numerous tools. The most common application of this market definition is the small auto repair service owner who works out of his home and trade vehicle and offers on-site tune-ups or lubrication service. Depending on your trade area, you might have to perform all these types of jobs or, preferably, specialize in one or two.

Let's say that based on your study of the local market, you determine that the best opportunity for you and your skills is to specialize in automotive radiator and cooling system repair. You look around and decide that there is enough work in your community to keep you busy for quite awhile, yet not so much as to attract lots of competition.

Okay, in this example, who are your customers? Your customers are those who own cars with water-cooled engines who want to repair existing problems or to avoid future problems with their radiators or cooling systems.

So how do you find out who needs these services? First, you break your business into two main service needs: emergencies and nonemergencies. If you are conveniently located, well known, and have a good reputation, the emergency service might come to you from car owners and other shops that don't perform radiator and cooling system services.

Let's consider how you can find customers for your nonemergency or maintenance work. Many such specialists take two tracks: one is to advertise to everyone knowing that, sooner or later, almost every car owner will need their service, and the other is to promote their service as a subcontractor to other auto repair services. That is, get other shops to refer work to them. Both tracks can be used at the same time.

Now it's time to approach your prospects. Build a database in your business notebook, a card file, or computer of noncompeting auto repair services in your area that might refer business to you or use you as a subcontractor. Then focus your attention on them with one goal: get them to recognize their need for your services and your qualifications to serve them.

Obviously, how you approach these prospects as a marque auto repair service will be somewhat different. Yet the principles will be the same. First determine whether there is sufficient opportunity for you to build your business and whether or not potential competitors are adequately serving this market. Then focus your attention and your marketing efforts on those who can best use your services. Learn who owns the specific brand of car in your trade area, and begin contacting them through mailings, telephone solicitations, and targeted advertising.

Depending on your specialty, you can subscribe to local or regional trade, business, and government publications that can keep you informed of opportunities.

Who are your customers? They are those recommended to you by other satisfied customers, those who have been influenced by your advertising or been solicited by your sales force. They are former customers, newcomers to the area, customers who need immediate emergency help, and your competitors' dissatisfied customers. They are businesses who have never before required auto repair services, as well as those who have decided to change suppliers because of price, quality, or service. Customers are your most valuable asset.

Don't limit your definition of a customer to individuals. Insurance companies, local businesses with company cars, trucking or transportation companies with large fleets, used-car dealers,and other firms can also be your customers. One of the largest users of automotive repair services in the United States is the American Automobile Association (AAA) located at 1000 AAA Dr., Heathrow FL 32746. Contact them or your local AAA office for information on how to become a contracted auto repair service. If you can serve recreational vehicles, contact the Good Sam Club at P.O. Box 500, Agoura CA 91376 to find out about serving their membership.

Here's another idea. Some startup auto repair services open their business by serving customers that cannot be served by their current or ex-employer. Work with them and you can reduce the amount of marketing you must do to develop customers. Most startup auto repair services then pay a marketing fee or a finders fee to these sources. It's another reason to maintain a good relationship with all of your past and current employers.

HOW TO GET MORE CUSTOMERS

Marketing is a science. It's not a perfect science; the answer to a given question is not always the same. It's a science based on data, information, knowledge, and wisdom. Data is easy to get and convert to information. From this information comes knowledge and, eventually, wisdom. Wisdom is what makes your business profitable. Marketing builds your business.

The purpose of marketing is to get more customers. That's it. If you're new to business, the purpose is to get your first customers. If you've established a substantial business, the purpose is to keep those customers that you have and attract more.

There are dozens of ways you can market your services to prospects and customers. They include the many forms of advertising, as well as literature, direct mail, and telephone marketing.

Advertising and promotion

Advertising tells potential customers why they can benefit from your services. The best way to do this is to let your existing customers tell your prospects about your service. That's called word-of-mouth advertising and it is the most valuable type of advertising there is. Unfortunately, it is also the slowest to develop. Your first satisfied client might, in conversations, mention your good service once or twice a month. When your client's friend is looking for your service, he might call you for your service. By that time you might be out of business due to lack of work.

Impressions Every time your prospect sees or hears your name, you make an impression. It might be something small like seeing your truck's sign on the freeway or seeing your sponsorship sign on a baseball field. Or it might be a listing in the yellow pages or a positive (or negative) comment about your last job made by a mutual acquaintance. Each contact makes an impression.

Each impression is cumulative. After numerous impressions, large and small, your prospect might bring your name into the "possible source" part of his or her brain. Then, when a legitimate need for your service arises, the prospect considers you as a supplier. Think about it. How many times did you see or hear about Ford or Jello or Mr. Coffee or Hawaii before you considered trying them. Probably dozens or even hundreds of impressions were made. And remember that any negative feelings about these products are also impressions. The point is that you will need to positively impress your prospects many times and in many ways before they can be upgraded to a customer.

Testimonials Of course, you can speed the process along by developing testimonials. That is, when you have a client who expresses satisfaction with your service, ask the client to write you a testimonial letter. The letter, on business stationery, should describe how professional your service is and how well you respond to the needs of customers.

Unfortunately, only a small percentage of those who say they will write a testimonial letter actually do so. But the problem isn't sincerity, it's time. Most customers just don't have the time to write such a letter. So some auto repair services hire a writer (check the local phone book for Writers or Resume Services) to interview the client and actually write the letter for the customer. You foot the bill. A well-written testimonial from a well-respected businessperson will be worth literally thousands of dollars in new business to you. Copy it and include it in with your brochure, quote from it in advertisements, and pass it out to prospects. It is your best form of advertising. If you use testimonials in advertising, be sure you have the customer's written permission to do so.

To encourage satisfied customers and their testimonials, some auto repair services establish and promote a policy of "satisfaction guaranteed." Any profits lost are usually replaced by the profits gained through this policy. It is a helpful persuasion tool when trying to close a sale.

Free advertising   There are numerous ways to advertise your new auto repair service at little or no cost. Exactly which methods you use depend somewhat on your specialization.

Once you have your business card printed, carry a stack of them with you wherever you go. Pass them out to anyone who might be or know of a prospect. When you stop for lunch, put your business card on the restaurant's bulletin board. Do the same if you stop at a local market for groceries: put your card on their bulletin board. All it costs is the price of a business card.

Many auto repair services overlook one of the best sources of free advertising: publicity. When you start your business, write a short article (called a press release) and take copies to your local newspaper, radio stations, shoppers, and other media. Include in it information about your business such as owners, experience, affiliations, background, expertise, purpose of the business, location, to whom the business sells its services, and how to contact the business. If your market is across an industry rather than a geographic area, send the press release to trade magazines or trade journals. If you're not comfortable writing a press release, hire a local freelance writer or publicist to do the job for you.

Your first brochure, which should describe your services and qualifications, might be a single sheet of paper, printed on both sides and folded. The cost is very small, especially if you can write and produce it yourself. Pass your brochure out at chambers of commerce meetings, at local tradesman meetings, anywhere where you would pass out your business card. Your brochure doesn't have to be slick and expensive, but spend a few dollars to make it neat and accurate. An attractive brochure might bring you many hundreds of dollars in new business. That's a good return on your investment. If you need help, contact a local "Desktop Publishing Service" through the yellow pages or a copy shop.

While business signs aren't free, they offer a "free" benefit in addition to their main purpose of providing information. They repeat your message whenever they are seen. So you want signs that are seen frequently. One excellent reason to select a delivery van rather than a pickup truck as your shop vehicle is that a van offers more space on its side for a large sign. Use a picture, a graphic image, or a logo on your sign to help viewers better identify and remember what you do. Some enterprising auto repair services park their work vehicles over the weekend at locations that offer high visibility, such as shopping centers, prominent industrial sites, and park-and-ride lots near major freeway off ramps. Make sure, though, that your vehicle is locked securely, especially if you keep any tools in it.

Traditional advertising   When most people think of advertising they think of billboards, large newspaper ads, catchy radio spots, and the like. Should auto repair services use this type of advertising to develop their business? In most cases, no. Why? Because the cost is typically too high for the results. Let's say that you purchase a quarter-page ad in your local daily newspaper and it's seen by 100,000 people for a price of just $500. That's just a half-cent-per-impression or reader. Pretty cheap. However, of those 100,000 people, only 50 are true prospects for your service. Then the price goes to $10 per impression. You could take each one to Burger King for about the same price. You'd be better off spending your money on an article that appears in the paper's business section, or mailing your brochures and a personalized letter to each of those 50 prospects.

Almost every home in the United States and Canada receives a newspaper. From the advertiser's point of view, newspaper advertising is convenient because production changes can be made quickly, if necessary, and you can often insert a new advertisement on short notice, depending on the frequency of the publication. Another advantage is the large variety of ad sizes newspaper advertising offers. The disadvantages to newspaper advertising include the cost of a large ad, which is required to make your message stand out from other large ads, the short throw-away life of a newspaper, and the poor printing quality of newspapers. If you decide to advertise in newspapers, establish a consistent schedule rather than a hit-and-miss advertising program. More importantly, ensure that the program is realistically within your budget.

Radio advertising Radio is a relatively inexpensive way to reach people. Radio has a more selective audience than newspapers because stations aim at specific age groups and genders as their primary target, while newspapers typically do not. However, a radio ad cannot be reviewed later. Once it is played, it is gone. So, during the 30- or 60-second length of the spot you must make sure that the listener hears something they can remember easily.

Television advertising Advertising on TV is financially impractical for most new auto repair services, unless you can use co-op or tag advertising. Let's say you carry a specific product for resale such as tires, batteries, or mufflers. The manufacturer of that product might share the cost of your advertising if you prominently mention their product. Even so, television co-op advertising is expensive. So some auto repair businesses find sources for tag advertising. A national supplier's television ad includes a tag line at the end of the commercial that says something like "Available at ABC Auto Repair Service."

Yellow pages advertising Depending on your specialty, an ad in the yellow pages might be one of your best sources of new business. In most locations, if you purchase a required business telephone line you will get a listing in one category of your local telephone book. In some areas, this is optional. The listing might be as simple as:

ABC Auto Repair Service, 123 Main St.---------555-1234

Or the firm name might be in capital letters such as:

ABC AUTO REPAIR SERVICE
123 Main St.-----------------------------555-1234

Or you can include information on your specialty, and even an alternate telephone number like this:

ABC Auto Repair Service
Specializing in Performance Tune-ups
    123 Main St.-----------------------------------555-1234
    If no answer------------------------------------555-2345

Many businesses upgrade their listings with space ads. A space ad is simply an advertisement that takes up more space than a line or two and is usually surrounded by a box.

To determine the size and cost of an appropriate space ad, check your local and nearby telephone book's yellow pages under headings for Automobile Repairing & Service, Automobile Engines (or other systems), and related topics. Look for your competitors. When a potential client looks in the yellow pages, which ads stand out? Which have the greatest eye-appeal? Which are easiest to read? Remember that you don't need the largest ad in the phone book, you need the one that is most cost-effective for you.

The last few pages in your yellow pages section frequently has information on how to select a space ad. You'll learn terms like "double half," "double quarter," and "triple quarter" as well as "columns." It's actually quite easy to follow. Most larger telephone books have four vertical columns per page; community phone books in rural areas are half-size with only two columns per page. So a "triple quarter" is three columns wide and a quarter page long; a "double half" is two columns wide and a half page long.

At the end of the yellow pages section, there often is a toll-free telephone number for ordering a space ad or listing. Or you might find the number in the front of the phone book under Business Telephone Service or a similar title. Also ask about the cost and availability of color in your ad. The firm that produces your telephone book can help you design and write your ad. Then they will supply a sample layout of the ad and a contract for you to sign. Most yellow pages listings or space ad contracts are for one year and can be paid in monthly installments.

Depending on your specialty, you might be able to get someone to help pay for your yellow pages ad. If you stock and sell or use a specific brand of supplies or equipment, the manufacturer or wholesaler might pay some of your advertising cost if you prominently display their name in your advertisement. This is called co-operative advertising or simply "co-op." Talk to your supplier about available co-op ad money.

Make sure you include any state or local licensing information in your yellow pages ad. Some include the phrase "Licensed—Bonded—Insured," while others include a state license board number such as "Professional License #12345." Some auto repair services also include information about affiliations, including the logo of trade associations.

Publicity

You can promote your business and get free advertising by offering to write a weekly newspaper column on auto repair in exchange for an ad in the paper. If you're not comfortable writing the column yourself, hire a writer or find an employee or relative who would enjoy writing the column for you.

If you're personable and comfortable doing it, offer to host a radio call-in talk show on auto care, or become a regular guest on someone else's talk show. The publicity can make you a local celebrity as well as an authority on auto care.

Cable TV also offers opportunities for auto repair service owners who want to market their business. Talk with your local cable operator about current and upcoming channels that might need your services.

WHERE TO FIND PROSPECTS

A prospect is a prospective customer, someone who might potentially use your service but hasn't done so yet. They might not have heard of your service, or they might not know enough about your service to determine its value, or they simply haven't been asked.

Who is a prospect for your auto repair service? That depends on what service you perform for customers. If your auto repair service specializes in electrical systems, your prospects are those who are repairing or upgrading their vehicle's electrical system. To turn prospects into customers you must first think like they think. For example, if your car had an electrical problem, how would you look for a qualified service person? Would you look at a local shopping center, follow a recommendation from your favorite mechanic, ask friends, check the yellow pages, or look for service ads in a local newspaper?

The United States Census Bureau is an excellent source of statistical data for market surveys. Based on the every-10-year census, the Bureau divides large cities into census tracts of about 5,000 residents within Standard Metropolitan Statistical Areas (SMSAs). Data on these tracts include income, housing, and related information that might be valuable to you. Results of the 1990 census are now available. For this and other market information, contact the Office of Business Liaison, U.S. Department of Commerce, Washington, DC 20230. The Bureau of the Census offers business statistics, data, and special demographic studies among its services.

QUALIFYING PROSPECTS

In some cases, qualifying is not necessary. Business comes to you when it's darn good and ready. While you are waiting, develop other qualified prospects in a variety of ways. If some of your business comes from referrals from other auto repair services, build a list of such services in your area, their owners, their level of business, their needs, and their potential for sending business your way. All of this can be done with a telephone call to noncompeting auto repair services in your local yellow pages.

Qualifying or determining the needs of prospects, of course, depends on your specialty. If you work primarily as an alarm and security system installer, you will have a different set of prospects: owners of newer, more expensive cars, especially that work or live in higher crime areas.

KEEPING TRACK

There are many ways to keep track of your prospects and customers. Some auto repair business owners use 3-x-5-inch file cards available at any stationery store. A completed card will include both basic information—name, owner, address, telephone number, business, etc.—as well as qualifying information and notes from prospecting contacts:

- 3/17: found out that Atlas Garage is selling out to Frank Smith who might want to use us for all their machine work.
- 3/21: Smith says that he wants proposal on wholesale prices for machine work.

Other new auto repair services use their business notebook, described earlier, to list prospect information and contacts.

If you're using a computer to automate your business records, there are diverse contact-management software programs that can help you keep track of prospects. These programs range in price from $50 for a simple system to $500 or more for a specialized prospecting system that can even help you write personalized sales letters. A good contact management program can give you standard "fields" or areas where you type the firm name, contact name(s), address, telephone and fax numbers, the names of mutual friends or associations, information about contacts, and can serve as a simple order entry form. If you're making regular telephone calls to prospects, the program might help you schedule call-backs, maintain records of conversations, and help you write personalized proposals that can be printed for mailing or even faxed to your prospect while they're still thinking about you.

CUSTOMER SATISFACTION

One of the most satisfying aspects of becoming a successful auto repair service is helping your customers solve problems. They might need cost-effective transportation that won't leave them and their family stranded on a vacation or along the freeway. In each case, they have a problem that requires a solution you offer.

The more customers you help, the more they can help you succeed. As you've learned, the best advertising is word-of-mouth, your satisfied customers tell your prospects about the value you give. That's the real key to keeping customers, keep them happy.

Of course, keeping your customers happy doesn't mean that you always have to agree with them or that they are always right, but they are always your customer and deserve your respect and best efforts.

Remember that, to many businesses, you are the customer. Your bank, your utility companies, your grocery and hardware stores, your suppliers, and other businesses want to keep you as their customer. How do they do it? Are they successful? What would it take for you to switch to the services of a competing business? What is the most important services these businesses give you? How do they make you feel as a customer? The golden rule of business success is to treat your customers as you wish your suppliers to treat you.

Your customers must be satisfied with the value of your service or they won't be your customers. You might have some customers who are temporarily dissatisfied, but they will get satisfaction from either you or one of your competitors. If you don't have any significant competitors, customer dissatisfaction might breed them. The point is that your auto repair business cannot afford dissatisfied customers.

So how do you continue to make sure that your customers are satisfied with your service? You listen to them. You watch how they pay their bills, you call them up for a friendly chat to learn what business problems they're facing, you ask other customers if they've heard of anyone who is dissatisfied with your services. Here are some of the questions that smart auto repair business owners periodically ask their customers.

- Is everything going well with our project?
- Have you seen anything that we can do better?

- Are there any of my employees that are doing an exceptional or an inadequate job for you?
- How can I get more great customers like you?

Why should a busy business owner take time out from his day to ask these questions of customers? Because if he doesn't someone else will and he might soon lose his valuable customers. Remember that it is much less expensive to keep an existing customer satisfied than to find a new one.

Repeat customers

A repeat customer is one who hires you for more than one job. If the customer is satisfied and needs your services again, you have a good chance of getting them as a repeat customer. You didn't have to go out and spend additional money on advertising, or work extra hours to promote your business. Your quality of business promoted itself.

The best way to get repeat business is to ask for it. When you call your clients to determine their satisfaction, also ask them questions like the following.

- Do you foresee any additional auto repairs in the future?
- Would you like us to give you a quote on them?
- What services do you expect to need from us in the coming year?
- Are there any related services that we could offer you in the future?

You can also build repeat business by continually trying to sell your services to customers. It is more productive to get more business from current customers than to find new ones. Here's how some successful auto repair services build repeat business.

- Monthly newsletter to all customers with new information on the industry (summarized from trade journals), as well as a listing of the jobs on which you are currently working and the services you offer.
- Perform extra services that other local auto repair services don't do for their customers, like vacuum out the car's interior, wash and wax the exterior, offer free pick-up and delivery of the car or owner.
- Serve as a consultant at no charge to clients, such as noncompeting auto repair shops who don't have expertise in your specialty.
- Send postcard or letter notices of services coming due on customer vehicles according to mileage: oil change, brake check, tune-up, etc.

Referral customers

Earning referrals is one of the most powerful types of business promotion. You get a referral when one of your satisfied customers sells your services to a prospective buyer. Prospects believe the word of a trusted businessperson more readily than the word of an unknown businessperson or salesperson.

So how do you get your customers to refer prospects to you? You ask them to do so. In fact, you should automatically ask: "Do you know anyone who might also need our services?" Ask it right after you close a sale, as you start a job, as you complete a job, and, especially, whenever anyone compliments an aspect of your work. Like this:

> "I really appreciate the way you found those parts and got them installed so quickly."
> "I'm glad to hear that. Is there anyone whom you know who might also need our services?"

In addition, once customers refer others to you, many feel a stronger obligation to continue to use your services. It cannot only help you enlarge your business, but can also help you keep the customers that you have.

WHAT CUSTOMERS WANT

One of the most important, and overlooked, aspects of keeping customers satisfied is to make sure you understand what they expect from you. Until you know, you won't be able to satisfy their needs. Here are some questions to ask about your customers.

- What are your customers expectations?
- Do customers expect immediate response to calls or do most customers need your services sometime in the next 30 days?
- Do customers expect instant credit from you or do they usually pay all or some of the costs in advance?
- Do customers expect you to be on call weekends or only during normal business hours?
- Do customers expect to talk to the boss when they call or can an office person handle most calls?
- Do your customers expect discounts for off-season jobs or for paying cash in advance?
- Do your customers expect to pay you in payments or within 30, 60, or 90 days of completion?
- Do your customers expect quotes that are priced by the hour, by the job, or another pricing structure?

How can you know what your customers expect? Ask them. Spend some time in person or on the phone with your customers, large and small, and ask them what they expect from you.

In fact, you can develop prospects into customers by telling them you are conducting a survey for your new auto repair business and would like to learn the expectations of potential customers. At the end of the conversation, ask, "Is your current auto repair service meeting your expectations?"

I'm certain that you, as a customer, are the same way. You have distinct expectations when you buy from someone. If you buy from a restaurant, you expect fast food at low cost from one type of take-out, and you expect quality food served well from a fine restaurant. From a supplier you want materials that are cost-effective and meet all codes and requirements. You might also want fast service or a broad inventory from which to choose. In fact, you might use one supplier for fast delivery of common materials and another for specialized materials.

Of course, the next question to ask yourself, and your customers and prospects is, "Are these expectations realistic?" That is, you might want to pay less than wholesale price for hard-to-get materials, but that isn't a realistic expectation. Or a customer might say that he expects you to be available 24-hours a day for questions about the job when you know that responding to questions within an hour during business hours is a realistic expectation.

Of course, if enough customers express the same unmet expectation, such as easy credit, you might consider meeting this expectation. By teaming up with an easy-finance broker you might be able to get discounted cash for your jobs from the broker while offering quick credit to your customers.

WHAT CUSTOMERS REQUIRE

An expectation is something that a customer would like to have happen. A requirement is something that a customer demands to have happen. A customer might expect that a job be done as quickly as possible, but requires that it be completed by a specific date.

So what does this have to do with a successful auto repair service getting and keeping customers? Plenty. In fact, unless you, as a service business, clearly define and understand your customer's requirements, you will not keep your customers. You are selling to your customer your clear understanding of what is required to do a job. In most cases, you will know the job's requirements more than your customer. The customer might hire you to rebuild his engine, but you must understand and furnish the specific requirements for the job to be a success.

How can you clearly define your customers' requirements? Again, by asking. Interview your prospect or customer to determine what they require as well as expect to complete the job. Of course, many requirements can be defined when your customer shows up at your door with a car that obviously needs repair. But you must probe past these obvious requirements to make sure that they accurately express the customer's perceived requirements. You might find that the plans, even when implemented, will not give the client what he requires or expects. It's your job, as a professional, to help the customer redefine his requirements and review his expectations. By doing so, you can help ensure the job's success as well as your own.

YOUR SUCCESS ACTION LIST

Customers for your auto repair business are everywhere, if you know where to look. This chapter offers ideas on how to find good customers and prospects, how to advertise your business, how to keep your customers happy, and how to get referral business. Here are some things that you can do right now to find and keep good customers for your auto repair service. Here's how to put this chapter into action.

_____ Review and revise how you earlier defined your auto repair service for completeness and accuracy.

_____ Define the typical customer you need for your auto repair service by vehicle, lifestyle, age, income, and buying habits.

_____ If appropriate, contact the AAA, Good Sam Club, or other automotive service contractors to learn about becoming a service provider.

_____ As soon as possible, develop testimonial letters that you can use to promote your auto repair service.

_____ Promote your business with business articles in local newspapers and regional business publications.

_____ Design a brochure that you can give to customers, prospects, or place on bulletin boards.

_____ Set up a small but consistent advertising program with the yellow pages and a local shopper or newspaper in your area.

_____ Learn as much as you can about your market and the people who live and shop in it.

_____ Decide how you plan to keep your customers happy and coming back to your business.

_____ Interview some of your customers or prospects to learn, in their own words, what they want and what they need.

The next chapter can show you how to reduce costs in your auto repair business to make it more profitable.

7
Reducing your costs

As we have discussed, the two secrets to making any business succeed are to: (1) increase sales, and (2) reduce costs. In the previous chapters, you learned how to start and run your auto repair business. Earlier chapters also provided ideas on how to increase sales. Now let's consider the other secret and learn how to reduce costs. Successful auto repair shop owners often learned the hard way how to analyze expenses, locate expenses that can be reduced, reduce overhead, increase discounts, schedule work efficiently, lease equipment, and save money when paying bills. They will share their knowledge and ideas with you in this chapter.

HOW TO REDUCE COSTS

The reason you reduce costs in your auto repair business is to increase profits. Increasing profits through cost reduction must be based on the concept of an organized, planned program. Unless adequate records are maintained through an efficient and accurate accounting system, there can be no basis for cost analysis.

Cost reduction does not mean slashing any and all expenses without order. The owner/manager of an auto repair service must understand the nature of expenses and how expenses relate to sales, inventories, overhead, gross profits, and net profits. Nor does cost reduction mean only the reduction of specific expenses. You can achieve greater profits by efficiently using your expense dollar. Some ways to do this are to increase the average sale per customer, get a larger return for your promotion and sales dollar, and improve your internal methods and procedures.

As an example, one small auto repair service was quite pleased when, in a single year, sales went from $200,000 to $1 million. However, at the end of the year, records showed that net profit the prior year, with lower sales, was actually higher than it was with increased sales. Why? Because the expenses of doing business grew at a rate faster than the income.

ANALYZE YOUR EXPENSES

Your goal should be to pay the right price for prosperity. Determining that price for your operation goes beyond knowing your expenses. Reducing expenses to increase profit requires that you obtain the most efficient use of your expense dollars.

After checking job records, you might determine that one of your employees is significantly less efficient than other employees performing the same tasks. Reduce expenses by increasing this employee's efficiency through training. Watch this employee perform his job and you can determine where the inefficiencies are and help him to overcome them. If done with consideration for the person, he or she will appreciate it and so will your profit line.

An understanding of the worth of each expense item comes from experience and an analysis of records. Adequate job and expense records tell what is happening. An analysis of these records provides facts that help you set realistic cost and profit goals.

Sometimes you cannot cut an expense item. But you can get more from it and thus increase your profits. When you analyze your expenses, use percentages rather than actual dollar amounts. For example, if you increase sales and keep the dollar amount of an expense the same, you have decreased that expense as a percentage of income. When you decrease your cost percentage, you increase your percentage of profit.

On the other hand, if your sales volume remains the same, you can increase the percentage of profit by reducing a specific item of expense. Your goal, of course, is to both decrease specific expenses and increase their productive worth at the same time.

Before you can determine whether cutting expenses will increase profits, you need information about your business. This information can be obtained only if you have an adequate recordkeeping system. Such records provide the figures needed to prepare an income statement, a budget, break-even calculations, and to evaluate your operating ratios as compared with those of similar types of business.

If you do much business-related traveling, an expense report (FIG. 7-1) or automobile travel log (FIG. 7-2) can help you keep track of costs. Blank forms that you can use are included in the appendix of this book.

A useful method for making expense comparisons is break-even analysis. Break-even is the point at which gross profit equals expenses. In a business year, it is the time at which your sales volume has been sufficient enough to enable your overall operation to start showing a profit. The two condensed income statement examples (TABLE 7-1) illustrate the point. In Statement A, the sales volume is at the break-even point and no profit is made. In Statement B, the sales volume is beyond the break-even point and a profit is shown. The percentage factors are the same in the two statements except for fixed expenses, total expenses, and operating profit. As shown in the example, once your sales volume reaches the break-even point, your fixed expenses are covered. Beyond the break-even point, every dollar of sales should earn you an additional profit percentage.

It is important to remember that once sales pass the break-even point, the fixed expenses percentage goes down as the sales volume goes up. Also, the operating profit percentage increases at the same rate as the percentage rate for fixed expenses decreases, provided that variable expenses are kept in line. In the illustration, fixed expenses in Statement B decreased by 5 percent and operating profit increased by 5 percent.

Locate reducible expenses

Your income statement provides a summary of expense information and is the record you should use to determine expenses that can be cut. For this reason, the information should be as current as possible. As a report of what has already been

ABC Auto Repair Service

123 Main Street, Yourtown USA 12345

Attach
Receipts

EXPENSE ACCOUNT OF: Bill Smith | For Period From: June 11, 19xx | To: June 17, 19xx

| DATE | TRAVELLED | | MI/KM | TRANS-PORT. | HOTEL | MEALS | | | PHONE | PARKING | MISC. | DAILY TOTAL |
	FROM	TO				BKFST.	LUNCH	DINNER			EXPLAIN BELOW *	
SAT												
SUN	Yourtown	Theirtown	229		$58.60		$7.90	$11.40	$4.15			$82.05
MON	Convention				$58.60	$8.19	$9.14	$12.10	$7.55		$46.50	$142.08
TUES	Convention				$58.60		$6.44	$23.12	$3.18			$91.34
WED	Theirtown	Yourtown	229				$4.78	$6.55				$11.33
THURS												
FRI												
TOTALS			458		175.80	12.97	30.03	46.62	14.88			$326.80

* EXPLANATION

MISC. June 16: Purchased management training tape at convention

ELAPSED BUSINESS MILES/KILOMETERS

Previous Total	
Current Week	458
Total to Date	458

CREDIT CARD BILLS

Bus. MI/KM
458 @ 0.2 = $91.60

TOTAL EXPENSE	$418.40
Less Advance	$400.00
Balance	**$18.40**

☐ Claimed   ☐ Refunded

Signature of Claimant:

Approved by:

Date:

7-1 The first step to reducing travel costs is to record and track them.

spent, an income statement alerts you to expense items that should be watched in the present business period. If you get an income statement only at the end of the year, consider having one prepared more often. A statement at the end of each quarter is usually sufficient for smaller firms. Larger auto repair services should receive the information on a monthly basis.

Regardless of the frequency, the best option is to prepare two income statements. One statement should report cumulative, year-to-date sales, expenses, and the profit/loss of your operations for the current business year. The other statement should report on the same items for the last complete month or quarter. Each of the statements should also carry the following information:

- This year's figures and each item as a percentage of sales.
- Last year's figures and the percentages.
- The difference between last year and this year, above or below.
- Budgeted figures and the respective percentages.
- The difference between this year and the budgeted figures, above or below.

- Average percentages for similar businesses (available from trade associations other sources listed earlier in this book).
- The difference between your annual percentages and the industry ratios, above or below.

This information allows you to locate expense variations in three ways:

- by comparing this year to last year;
- by comparing expenses to your own budgeted figures; and
- by comparing your percentages to the operating ratios for similar businesses.

The important basis for comparison is the percentage figure. It represents a common denominator for all three methods. After you have indicated the percentage variations, study the dollar amounts to determine what type of corrective action is needed.

Because your cost cutting will come largely from variable expenses, make sure that they are indicated on your income statements. Variable expenses are those that fluctuate with the increase or decrease of sales volume. Some of them are overtime, subcontractors, advertising, sales salaries, commissions, payroll taxes. Fixed expenses are those that stay the same regardless of sales volume. Among them are your salary, salaries for permanent employees, depreciation, rent, and utilities.

When you have located a problem expense area, the next step obviously is to reduce that cost in order to increase your profit. A key to the effectiveness of your cost-cutting action is the worth of the various expenditures. As long as you know the worth of your expenditures, you can profit by making small improvements to expenses. Keep an open eye and an open mind. It is better to do a spot analysis once a month than to wait several months and then do a detailed study.

Take action as soon as possible. Refine your cost-cutting action as you go along. Be persistent. Results typically come slower than you might like. Keep in mind that only persistent analysis of your records and constant action can keep expenses from eating up profit.

Reduce overhead

Business overhead is the costs of keeping your doors open. If your auto repair business is located in your home, overhead costs are probably small. But if you have a shop, an office, and office personnel, your overhead is greater. Overhead also might be large if you have high debt to banks, suppliers, and backers.

The suggestion made earlier in this book was to start out small and let your growing business force you into larger quarters. That is, depending on your auto repair specialty, start with a small shop in your home's garage or in a building shared with a noncompeting auto repair service. Then, as business grows, take on greater obligations for additional overhead. If you build a perception of quality in your customer's mind, you won't have to maintain impressive offices or shops. Few customers will decide not to do business with you because your service area is in your house's garage or a small shop.

You can also reduce overhead by carefully watching the costs of supplies. Printed stationery is an excellent way to promote the quality of your business, but you don't need printed notepads unless the customer sees them. For the price of

Monthly Summary Sheet

| **Date:** | July 31, 19xx |

123 Main Street, Yourtown USA 12345

AUTOMOBILE INFORMATION

Make of Auto: Ford

Year & Model: 1991 F-150 Pickup Truck

Vehicle I.D. Number: 1234567890-2345678901

Driver of Vehicle: Mack Smith

Odometer   End of month: 37,283.00

                Beginning of month: 35,421.00

Total Miles Driven: 1,862.00

Qualified Business Miles Driven: 1,219.00

Allowable Reimbursement Rate: 1,219.00   x $ 0.28 /mi

Total Expense $ $341.32

YEAR TO DATE - INFORMATION

	BUSINESS MILES	TOTAL MILES
Prior YTD	6,912	10,479
Current Month	1,219	1,862
New YTD	8,131	12,341

DATE: _____   SIGNATURE : _____

APPROVAL : _____

7-2 Use an Automobile Travel Log to reduce business mileage on a personal vehicle.

Table 7-1   Two condensed income statements.

	A		B	
	Break-even amount	Percent of sales	Profit amount	Percent of sales
Sales	$500,000	100	$600,000	100
Cost of sales	300,000	60	360,000	60
Gross profit	200,000	40	240,000	40
Operating Expenses:				
Fixed	150,000	30	150,000	25
Variable	50,000	10	60,000	10
Total	200,000	40	210,000	35
Operating Profit	$ None	0	$ 30,000	5

generic ink pens you can often get ones that include your business name and phone number. But don't buy so many that they wind up costing more than quality ink pens because you've changed your address or phone number. Buy supplies in quantity if you can, but don't buy more than you can use in three to six months unless you're certain that they won't become out-of-date.

Manpower can quickly eat away the profits of a small auto repair business. Don't hire an office manager or secretary until you absolutely must. It's more profitable to do the required filing and office functions yourself after normal business hours or on weekends. Or ask a spouse or older child to help you and then put them on the payroll as soon as your business can afford it.

Some small auto repair services use temporary help or outside services rather than hiring employees and assuming all the taxes and records that come with them. Their records are kept by a bookkeeping or accounting service, office cleaning is done by a janitorial service (or the boss), telephones are answered by an answering service, correspondence is performed by a secretarial service. Auto repair jobs that the owner can't handle are subcontracted out to other auto repair services. These business owners know that the complexity of regulations and taxation is endlessly multiplied when the first employee is hired, so they avoid hiring anyone until their success requires them to do so.

Long distance phone calls can quickly add to your expenses and cut into your profits, especially when they are personal calls made by employees. Many successful auto repair services use a telephone call record (FIG. 7-3) to keep track of long distance calls and then compare the report with the monthly phone bill. Calls not listed on the report are assumed to be personal calls and should be checked out.

Earn discounts

Every businessperson wants to take advantage of discounts. If your gross profit is 5 percent of sales, a 10 percent discount on materials can dramatically increase overall profits. So how do you ensure that you are getting the best price for the materials and equipment you buy? You ask!

ABC Auto Repair Service

TELEPHONE CALL RECORD

123 Main Street, Yourtown USA 12345

TIME PERIOD FROM: June 1   TO: June 30, 19xx

Date	Caller	Call To	Company and Location	Code	Phone #	Charges
June 7	Bob	Phoenix	Southwest Auto Parts		555-678-9012	$6.37
June 12	Bob	Des Moines	Lube N Go Franchise		555-123-4567	$9.25
June 14	Hank	Ottawa	Murphy Tool Company		555-987-6543	$11.67
June 23	Bob	Des Moines	Lube N Go Franchise		555-123-4567	$8.22
June 28	Larry	Theirtown	Skeeter's Transmission		555-444-5555	$3.45

NOTES OR COMMENTS:

7-3 Record long distance calls on a Telephone Call Record.

Let's say that you order parts through a specific parts house in your area. Do you know what discounts are available to you for cash in advance? Do you know what discounts can be earned by ordering all of your materials through a single parts house? Or can you receive materials at no charge because ordering a few more of a component will lower your per-unit charge enough to pay for the extra materials? Can you receive higher discounts from the supplier's competitor for all materials you buy from them? How about if you buy only materials in which they specialize? Here are a few ways that you can ensure that you are earning the greatest available discounts.

- Pool your purchases with other friendly competitors in order to earn greater quantity discounts.
- Order through a single clerk, especially one that works on commission, and always ask for best pricing and available discounts.
- Ask if there are any discounts or price breaks that you should be aware of.
- If necessary, sign a contract with a single supplier to give them all of your business if you can get an additional 3 or 5 percent discount, as long as their standard prices are equal to or less than those of other suppliers.

- Ask if members of any local or national trade associations earn additional discounts.
- Find out if your supplier allows a discount for cash and carry.
- Even if you have a favorite supplier, always continue to shop around for better pricing, discounts, and terms.

Keep in mind, though, that some suppliers charge a little more because they offer services that are worth the difference in price. As an example, a crosstown supplier can give you immediate delivery of hard-to-find supplies that you often need, but can't afford to stock in quantity. The loss of a 5 percent discount might be small compared to the cost of stocking them or having to stop what you're doing to pick them up. Remember, you don't want the lowest price, you want the one that is most profitable to you in the long term. Of course, that means you don't want cheap, you want quality at the best price. That's also what your customers want!

Also be aware of the commission salesman who says, "Take a few hundred more units and I'll give you another 4 percent discount." If you use 100 units a week, this might be a good deal. But if it will take you a year or more to use the units, a 4 percent return on your cash is not a good discount.

SHOULD YOU HIRE AN ACCOUNTANT?

Believe it or not, an accountant can help you reduce your business costs. Not only can an accounting service mean that you don't have to hire an employee to manage your records, but a good accountant can help you find ways to reduce your costs of doing business.

Of course, with any investment, you cannot show a profit unless what you receive is worth more than what you pay. So only hire an accounting service for those functions you cannot do yourself or as an auditor of your records. When you interview accountants, look for one with experience in your trade who can offer you valuable ideas on how to save money in your auto repair business. When do you need to hire an accountant or accounting service for your auto repair business? Anytime.

When you start   The best way to start off on the right road is to get a quality map. An accountant can help you draw such a map based on his or her knowledge and experience as well as the experience of others. This map might show the potholes that auto repair services typically find on their road to success: cash flow, recordkeeping, taxation, payroll, etc. Just as important, an accountant can help you smooth out the road by offering techniques to increase the inflow of cash during the critical first few months of business, by setting up an easy-to-use recordkeeping system, and by marking your calendar with important dates when tax forms must be submitted.

When you grow   An accountant can help you as your business picks up speed. He or she can help you make informed decisions about hiring employees, hiring subcontractors, investing excess cash, purchasing capital assets, collecting bad debts, signing large contracts, purchasing supplies and materials, improving balance sheet ratios, applying for loans, and preparing tax forms.

When you change your business structure   Your accountant can also be a valuable adviser when you are considering taking on a partner, forming a limited partnership, or incorporating your auto repair business. The accountant can help you prepare required balance sheets and income statements, hire an independent auditor, and outline the tax advantages and disadvantages involved. A good accountant is like a navigator. You are at the helm steering the appropriate course, but your accountant/navigator is the one who tells you where the shallow water is and how to stay in the shipping lane.

PROFITABLY SCHEDULE YOUR WORK

How does scheduling your work help you reduce the costs of doing business? In many ways. By prioritizing your jobs into most-important, less-important, and least-important, you can make sure that you are always doing what is most valuable to your business. A most-important job is one with the shortest deadline, the quickest pay out, the most important customer, and the greatest opportunity for your auto repair firm.

Of course, this doesn't mean that any of your customers are less important than any other. All have equal potential for helping your business succeed either from work they hire you to complete or from other customers they bring you. But the cash customer stranded on vacation with car problems has a greater need for your services than the customer who needs you to perform an oil change this week. Prioritize your work based on the customer's need as well as your own.

Many successful auto repair service owners reduce costs by scheduling each job to balance both the customer's need and their own. How do they do so? They first take care of the jobs that require the quickest inspections or sign-offs.

If possible, group together similar jobs during the same time period, such as welding tail pipes, to reduce the time needed to get the welding system set up.

When available, give highest priority to jobs that provide your business with the greatest cash flow (cash, net 15 days, etc.) rather than slow-pay jobs (insurance jobs, net 90 days, etc.).

If workable, give high priority to those jobs that improve your relations with customers (special favors, rechecking a job, offering no-charge advice or assistance, etc.).

Plan for problems. We all know that problems arise, a critical tool breaks or disappears, so assume that they will happen and plan for them as part of every job. How? By making sure that you have sufficient parts as well as a quick source for more, that plans have been checked in advance for accuracy, and that backups are available for your most critical equipment.

A monthly planner (FIG. 7-4) can help with long-term planning and help you develop your daily planner (FIG. 7-5) or list of things to do (FIG. 7-6).

DEPRECIATION

You can reduce your annual tax obligation for a major expense over more than one tax year by using depreciation. Depreciation is a method of spreading out the expense of a purchase over time. In order to depreciate or slowly charge off the cost, the purchase must be for a fixed asset (other than land) that you will use in your business for more than one year. Examples include buildings, vehicles, equipment, tools, furniture, and fixtures.

ABC
Auto Repair
Service

123 Main Street, Yourtown USA 12345

PERSON: Bill Smith
FROM: July 1, 19xx
TO: July 31, 19xx

PRIORITIES	Monday	Tuesday	Wednesday	Thursday	Friday	Saturday	Sunday
1 Orient new employee	Introduce Bob Review job	Staff mtg @ 9am	Review resources	Call suppliers	Meet with Bob	Golf with Frank	
2 Purchase new equipment for high-performance services	Demonstrations		Jake's Tools @ 3pm	MagnaTools @ 11am			
3 Train employees on high-performance services		High-Perf class 9-10am	High-Perf class 1-2pm	High-Perf class 3-4pm		Theirtown	Theirtown
4 Market new high-performance services	Theirtown		Shopper ad mgr @ 10am	Newspaper ad mgr @ 11am		Golf Tournament	Golf Tournament
5							

7-4 A Monthly Activity Planner can help you plan for the future.

Most small businesses don't have enough fixed assets to worry about depreciation more than once a year, typically when the year's books are closed. So what do you need to know about depreciation? First, keep in mind that nothing is certain while Congress is in session. Any current rules of depreciation might be invalid as long as Congress and the IRS can change the tax laws. So check with your accountant about setting up a depreciation system for your business based on current rules and guidelines. Here's what's current as this book is written.

MACRS (Modified Accelerated Cost Recovery System) *allows all fixed assets placed in service after 1986 to be assigned a "recovery period" over which the expense can be spread. The length of the recovery period depends on the type of fixed asset. The current schedule allows for 3-, 5-, 7-, 10-, 15-, 20-, 27.5-, and 31.5-year recovery periods. Under the MACRS rules, the entire cost of an item is recovered. There is no "salvage value" at the end of the recovery period as there was with prior depreciation methods.*

To make things somewhat more confusing, there are three methods of depreciation depending on the type of asset and its recovery period. Shorter recovery periods (10 years or less) use the "200 percent declining balance" method; 15- and 20-

123 Main Street, Yourtown USA 12345

DAY OF THE WEEK:
Tuesday, 17th
MONTH AND YEAR:
June, 19xx

TIME	TO DO	NOTES
8:00 - 9:00	Training Session--Brake Systems	
9:00 - 10:00	Bev Jenkins: '84 Honda--Tune-up, Lube	
10:00 - 11:00	John's Nursery: '92 GMC--Differential	Take Bill back to nursery; PU at 5pm
11:00 - 12:00	Mike McLain: '91 Ford Taurus--Clutch	
12:00 - 1:00	Lunch --Kiwanis	
1:00 - 2:00	McLain Taurus	
2:00 - 3:00	Jim Jenkins: '86 Toyota Pick-up--Diagnostics	Doesn't start when cold
3:00 - 4:00		
4:00 - 5:00		
5:00 - 6:00	Bill will pick up John's Nursery truck	
6:00 - 7:00	Dinner with family	
7:00 - 8:00	Payroll taxes	
8:00 - 9:00		
9:00 - 10:00		
10:00 - 11:00		
11:00 - 12:00		

7-5 A Daily Planner let's you know what needs to be done each day.

year recovery periods use the "150 percent declining balance" method. Longer periods are used only for real estate and employ the "straight-line" method. To help you understand how to reduce business costs, here are definitions for the preceding three depreciation methods:

ABC Auto Repair Service

Things To Do

Date: June 30, 19xx

1 Discuss new duties with office manager ☐

2 Pick up special parts for Jefferson repair ☐

3 Lunch with Jim of Morgan Racing ☐

4 Begin preparing estimated taxes ☐

5 Call for more info on this year's convention ☐

6 Sign up for certification program ☐

7 Preventive maintenance on generator ☐

8 ☐

9 ☐

10 ☐

11 ☐

12 ☐

7-6 Organize yourself with a Things-To-Do List.

The straight line method   This method is quite simple. A $10,000 fixed asset with a 5-year recovery rate is depreciated at $2,000 (1/5 or 20 percent) per year.

The declining balance method   This method accelerates the amount of depreciation taken in the early years and reduces the amount taken in later years. The 200 percent declining (or double declining) balance approach depreciates the $10,000 asset by $4000 (⅖ or 40 percent) the first year, then $2400 the second year ($10,000–$4000 = $6000 × 40 percent), $1440 the third year ($6000 – $2400 = $3600 × 40 percent), $864 the fourth year ($3600 – $1440 = $2160 × 40 percent), and $518.40 the final year ($2160 – $864 = $1296 × 40 percent). In our example, the 150 percent declining balance method depreciates 30 percent (150 percent of ⅕) of the remaining balance per year.

Expensing depreciable assets   You can elect the method you use. Depending on your cash flow and tax liability, you can elect to "expense" the purchase of a fixed asset (up to $10,000) during the year in which it is purchased. In the above example of a $10,000 purchase, you could write off the entire $10,000 as an expense during the year it was purchased. No depreciation is necessary. The only requirement is that your business must show a profit. That is, the expense must not force your business into a loss for the year. Many small businesses who have few fixed assets, who typically show a profit, and who don't want to mess with depreciation, will expense the purchase of fixed assets up to $10,000, or any lower limit they set for themselves. This helps lower their current-year taxes.

As this book is being written, Congress is considering increasing the limit of depreciable assets that can be expensed in a fiscal year. Check with your tax advisor or accountant for the latest information.

INCREASE CASH FLOW

Every time you purchase on credit, you add interest costs to your business. The more cash you have the more interest expense you can save. For this and other reasons, you can reduce your costs by increasing cash flow.

The cash-flow forecast (FIG. 7-7) identifies when cash is expected and when it must be spent to pay debts. This document shows how much cash you will need to pay expenses and when you will need it. It also allows you to identify the source of the income. For example, will the funds you need to purchase new tools come from the collection of accounts receivable or must it be borrowed?

The cash-flow statement is an estimate of sales and expenses. It indicates when money will flow into and out of your business. It enables you to plan for shortfalls in cash resources so short-term working-capital loans, or a line of credit, might be arranged in advance. It allows you to schedule purchases and payments so you can borrow as little as possible. Because not all sales are cash sales, you must be able to forecast when accounts receivable will be cash in the bank, as well as when regular and seasonal expenses must be paid.

You can also use the cash-flow statement as a budget to help you increase your control over your business by comparing actual receipts and payments against forecasted amounts. This comparison helps you identify areas where you can manage your finances even better.

Closely watch the timing of cash receipts and payments, cash on hand, and loan balances, and you can identify potential shortages in collecting receivables, unreal-

ABC Auto Repair Service

123 Main Street, Yourtown USA 12345

DATE: June 30, 19xx	
FOR TIME PERIOD: Second Quarter	
APPROVED BY:	
PREPARED BY:	

	Date: April 30		Date: May 30		Date: June 30	
	ESTIMATE	**ACTUAL**	**ESTIMATE**	**ACTUAL**	**ESTIMATE**	**ACTUAL**
Opening Balance	11,234.00	10,934.00	11,531.00	11,731.00	12,225.00	12,334.00
Collections From Trade	5,280.00	4,921.00	5,667.00	5,822.00	5,950.00	5,123.00
Misc. Cash Receipts	1,258.00	1,715.00	1,520.00	1,433.00	1,620.00	1,559.00
TOTAL CASH AVAILABLE	**$17,772.00**	**$17,570.00**	**$18,718.00**	**$18,986.00**	**$19,795.00**	**$19,016.00**
DISBURSEMENTS						
Payroll	1,945.00	1,955.00	1,945.00	1,936.00	1,945.00	1,989.00
Trade Payables	2,111.00	1,945.00	2,200.00	2,111.00	2,300.00	1,980.00
Other	786.00	765.00	822.00	754.00	833.00	875.00
Capital Expenses	789.00	899.00	800.00	812.00	820.00	844.00
Income Tax	2,123.00	2,192.00	2,123.00	2,146.00	2,123.00	2,111.00
Bank Loan Payment	567.00	567.00	567.00	567.00	567.00	567.00
TOTAL DISBURSEMENTS	**$8,321.00**	**$8,323.00**	**$8,457.00**	**$8,326.00**	**$8,588.00**	**$8,366.00**
Ending Balance	$9,451.00	$9,247.00	$10,261.00	$10,660.00	$11,207.00	$10,650.00
Less Minimum Balance	$10,000.00	$10,000.00	$10,000.00	$10,000.00	$10,000.00	$10,000.00
CASH AVAILABLE	**($549.00)**	**($753.00)**	**$261.00**	**$660.00**	**$1,207.00**	**$650.00**

(FOR INTERNAL USE ONLY)

7-7 A Cash Flow Forecast identifies when cash is expected.

istic trade credit, or loan repayment schedules. You can also identify surplus cash that might be invested for a greater return on your investment. In addition, the cash-flow statement can help you convince your banker that you need a certain loan and how you expect to pay it off.

A cash-flow statement or budget can be prepared for any period of time. However, a one-year budget that matches the fiscal year of your business is the most useful. Many successful auto repair services prepare their cash-flow statements on a monthly basis for the next year. It should be revised no less than quarterly to reflect actual performance in the previous three months of operations to verify projections.

A cash-flow statement includes sales budgets, selling expenses, direct labor expenses, and other vital components. The result of all this budgeting is the cash budget.

All businesses, no matter how small or large, function on cash. Many businesses become insolvent because they don't have enough cash to meet their short-term obligations. Bills must be paid in cash, not potential profits. Sufficient cash is, therefore, essential to maintaining a successful business. You must understand how cash moves or flows through your business and how planning can remove some of the uncertainties about future requirements.

Cash cycle

Auto repair services face a continual cycle of events that might increase or decrease the cash balance. Cash is decreased when you acquire materials and services. It is reduced when you pay off the amounts owed to suppliers (accounts payable). Money is generated when services or inventory is sold and the sales generate money owed by customers (accounts receivable). When customers pay, accounts receivable are reduced and the cash account is increased. However, cash flows are not related necessarily to the sales in that period because customers might pay in the next period.

Auto repair services must continually be alert to changes in working capital accounts, the cause of these changes, and their implications for the financial health of the company.

Net working capital

As discussed earlier in this book, current assets are those resources of cash and those assets that can be converted to cash within one year or within a normal business cycle. These include cash, marketable securities, accounts receivable, and inventories. Current liabilities are obligations that become due within one year or a normal business cycle. Those include accounts payable, notes payable, and accrued expenses payable. Consider current assets as a source of funds that can reduce current liabilities.

One way to measure the flow of cash and the firm's ability to maintain its cash or liquid assets is to compute working capital. It is the difference between current assets and current liabilities. The change in this value from period to period is called net working capital (TABLE 7-2). Net working capital in the example increased during the year, but we don't know how. It could have been all in cash or all in inventory. Or, it might have resulted from a reduction in accounts payable.

Table 7-2
Calculating net working capital.

	Year 1	Year 2
Current assets	$110,000	$200,000
Less current liabilities	−70,000	−112,000
Working capital	40,000	88,000
Net working capital increase	$48,000	

CASH-FLOW STATEMENT

While net working capital shows only the changes in the current position, you can develop a "flow" statement to explain the changes that have occured in any account during any time period. The cash-flow statement is an analysis of the cash inflows and outflows.

When you have the ability to forecast cash requirements you will be a more efficient auto repair service owner/manager. If you can determine your cash requirements for any period, you can establish a bank loan in advance, or you can reduce other current asset accounts so that the cash will be available. Also, when you have excess cash, you can put this cash to productive use to earn a return.

You can determine changes to your cash flow if you know your net working capital, and the changes to current liabilities and current assets other than cash. Net working capital is the difference between the change in current assets and current liabilities :

$$NWC = CA + cash - CL$$
$$cash = NWC - CA + CL$$

This relationship states that if you know the net working capital (NWC), the change in current liabilities (CL), and the change in current assets less cash (CA − cash), you can calculate the change in cash. The change in cash is then added to the beginning balance of cash to determine the ending balance. If you forecast an income increase for your auto repair business, the following also will change:

- Accounts receivable increase by $25,000.
- Inventory increases by $70,000.
- Accounts payable increase by $30,000.
- Notes payable increase by $10,000.

Using net working capital of $48,000, what is the projected change in cash?

$$cash = NWC - CA + CL$$
$$= 48,000 - 25,000 - 70,000 + 30,000 + 10,000$$
$$= -7,000$$

The answer is that, over this period of time, under the condition of increasing sales volume, cash decreases by $7,000. Is there enough cash to cover this decrease? This will depend on the beginning cash balance.

At any given level of sales, it's easier to forecast the required accounts payable, receivables, and inventory, than the net working capital. To forecast the value of the net working capital account, trace the sources and application of funds. Sources of funds increase working capital. Applications of funds decrease working capital. The difference between the sources and applications of funds is net working capital.

The following calculation is based on the fact that the balance sheet is indeed in balance. That is, total assets equal total liabilities plus owner's equity.

current assets + noncurrent assets + retained earnings = current liabilities + long-term liabilities + equity

or,

current assets − current liabilities = long-term liabilities + equity − noncurrent assets − retained earnings

Because the left side of the equation is working capital, the right side must also equal working capital. A change in either side is the net working capital. If long-term liabilities and equity increase or noncurrent assets decrease, net working capital increases. This change would be a source of funds. If noncurrent assets increase or long-term liabilities and equity decrease, net working capital decreases. This change would be an application of funds.

Typical sources of funds or net working capital are funds provided by operations, disposal of fixed assets, issuance of stock, and borrowing from a long-term source.

To obtain the figure for "funds provided by operations," subtract all expense items that require funds from all revenues that are sources of funds. You also can obtain this result by adding back expenses that don't result in inflows or outflows of funds to reported net income.

The most common nonfund expense is depreciation, the allocation of the cost of an asset as an expense over the life of the asset against the future revenues produced. Adjusting net income with depreciation is simpler than computing revenues and expenses that require funding. Again, depreciation is not a source of funds.

The typical applications of funds or net working capital are purchase of fixed assets, payment of dividends, retirement of long-term liabilities, and repurchase of equity.

PLAN FOR CASH FLOW

Use cash flow to determine how cash moves through your business and as an aid to determine an excess or shortage of cash. Suppose your analysis of cash flow forecasts a potential cash deficiency. You might then do a number of things, such as increase borrowing (loans, stock issuance), reduce current asset accounts (receivables, inventory), and reduce noncurrent asset accounts (sell fixed assets, postpone expansion).

Use your cash-flow statement to determine if sufficient funds are available from financing activities, to show funds generated from all sources, and to show how these funds are applied. Using and adjusting the information gained from this cash flow analysis can help you know in advance if there will be enough cash to pay suppliers' bills, bank loans, interest, and dividends.

Increase cash flow

As you can see, you need cash to enlarge your auto repair business. Once you've analyzed cash flow and determined that you need more of it, what can you do? Depending on the specific type of auto repair business you own, you can find increased cash in your accounts receivable and in your inventory.

Accounts receivable represent the extension of credit to support sales. In your business, the types and terms of credit you grant are set by established competitive practices. As an investment, accounts receivable should contribute to your overall return on investment (ROI).

Excessive investment in accounts receivable can hurt our ROI by unnecessarily tying up funds. One good way to judge the extent of accounts receivable is to compare your average collection period with that of rivals or the industry average. If your average collection period is much higher than your competitors' or the industry norm, your accounts receivable might be excessive.

If your accounts receivable are excessive, it might be that you are not collecting from late payers. Check this by developing an aging schedule. An aging schedule shows whether accounts receivable are being paid on time or late (FIG. 7-8).

123 Main Street, Yourtown USA 12345

Period Ending: June 30, 19xx

Invoice Date	Invoice #	Acct #	Customer Name	30 days	60 days	90+ days	Total
February 11	12345-67	1111	Jim Johnson	110.00	110.00	110.00	$330.00
March 19	23456-78	2222	Smith Taxi Service		465.00		$465.00
April 2	34567-89	3333	William Jones	292.20			$292.20
April 23	45678-90	4444	Betty Doe	121.92			$121.92
				TOTALS	524.12	575.00	110.00	$1,209.12

GRAND TOTAL DUE $2,418.24

7-8 An Aging of Accounts Receivable report tells you who is late paying money owed you.

Failure to monitor late payments ties up investments and weakens profits. The more overdue accounts become, the greater the danger that they will be uncollectable and will have to be written off against profits.

If the aging schedule does not reveal excessive late accounts, your average collection period might be out of line simply because your credit policy is more liberal than most. If so, it should translate into more competitive sales and greater profits. Otherwise, you should rethink your credit program.

Not all auto repair services have significant inventory, or even require inventory. Those that do can improve cash flow by improving their management of inventory. Excessive inventory reduces your ROI. One way to determine whether your inventory level is excessive is to compare your inventory turnover ratio with the industry norm. If your inventory turnover (the times per year that you replace your inventory) is much lower than the average, your ROI obviously will suffer.

If inventory is much higher than it should be for your level of sales, it might be that you are holding items that are obsolete or that simply don't move fast enough to justify their cost. You might also be speculating on price increases. Or perhaps, for competitive reasons, you think a full line of inventory items is essential, even if some items are in low demand. In any case, reevaluate your policy and make sure that the gains outweigh the costs of the higher investment. Which is more valuable to the success of your business: the excess inventory or the equivalent cash.

When you consider your level of inventory, consider the cost associated with maintaining inventory. Carrying costs are the expenses associated with inventory storage, handling, and insurance. Ordering costs are the clerical and administrative costs incurred when an order is placed for an item in inventory. If you expect to use 600 quarts of 10W-40 oil over the next 30 days, you could buy it all now and carry it in inventory until it is all used up. Or you could buy 200 quarts every 10 days. The more frequently you place orders for inventory, the less inventory you have to keep on hand and the less carrying cost you have. But more frequent orders also result in greater ordering costs. Remember, the bottom line is the bottom line.

Paying bills

Another way to increase cash flow is to review every invoice you receive to ensure its accuracy before you pay it. Some invoices inadvertently include misdirected charges. Others incorporate service charges that are unearned. A few dishonest people make a living by sending bogus invoices to thousands of businesses each month, hoping that a few will pay without reviewing them.

Set aside a time each week to review your invoices against your records. When you incur any charges, write them in a notebook or slip a note into a box so each one can be verified. If you have a staff that prepares your bills for payment, you'll need more complete records so that they or you can verify each invoice or statement to your records.

Some businesses use a rubber stamp for invoices that require a checkoff for charge created, invoice checked, and invoice paid. Larger firms use formal purchase orders for every charge created, other than those paid with petty cash.

When you call accounts payable and ask questions about their invoices, you will find that companies will attempt to be more accurate on future invoices. They know that you review your invoices. They might be perfectly honest, but still make honest mistakes, which might be reduced if they know you will call them to ask about any questionable charges. This is especially true if you tell them that you will set the invoice aside for later payment if you find any questionable charges.

SHOULD YOU LEASE EQUIPMENT?

Raising capital is difficult for small businesses. That's no secret. This difficulty has caused many small businesses to look at leasing as an alternative financing arrangement when acquiring assets. All types of equipment used by auto repair services, from vehicles to computers to equipment to office furniture, have become easier to lease. Smart business owners are learning more about leases and how this option helps them efficiently manage their business.

A lease is a long-term agreement to rent equipment, land, buildings, or any other asset. In return for most, but not all, of the benefits of ownership, the user (lessee) makes periodic payments to the owner of the asset (lessor). The lease payment covers the original cost of the equipment or other asset and provides the lessor a profit.

Types of leases

There are three major types of leases: the financial lease, the operating lease, and the sale and leaseback lease.

Financial leases These are the most common by far. A financial lease is usually written for a term shorter than the economic life of the property or equipment. A financial lease usually requires that periodic payments be made, that ownership of the asset reverts to the lessor at the end of the lease term, that the lease is non-cancelable with the lessee having a legal obligation to continue payments to the end of the term, and that the lessee agrees to maintain the asset.

Operating or maintenance lease These leases usually can be canceled under conditions spelled out in the lease agreement. Maintenance of the asset is usually the responsibility of the owner or lessor. Computer equipment is often leased under this kind of arrangement with the lessor taking care of maintenance or repairs to the computer as required.

Sale and leaseback These are similar to the financial lease. The owner of an asset sells it to another party and then leases the asset back for a specified term. This arrangement lets you free up money for use elsewhere that would otherwise be tied up. Buildings are often leased this way. Your corporation buys a building then leases it back to you.

You might also hear leases described as net leases or gross leases. With a net lease, the lessee is responsible for expenses such as maintenance, taxes, and insurance. The lessor pays these expenses under a gross lease. Financial leases are usually net leases.

Finally, you might run across the term "full pay-out lease." With a full pay-out lease, the lessor recovers the original cost of the asset during the term of the lease.

Types of lessors

As the use of leases has increased, the number of companies in the leasing business has increased dramatically. Leasing is now a billion dollar industry. Commercial banks, insurance companies, and finance companies do most of the leasing. Many of these organizations have formed subsidiaries primarily concerned with equipment leasing. These subsidiaries usually are capable of making lease arrangements for almost anything. Ask your primary bank or lender whether they offer leases for equipment you require.

In addition to financial organizations, there are companies that specialize in leases. Some are engaged in general leasing, while others favor particular equipment, such as electronic diagnostic equipment, computers, or auto repair equipment.

Some equipment manufacturers are also in the leasing business. They often lease their equipment through their sales reps. When you consider leasing equipment, ask your auto repair equipment sales rep about leases available through the manufacturer.

Advantages and disadvantages to leasing

The obvious advantage to leasing is acquiring the use of an asset without making a large initial cash outlay. A lease usually requires little or no down payment, no restriction on a company's financial operations, spreads payments over a longer period than most loans, and provides protection against the risk of equipment obsolescence.

There also might be tax benefits to leasing. Lease payments are deductible as operating expenses if the arrangement is a true lease (as defined by the Internal Revenue Service). Ownership, however, usually has greater tax advantages through depreciation. Naturally, you need to have enough income and resulting tax liability to take advantage of these two benefits.

Firms that specialize in equipment used by auto repair services have considerable knowledge about the kinds of equipment they lease. Thus, they can provide expert technical advice based on experience with the leased equipment.

Finally, there is one further advantage to leasing that you hope won't ever be necessary. In the event your firm files for bankruptcy, the lessor's claims to your assets are more restricted than those of general creditors.

So what's the downside of leasing? In the first place, leasing usually costs more because you lose certain tax advantages that go with asset ownership. Leasing might not cost more if you can't take advantage of these tax benefits because you don't have enough tax liability for them to come into play.

Obviously, you also lose the economic value of the asset at the end of the lease since you don't own the asset. Lessees have been known to grossly underestimate the salvage value of an asset. If they had known this value from the outset, they might have decided to buy instead of lease.

Finally, never forget that a lease is a long-term legal obligation. Usually you can't cancel a lease agreement. So if you were to end an operation that used leased equipment, you might find you'd still have to pay as much as if you had used the equipment for the full term of the lease.

Leases and taxes

Full lease payments are deductible as operating costs. You can make these deductions only if the Internal Revenue Service finds that you have a true lease. You cannot take a full deduction for a lease that's really an installment purchase.

Although each lease arrangement might be different, here are some general guidelines.

- In no way should any portion of the payment be construed as interest.
- Lease payments must not be large compared to the cost of purchasing the same asset.
- Any renewal option at lease end must be on terms equivalent to what a third party would offer.
- Purchase options must be at amounts comparable to fair market value.

Accounting for leases

Historically, financial leases were "off-the-balance-sheet" financing. That is, lease obligations often were not recorded directly on the balance sheet, but listed instead in footnotes. Not explicitly accounting for leases sometimes results in a failure to state fairly operational assets and liabilities.

In 1977, the Financial Accounting Standards Board (FASB), the rule-making body of the accounting profession, required that capital leases be recorded on the balance sheet as both an asset and a liability. This was in recognition of the long-term nature of a lease obligation.

Cost analysis

You can analyze the cost of a lease versus purchase through discounted cash flow analysis. This analysis compares the cost of each alternative by considering the timing of the payments, tax benefits, the interest rate on a loan, the lease rate, and other financial arrangements.

Even if you plan to have your accountant work up these numbers for you, follow through on this exercise so that you can better understand what this cost analysis tells you about buying versus leasing equipment. After all, it's you not your accountant who will make the decision.

Table 7-3   Sample problem assumptions.

Equipment cost	$60,000
Estimated economic life	10 years
Lease terms	8 annual* payments of $10,363.94 (Apr 10.5%). First payment due upon delivery. Investment tax credit to lessor. Lessee maintains equipment.
Loan terms	5 years, 75% financing at 10% (Apr). 5 annual* payments of $11,870.89. First payment due at end of first year.
Taxes	Lessee tax rate 50%. Method of depreciation for tax purposes is straight line.
Other	Equipment needed for term of lease, 8 years. If firm purchases equipment, it can be sold at end of 8 years for book value. Average after tax cost of capital for lessee is 9%.

*Payments have been annualized to simplify calculations. Payments are usually made monthly.

Table 7-4 Lease analysis.

(1) End of year	(2) Lease payment	(3) (0.52 × 2) Tax saving	(4) (2–3) Net cash outlay	(5) Discount factor	(6) (4 × 5) Net present value
0	$10,363.94	$5,181.97	$5,181.97	1.000	$5,181.97
1	10,363.94	5,181.97	5,181.97	0.952	4,933.24
2	10,363.94	5,181.97	5,181.97	0.907	4,700.05
3	10,363.94	5,181.97	5,181.97	0.864	4,477.22
4	10,363.94	5,181.97	5,181.97	0.823	4,264.76
5	10,363.94	5,181.97	5,181.97	0.784	4,062.66
6	10,363.94	5,181.97	5,181.97	1.746	3,865.75
7	10,363.94	5,181.97	5,181.97	1.710	3,684.38
8	—	—	—	—	—
Net present value of costs of leasing					**$35,170.03**

To make the analysis you must first make certain assumptions about the economic life of the equipment, its salvage value, and depreciation. Let's work through a sample problem to illustrate the process. The assumptions for the sample problem are included in TABLE 7-3. TABLE 7-4 is the analysis of the lease alternative. TABLE 7-5 is an analysis of the borrow-and-buy option.

To evaluate a lease you must first find the net cash outlay (not cash flow) for each year of the lease term. You find these amounts by subtracting the tax savings (at 50 percent in our example) from the lease payment. This calculation gives you the net cash outlay for each year of the lease.

Each year's net cash outlay must next be discounted to take into account the time value of money. This discounting gives you the *present value* of each of the amounts.

The present value of an amount of money is the sum you would have to invest today at a stated rate of interest to have that amount of money at a specified future date. As an example, if someone offered to give you $100 five years from now, how much could you take today and be as well off? Common sense tells you that you could take less than $100 because you'd have the use of the money for the five-year period. Naturally, how much less you could take depends on the interest rate you thought you could get if you invested the lesser amount. To have $100 five years from now at 6 percent compounded annually, you'd have to invest $74.70 today. At 10 percent, you could take $62.10 now to have the $100 at the end of five years.

Thus, the present value of the net outlay under the lease ($5,181.97 after tax savings) at the end of year six of the lease term, for example, is something less than $5,181.97. Here, we will use 5 percent as the appropriate interest rate for discounting the lease payment (after tax cost of 50 percent times the loan interest of 10 percent). This low rate of interest is used because of the certain nature of the payments with a lease contract. So, at an annually compounded 5-percent interest rate, you would have to invest $3,865.75 today to have $5,181.97 at the end of six years.

Table 7-5 Borrow-and-buy analysis.

(1) End of Year	(2) Payment	(3) Interest	(4) (2-3) Principal repayment	(5) (5-4) Outstanding balance	(6) Depreciation	(7) .05 × (6+3) Tax savings	(8) (2-7) Net cash flow	(9) Discount factor	(10) (8 × 9) Net present value
0	$15,000.00			$45,000.00		$6,000.00*	$ 9,000.00	1.000	$ 9,000.00
1	11,870.89	$4,500.00	$ 7,370.89	37,629.11	$6,000.00	5,250.00	6,620.89	0.952	5,303.09
2	11,870.89	3,726.91	8,107.98	29,521.13	6,000.00	4,881.46	6,989.43	0.907	6,339.41
3	11,870.89	2,952.11	8,918.78	20,602.35	6,000.00	4,476.06	7,394.83	0.864	6,389.13
4	11,870.89	2,060.24	9,810.66	10,791.69	6,000.00	4,030.12	7,840.77	0.823	6,452.95
5	11,870.86	1,079.17	10,791.69		6,000.00	3,539.59	8,331.27	0.784	6,531.72
6					6,000.00	3,000.00	(3,000.00)	0.746	(2,238.00)
7					6,000.00	3,000.00	(3,000.00)	0.711	(2,133.00)
8	(12,000.00)**				6,000.00	3,000.00	(3,000.00)	0.677	(2,031.00)
							(12,000.00)	0.502***	(6,024.00)

Net present value of cost of purchasing $28,590.30

* Investment tax credit = 0.10 × $60,000 − $6,000.

** Salvage value = book value = $60,000 − 8 × $6,000 = $12,000.

*** Discount factor using average after tax cost of capital.

Fortunately, there are tables that provide the discount factors for present value calculations (TABLE 7-6). The factor for the present value of $1 six years from now at 5 percent is 0.746. This factor (.746) times the after-tax lease payment outlay ($5,181.97) equals $3,865.75, or exactly the amount you would have to invest today at 5-percent interest compounded annually to have $5,181.97 six years hence. There also are relatively inexpensive business calculators and computer spreadsheets programmed to make these calculations for you.

Table 7-6   Discount factors for present value calculations.

Year*	1%	2%	3%	4%	5%	6%	7%	8%	9%	10%
1	.990	.980	.971	.962	.952	.943	.935	.926	.917	.909
2	.980	.961	.943	.925	.907	.890	.873	.857	.842	.826
3	.971	.942	.915	.889	.864	.840	.816	.794	.772	.751
4	.961	.924	.889	.855	.823	.792	.763	.735	.708	.683
5	.951	.906	.863	.822	.784	.747	.713	.681	.650	.621
6	.942	.888	.838	.790	.746	.705	.666	.630	.596	.564
7	.933	.871	.813	.760	.711	.665	.623	.583	.547	.513
8	.923	.853	.789	.731	.677	.627	.582	.540	.502	.467
9	.914	.837	.766	.703	.645	.592	.544	.500	.460	.424
10	.905	.820	.744	.676	.614	.558	.508	.453	.422	.386

* Periods can be any time period; they do not have to be years.

Why bother to make these present-value calculations? They are necessary in order to compare the actual cash flows over the time periods. You can't realistically compare methods of financing without taking into account the time value of money. It might seem confusing and complex at first, but if you work through the example, you'll begin to see that the technique isn't difficult, just sophisticated.

Let's consider the present-value calculations over the full term of the proposed lease. The sum of the discounted cash flows, $35,170.03, is called the *net present value of the cost of leasing*. It is this figure that is compared to the final sum of the discounted cash flows for the loan and purchase alternative.

Evaluation of the borrow/buy option is a little more complicated because of the tax benefits that go with ownership through loan interest deductions and depreciation. The steps in the calculation are shown above each column head. The interest portion of each loan payment is found by multiplying the loan interest rate (10 percent in the example) by the outstanding loan balance for the preceding period.

Note that in the last three years of the analyzed period the cash flow is positive, coming from the tax savings on depreciation and, in the eighth year, from depreciation and the assumption that the asset could be sold for a salvage value of $12,000. Since these amounts in the last three years are coming in, they are subtracted after discounting from the amounts in the first five years (cash flowing out) to get the *net present value of costs of purchasing*.

As noted earlier, the salvage value is one of the advantages of ownership. It must be considered when making the comparison. However, it is discounted at a higher rate (the firm's assumed average cost of capital, 9 percent). This rate is used because the salvage value is not known with any certainty, as are the loan payment, depreciation, and interest payments.

When you compare the two alternatives you see that the buy option looks like the least costly approach. The major difference in cost, of course, comes from the salvage value. If you ignore that value, the alternatives are very close in their net present value of costs. Naturally, it's possible that salvage cost for real assets could be very high or be next to nothing. So salvage value assumptions need to be made carefully because they can impact greatly your decision.

Thus, while this sort of analysis is useful, you can't make a lease/buy decision solely on cost-analysis figures. The advantages and disadvantages, while tough to qualify, might outweigh the differences in cost. This is especially true if the costs between leasing and buying are reasonably close.

Signing a lease

A lease agreement is a legal document. It carries a long-term obligation. You must be thoroughly informed of the commitment you're making. Find out the lessor's financial condition and reputation. Be reasonably sure that the lease arrangements are the best you can get, that the equipment is what you need, and that the term is what you want. Remember, once the agreement is signed, it is just about impossible to change it.

The lease document spells out the precise provisions of the agreement. These provisions might include the specific nature of the financial agreement, the payment amount, terms of the agreement, disposition of the asset at the end of the term, schedule of asset value (for insurance and settlement purposes in case of damage or destruction), who is responsible for maintenance and taxes, renewal options, and cancelation penalties. In addition, the lease might include special provisions required by either you or the lessor.

As with any legally binding document, make sure that your attorney, and even your accountant, review it before you sign it to ensure that they don't have to defend it later.

YOUR SUCCESS ACTION LIST

The more you reduce costs, the more your auto repair business profits. There are many things that you can do to analyze expenses, locate reducible expenses, reduce overhead, increase discounts, schedule work efficiently, increase cash flow, and save money when paying bills. You can also reduce your capital requirements with leases. Following are some of the actions you can take now. The next chapter tells you how to reduce potential costs by reducing risks.

_____ Analyze your operating expenses to determine if any seem excessive or have dramatically increased from the previous report.

_____ Calculate your auto repair business' break-even point.

_____ List all discounts available to your business and what would be required to earn or increase them.

_____ Consider hiring an accountant or consulting with a SCORE volunteer for an efficient review of your operation to look for reducible expenses.

_____ Review your business' methods of scheduling work to determine if it can be more efficient or more profitable.

_____ Verify that you use the appropriate depreciation method for your equipment and other assets.

_____ Compile a cash-flow statement for the next 6 and 12 months for your business.

_____ Make sure you carefully review all incoming invoices and manage payments for greatest profits.

_____ List the opportunities that your auto repair service has for leasing, and consider each one as an option to purchasing.

8
Reducing your risks

Business is legalized gambling. You place your bet and you take your chances. The odds are much better in business, especially if you know how to reduce normal business risks. This chapter is about reducing the risks you'll face in this industry.

On the following pages, you'll learn about the risks you take as you start and manage your auto repair service. You'll discover how other successful businesspeople minimize these risks and actually turn them into opportunities.

COMMON RISKS

You've learned how to increase sales and reduce expenses for your auto repair business. But even when your business grows and profits, you can still lose money. How?

- An employee is injured on the job and sues you.
- An employee steals money from your business.
- A fire or flood wipes out your office, tools, machinery, and important records.
- A partner in your business files bankruptcy and the courts attach your business.
- The local economy goes sour and you can't find any profitable jobs for six months or more.
- A business for which you subcontract work files bankruptcy or is subject to a large lien and you don't get paid what's owed to you.
- A business partner is involved in a divorce settlement and business assets must be sold to meet a court order.
- The IRS comes after you for a large tax bill they think you owe them and takes over your bank account until everything is resolved.

The list goes on. What can you do about these risks? First, you can make sure you understand the risks involved in your business. Second, you can take precautions to ensure that the risks are minimal. They will never go away, but through smart risk management, you can minimize them and prepare for the worst.

WHAT RISKS YOU FACE

It's obvious that the best time to minimize the risk of business disasters is before they happen. And the first step to minimizing risk is to identify the risks that can occur. Business risks that auto repair services typically face are:

- acts of nature (fire, flood)
- acts of man (theft, vandalism, vehicle accidents)
- personal injury (employee or user)
- legal problems (liens, unfair trade practices, torts)
- financial (loss of income, funding, or assets)
- taxation (judgments, tax liens)
- management (loss of owner's capacity to manage or partner's ownership)

Of course, every method to reduce risk—attorneys, bonds, insurance, binding agreements, security systems, fire alarms, etc.—cost money. So when is it more cost-effective to accept the risk rather than pay for products or services that eliminate the risk? It's a simple question with a simple answer: it all depends.

Actually, the best time to minimize risk to your business is right now. The real answer lies in balancing the cost of loss against the cost of security. For example, if your work vehicle is a beat-up 1972 Ford van with a pinto paint job, collision insurance that costs an extra $300 a year is more expensive than absorbing the cost of body damage from minor accidents.

Reduce the risks involved in owning and operating your auto repair business by using the knowledge and skills of others. Select an insurance agent, an attorney, and an accountant whom you trust and let them guide you toward cost-effective methods that can minimize risks without spending too much time and money.

Insurance agent

A good insurance agent is as valuable to your success as any other professional consultant. A good insurance agent can both ensure that your exposure to risk is low and keep your insurance costs to a minimum.

Ask other auto repair services and professionals to recommend a good insurance agent. If possible, search for one who primarily serves the business community rather than families or individuals. They will better know your problems and concerns.

Ask prospective agents for advice on a specific problem. Don't tell them what you think the solution is. Their responses can help you determine who is the best at cost-effective problem solving.

There are some things you can do to reduce insurance costs. For example, you can save money over the long-term by increasing your vehicles' deductible. In fact, the best way to save on all insurance costs—auto, fire, theft, health—is to increase your deductible to a manageable amount. Determine if paying the higher annual deductible would significantly change your premiums. That is, if your deductible increases from $50 to $200, would you save the $150 in annual premiums?

Attorney

To find an attorney who is familiar with businesses of your size and trade, ask for a referral from a business colleague, your accountant, your banker, your local chamber of commerce, or other auto repair services in your area. Some local bar associations run an attorney referral and information service. Check your local telephone book's yellow pages under Attorneys' Referral & Information Services. Many referral services give you only names and phone numbers; a few will give information on experience and fees to help you match your needs to an attorney's background and charges.

As discussed earlier, an attorney can help you decide which is the most advantageous business structure to reduce risks. He or she can also help you with zoning, permit, or licensing problems, unpaid bills, contracts and agreements, trademarks, and some tax problems.

Because there is always the possibility of a lawsuit, claim, or other legal action against your business, it is wise to have an attorney who is already familiar with your business lined up before a crisis arises. An attorney with experience serving auto repair businesses can also advise you on federal, state, and local laws, programs, and agencies to help you obtain loans, grants, procurement set-asides, and solve tax problems. Your attorney might be able to advise you about unexpected legal opportunities and pitfalls that might affect your business.

When choosing an attorney, experience and fee should be related. One attorney might charge an hourly rate that, at first glance, looks cheaper than another attorney's. However, because of a lack of experience solving legal problems for auto repair services, the less expensive attorney might cost more to solve the same problem. If you feel overwhelmed with the selection process, take a trusted friend to your initial meeting with the attorney to help you keep on track as you interview the attorney about services and fees.

If you retain a law firm, be sure you understand who will work on your projects and who will supervise the work. If junior attorneys handle your work, the fees should be lower. That's okay as long as you know that an experienced attorney will review and be ultimately responsible for the work done.

Let your attorney know that you expect to be informed of all developments and consulted before any decisions are made on your behalf. You might also want to receive copies of all documents, letters, and memos written and received regarding your project. If this isn't practical, you should at least have the opportunity to read such correspondence at your attorney's office.

Whenever giving your attorney a project—defending a lawsuit, reviewing a contract, consulting on tax matters—ask him or her to estimate the costs and time required to adequately complete the project. You might want to place a periodic ceiling on fees, after which your attorney needs to call you before proceeding with work that will add to your bill.

One way to reduce the need to file a lien against a job is to never let a customer go past 90 days overdue without taking some sort of action. Talk to your attorney or to a collection service about your options and the process.

One more point when working with an attorney. If you hire an attorney on retainer, make sure that you have a written agreement between you that clearly describes just what you and the attorney expect from each other.

Save attorney fees

Everybody loves to save money! Especially when the money saved is significant. Here are some ideas on how you can save money as you work with your attorney.

First, talk about fees up front, making sure that you are clear on what will be charged and when. The fees might be established by the hour, by the job (flat fee), or on a contingency fee (ranging from 25 to 50 percent). If you expect to use a specific number of hours of your attorney's time during the coming year, you might be able to contract for that minimum at a lower rate. In most cases, out-of-pocket expenses such as long distance phone calls, filing fees, and transcripts are paid by the client unless agreed upon in advance. You can also reduce your attorney's research costs by bringing all pertinent information and documents with you to your meeting.

Second, negotiate each transaction separately. That is, some legal matters can be handled with just a few hours of your attorney's time while others might require extensive time and research. Obviously, the first matter should be negotiated as an hourly or flat fee while the large job should be negotiated as a flat fee or a contingency project. Make sure you get a monthly itemized bill.

Third, if possible, settle a case rather than go through litigation. Even litigation will typically not get you every last dollar. Often the end result will be negotiated. Besides, the legal system might take years to resolve your dispute.

Finally, treat your attorney as a professional counselor who works for you. If your budget is tight, inform him or her. If you're not clear why you should take their advice, ask. In other words, keep the lines of communication open.

Finding an accountant

An attorney is a valuable resource as you start and build your business, but a good accountant is even more so. Most businesses fail not for lack of good ideas or good intentions, but rather for lack of financial expertise and planning.

Look for an accountant as you would an attorney. Get referrals from trusted friends, business associates, professional associations, and other auto repair services. Discuss fees in advance and draw up a written agreement about how you will work together. Your accountant can advise you about initial business decisions, can help you set up your records, draw up and analyze income statements, advise on financial decisions involving the purchase of capital assets, and give advice on cash requirements for the successful continuation of your venture. He or she can make budget forecasts, help prepare financial information for a loan application, and handle tax matters.

Accounting firms offer a variety of services. If this is not an easy area for you, the fees you pay will be well worth the value. Most accounting firms can maintain books of original entry, prepare bank reconciliation statements and post the general ledger, prepare quarterly and semi-annual balance sheets and income statements, and design and implement various accounting and recordkeeping systems.

Accounting firms can also get your federal and state withholding numbers for you, instruct you on where and when to file tax returns, prepare tax returns, and do general tax planning for your small business.

Your accountant is your key financial adviser. He or she should alert you to potential danger areas and advise you on how to handle growth spurts, how to best plan for slow business times, and how to financially mature and protect your business future from unnecessary risk.

WHAT "RISK-MANAGEMENT" IS

Risk management consists of identifying and analyzing the things that might cause loss, and choosing the best way to deal with each of these potentials for loss. You've worked hard to build your business. You've poured a lot of time, effort, and money into building it up. Spend some time looking at the best ways to reduce risk.

The best way to reduce risk to your growing auto repair business is to continue the learning process. You've been a student for all of the years you've worked in your trade, learning how to do your job better, faster, and more efficiently. Now you're starting your own business and have learned about dozens of new topics.

Here are three things you can do to continue the learning process, increase your knowledge, reduce risks, and expand your business.

First, work closely and creatively with your professional advisers—your attorney, your accountant, and your insurance agent. As you periodically review your business records, you will see ways that you can do things better the next time. You will begin to develop your skills in planning and managing your business.

Second, continue to learn about all aspects of business operations; constantly acquire new ideas and new skills. Sign up for beginning, intermediate, and advanced business courses at your local community college or through seminars sponsored by regional business development centers. Also, continue to learn more and more about the auto repair trade through association books, tapes, seminars, courses, and conventions.

Third, get to know other business owners with similar needs or problems. Your business has little in common with retailers, but you have much in common with other service businesses. Talking with others can help you keep from repeating mistakes they have made. You can benefit from their experiences and they from yours. Local and national associations offer membership, social events, networking opportunities, newsletters, and seminars for auto repair services. Some organizations enable you to advertise your product or service to potential customers. They also provide a way to learn about services you might need, such as accounting, advertising, or secretarial services. These organizations offer updates in such areas as taxes and zoning in their newsletters and workshops.

Exposures to loss

Identifying exposures to loss is a vital step to reducing your risks. Until you know the scope of all possible losses, you won't be able to develop a realistic, cost-effective strategy for dealing with them. The last thing you want is to come up with a superficial Band-Aid approach that might cause more problems than it solves.

It's not easy to recognize the hundreds of hazards or perils that can lead to an unexpected loss. Unless you've experienced a fire, for example, you might not realize how extensive fire loss can be. Damage to the building and its contents are obvious exposures. But related losses include damage or destruction caused by smoke and water, damage to employees' personal property, damage to customers' or suppliers' property, the loss of income during the time it takes to get the business back to normal, and the loss to competitors of customers who might not return when you reopen for business.

What's the solution? Begin the process of identifying exposures by taking a close look at each of your business operations and asking yourself these questions.

- What could cause a loss to my business operation?
- How serious is that loss to the continuation of my business?

Many business owners use a risk analysis questionnaire or survey as a checklist. These are available from insurance agents, most of whom can provide the expertise to help you with your analysis. With their knowledge and experience, you're less likely to overlook any exposures. Most risk analysis questionnaires and surveys look at potential for property losses, business-interruption losses, liability losses, key person losses, and automobile losses.

Property losses

Property losses stem from physical damage to property, loss of use of property, or criminal activity.

Physical damage Property damage can be caused by many common perils: fire, windstorm, lightning, and vandalism might be the first that come to mind. And it's a rare business that doesn't buy insurance to protect against these. But to cope effectively with the possibility of physical damage to property, you should consider more than just damage to or destruction of a building.

Contents might be even more susceptible to loss. Your auto repair business could lose valuable accounting records, making it difficult to bill customers or to collect from customers who owe money. Vital tools and equipment might become unusable because of fire and, if replacements can't be found and installed immediately, your business might be forced to shut down temporarily. Unless you continue to pay employees, a shutdown can force experienced employees to find work elsewhere, maybe with a competitor.

Loss of use Your business could lose the use of property without suffering any physical damage. A government agency can close a client's office down as part of a lawsuit, for delinquent taxes, or other causes.

Criminal activity Small businesses are very susceptible to crimes committed by others. Burglary and robbery are obvious perils, but don't overlook possible exposure to white-collar crime, employee theft, embezzlement, or forgery. An experienced insurance agent can help you define the types of risks your auto repair business faces in your locality.

Business-interruption losses

You've already seen how a direct loss from a fire can temporarily shut down your business. Although property insurance provides money for repairing or rebuilding physical damage that is a direct result of a fire, most property policies don't cover indirect losses such as the income lost while your business is interrupted for repairs.

A special kind of insurance covers indirect losses that occur when a direct loss forces a temporary interruption of business. For example, an auto repair service owner whose critical equipment and tools were stolen during the height of his busiest season lost nearly a month's income because they weren't available to him.

Business-interruption insurance reimburses policyholders for the difference between normal income and the reduced income earned during the enforced shutdown period.

Not only is income reduced or cut off completely during such interruptions, but many business expenses continue such as taxes, loan payments, salaries to key employees, interest, depreciation, and utilities. Without income to pay for these expenses, your business is forced to dip into reserves.

In addition, business interruption often triggers extra expenses. For example, you might have to authorize overtime to shorten the interruption period, or you might have to rent shop space or equipment for the period in order to perform your services. These extra expenses put an additional strain on finances at a time when little if any income is being produced.

An auto repair business owner can even buy business-interruption coverage to protect against interruptions triggered by direct loss on someone else's property. If your key supplier is shut down by fire and can't deliver required materials to you, you could suffer a business loss. Or if your tools and equipment are stored at the customer's job site and it suffers physical or criminal damage, you can lose income as if it were a direct loss to you.

Key-person losses

What would happen to your business if an accident or illness made it impossible for you to work? What if one of your partners or your shop manager were to die suddenly? Most of us would rather not think about such a "what if." Nevertheless, it is important for you to prepare your business for survival, long before a key person dies or is disabled. Unfortunately, it is a step that is often overlooked.

Here are some of questions you should consider regarding the loss of people key to your auto repair business.

- How will your business survive if you become seriously ill or disabled?
- What will be your source of income?
- Who would take over his job so the business can continue?
- What if the heir is not qualified or is a minor?
- What will happen to the business if you die?
- If a will is not in place before you die, what happens to the business?
- If your life savings have been invested in the business, will your surviving family members receive any cash to help them continue?
- What will the surviving family's source of income be while the future of the business is being decided?
- If the business is to be sold, where will working capital come from for the transition period?

- How will the fair market value of the business be determined?
- Would the business' fair market value be apt to change because of the loss of a key person?
- If the business forms the bulk of the estate, what are the income and inheritance tax implications for the surviving spouse and heirs?
- Is there some pre-death strategy that could minimize that tax liability?
- If the business is a partnership, is their a binding agreement in place that will allow a continuation of the business?
- What are the duties of the surviving partner regarding wrapping up the affairs of the partnership?
- Will the surviving partner be personally liable for losses that the business's assets are insufficient to cover.
- If your business is a corporation, how does the death or disability of a major stockholder affect your business?

Once again, planning is essential. Your attorney, accountant, and insurance agent can develop a legally binding and cost-effective strategy to reduce losses and to prevent outsiders from taking over your business during a catastrophe.

LOSS CONTROL

There are a number of ways you can keep your losses to a minimum. They include preventing or limiting exposure to loss, risk retention, transferring risk, and insurance.

One principle of loss prevention and control is the same in business as it is in your personal life: avoid activities that are too hazardous. For example, don't place vehicles on your service rack that are heavier than the rated lift.

An auto repair business owner might decide that the firm can afford to absorb some losses, either because the frequency and probability of loss are low or because the dollar value of loss is manageable. Maybe your auto repair business owns several older vehicles and their drivers have excellent safety records so you decide to drop the collision insurance on these vehicles, but retain it on newer vehicles.

Another way to manage exposure to loss is to transfer the risk. Although many businesses do this by buying insurance, thus transferring some of the risk to the insurance company, there are other options. Your firm might decide to eliminate collision exposure completely by hiring subcontractors (such as a towing service) who supply their own vehicles, rather than hiring employees. Or you might decide not to stock an inventory of parts or equipment, but rather to purchase materials only as you need them and to have them delivered to your shop.

WHAT INSURANCE YOU NEED

The most common method of transferring risk is purchasing insurance. By insuring your business and equipment you transfer much of the risk of loss to the insurance company. You pay a relatively small amount in premium rather than run the risk of not protecting yourself against the possibility of a much larger financial loss.

Of course, you can be overinsured or pay more than is necessary for the amount of risk that you transfer. Only you can decide which exposures you absolutely must insure against. Some decisions, however, are already made for you, such as those required by law and those required by others as a part of doing business with them. Workers' compensation insurance is an example of insurance that is required by law. Your bank probably won't lend you money for equipment, real estate, or other assets unless you insure them against loss.

Today, very few businesses, and especially auto repair services, have sufficient financial reserves to protect themselves against the hundreds of property and liability exposures that they face. What those exposures are, what their dollar value is, and how much is enough, are difficult questions. That's why, as you build a team of business professionals to help you effectively manage your business, you should hire an insurance professional.

The insurance agent The agent is the insurance industry's primary client representative. Typically, the independent agent is a small business owner and manager. By using this distribution system, insurance companies are represented by agents who receive a commission for selling the companies' products and services. An independent agent may represent more than one insurance company.

The professional insurance agent has been trained in risk analysis. She or he is familiar with the insurance coverages and financial strategies available in your state, and with regulations that govern them. With this experience, the agent can point out exposures that you might otherwise overlook.

Finally, your insurance professional can help you develop possible solutions. You make the final decisions, but your agent can suggest options from a vast menu of risk-management strategies. He or she has the technical knowledge to amend a basic policy by adding special coverages and endorsements. The resulting policy can be custom-tailored to your business' unique protection needs.

The insurance company There are a number of related services that insurance companies provide to policyholders. As a small businessperson who wants to reduce both risk and costs, you should consider using these services.

Liability insurance coverages, particularly for property damage and bodily injury, usually include legal defense at no additional charge when the policyholder is named as a party to the lawsuit that involves a claim covered by the policy. Litigation is costly, whether the claimant's suit is valid or frivolous. The legal defense provision greatly reduces these costs to you.

Insurance companies that write a lot of workers' compensation insurance might have extensive rehabilitation services available. Generally, these services help return injured workers to useful employment and, in some cases, might even help train the worker for a different job.

Essential insurance coverage

Four kinds of insurance are essential to your business: fire, liability, automobile, and workers' compensation insurance. Selecting from among the dozens of available policies and options can be somewhat confusing. However, the following information can help you make the right decisions for the right reasons.

Fire insurance Here are some tips on buying fire insurance coverage. You can add other perils, such as windstorm, hail, smoke, explosion, vandalism, and malicious mischief, to your basic fire insurance for a relatively small additional fee.

If you need comprehensive coverage, your best buy might be one of the all-risk contracts, such as the $1 million umbrella policy, that offer the broadest available protection for the money.

Remember that the insurance company might compensate your losses by paying actual cash value of the property at the time of the loss, it might repair or replace the property with material of like kind and quality, or it might take all the property at the agreed or appraised value and reimburse you for your loss.

You can insure property that you don't own, such as a shop or job site, for potential loss of assets at that site.

You cannot assign an insurance policy along with property you sell unless you have the permission of the insurance company.

Even if you have several policies on your property, you can still collect only the amount of your actual cash loss. All the insurers share the payment proportionately.

Special protection other than the standard fire insurance policy is needed to cover the loss by fire of accounts, bills, currency, deeds, evidence of debt, and securities.

If you increase the hazard of fire, the insurance company might suspend your coverage even for losses not originating from the increased hazard (such as renting part of your building to a cleaning plant).

After a loss, you must use all reasonable means to protect the property from further loss or run the risk of having your coverage canceled.

In most cases, to recover your loss you must furnish within 60 days a complete inventory of the damaged, destroyed, and undamaged property showing in detail quantities, costs, actual cash value, and amount of loss claimed.

If you and your insurer disagree on the amount of the loss, the question might be resolved through special appraisal procedures provided for in the fire insurance policy.

You may cancel your policy without notice at any time and get part of the premium returned. The insurance company also may cancel at any time within a specified period, usually five days, with a written notice to you.

You can substantially reduce premiums by accepting a co-insurance clause in your fire insurance policy. A co-insurance clause states that you must carry insurance equal to 80 or 90 percent of the value of the insured property. If you carry less than this, you cannot collect the full amount of your loss, even if the loss is small. What percent of your loss you can collect will depend on the percentage of the full value of the property for which you have insured it.

If your loss is caused by someone else's negligence, the insurer has the right to sue this negligent third party for the amount it has paid you under the policy. This is known as the insurer's right to subrogation. However, the insurer usually waives this right upon request. For example, if you have leased your insured building to someone and have waived your right to recover from the tenant for any insured damages to your property, you should have your agent request that the insurer waive the subrogation clause in the fire policy on your leased building.

A building under construction can be insured for fire, lightning, extended coverage, vandalism, and malicious mischief.

Liability insurance Here are some important things to consider when you purchase liability insurance.

You might be legally liable for damages even in cases where you used "reasonable care."

Under certain conditions, your business might be subject to damage claims even from trespassers.

Most liability policies require you to notify the insurer immediately after an incident on your property that might cause a future claim. This holds true no matter how unimportant the incident might seem at the time it happens.

Even if the suit against you is false or fraudulent, the liability insurer pays court costs, legal fees, and interest on judgments in addition to the liability judgments themselves.

You can be liable for the acts of others under contracts you have signed with them, such as subcontractors. This liability is insurable.

Automobile insurance   One of the most common types of risk transference is automobile or vehicle insurance. Here are some pointers to help you make an informed decision.

When an employee or a subcontractor uses their vehicle on your behalf, you can be legally liable even though you don't own the car or truck.

Five or more automobiles, trucks, or motorcycles under one ownership and operated as a fleet for business purposes can generally be insured against both material damage to the vehicles and liability to others for property damage or personal injury under a low-cost fleet policy.

You can often get deductibles of almost any amount—$250, $500, $1,000—and thereby reducing your premiums.

Automobile medical-payments insurance pays for medical claims, including your own, arising from vehicular accidents regardless of the question of negligence.

In most states, you must carry liability insurance or be prepared to provide a surety bond or other proof of financial responsibility when you're involved in an accident.

You can purchase uninsured motorist protection to cover your own bodily injury claims from someone who has no insurance.

Personal property stored in a car or truck and not attached to it is not covered under an automobile policy.

Workers' compensation insurance   Workers' comp is required in most states if you have employees. You can reduce the cost of this mandatory insurance by knowing the following information.

Federal laws require that an employer provide employees a safe place to work, hire competent fellow employees, provide safe tools, and warn employees of existing danger. If an employer fails to provide these things, he is liable for damage suits brought by an employee and possible fines or prosecution.

State law determines the level or type of benefits payable under workers' compensation insurance policies. Not all employees are covered by workers' compensation insurance laws, however. The exceptions are determined by state law and therefore vary from state to state.

You can save money on workers' compensation insurance by seeing that your employees are properly classified. Rates for workers' compensation insurance vary from 0.1 percent of the payroll for "safe" occupations to about 25 percent or more of the payroll for very hazardous occupations.

Most employers can reduce their workers' compensation insurance premium by reducing their accident rates below the average. They do this by using safety and loss-prevention measures established by the individual state.

Desirable insurance coverage

Some types of insurance coverage, while not absolutely essential, can add greatly to the security of your business. These coverages include business-interruption insurance and crime insurance. Whether these coverages are vital to your business depends on how and where your business operates. A small firm with two partners who have identical skills might not require business-interruption insurance. But a million dollar one-man-band might require extensive insurance against business interruption. The same applies to crime insurance, some business locations require it while others might not.

Business-interruption insurance You can purchase insurance to cover fixed expenses that will continue if a fire shuts down your business, such as salaries to key employees, taxes, interest, mortgage, and utilities, as well as the profits you will lose.

Under contingent business-interruption insurance, you can also collect if fire or another peril closes down the business of a supplier or customer and this interrupts your business.

The business-interruption policy provides payments for amounts you spend to hasten the reopening of your business after a fire or other insured peril.

You can get coverage for the extra expenses you suffer if an insured peril seriously disrupts your business rather than closes it down.

Some business-interruption policies indemnify you if your operations are suspended because of failure or interruption of the supply of power by a public utility company.

Crime insurance Crime insurance is a cost of doing business to nearly every area of this country. Unfortunately, in some areas it is a major expense. Here are some facts to consider before you purchase crime insurance for your auto repair business.

Burglary insurance excludes such property as accounts receivable files. If you lose them to a burglar, you will have problems collecting from your accounts or from your insurance company.

With many policies, coverage is granted under burglary insurance only if there are visible marks of the burglar's forced entry. If he somehow found your keys, you might not be protected.

Burglary insurance can be written to cover, in addition to valuables stolen, damage incurred in the course of a burglary. It also covers theft on your property, as well as loss of property, money, and other assets by force, trickery, or threat of violence on or off your premises.

Consider purchasing a comprehensive crime policy written specifically for small business owners. In addition to burglary and robbery, it covers other types of loss by theft, destruction and disappearance of money and securities, and theft by employees.

If your business is located in a high-risk area and cannot get insurance through normal channels without paying excessive rates, you might be able to get help through the federal crime insurance plan. Your agent or state insurance commissioner can tell you where to get information about these plans.

REDUCE BAD DEBTS

As discussed earlier, one excellent way to reduce bad debts is to require payment on delivery of services. Payment can be cash, verified check, or credit card. Or establish a working relationship with a financial services business that can carry the loan and give you up-front cash for the job.

For competitive reasons you might decide to offer credit. A primary cause for bad debt loss is a credit decision based on an inadequate credit investigation. Yet, prompt repair service is essential. Your credit checking method should be geared for speed and efficiency to enhance order flow and reduce bad debts.

The depth of your investigation into a customer's credit depends on many factors: the size of the repair order and the potential for future orders, the status of the present account, whether the account is seasonal, the amount of time required to complete the job, relationship of the order to the total credit exposure of the customer, and whether a deposit is required.

Sources for credit information include local credit research services, Dun & Bradstreet Reports, NACM Credit Interchange, and Industry Credit Reports. If you need to extend credit to customers, test the services of credit research and reporting firms listed in your local telephone book's yellow pages. The right vendor for you will be one who can give you both accurate and prompt reports at a reasonable cost.

Use credit card services such as Visa, MasterCard, American Express, and Discover, to transfer bad debt problems to others and increase cash flow for your business. There is an initial setup cost and ongoing service charges for these services. Talk with your banker about offering your customers the option of paying for services with their credit card. Service-station-connected shops can accept gasoline credit cards in payment for many repairs.

If you don't get your money when it is expected, make sure the customer is notified that the payment is past due (FIG. 8-1). This record can make future legal action or the selling of the account to a collection agency easier.

YOUR SUCCESS ACTION LIST

As you've seen, you can reduce the typical risks that your auto repair service faces. Doing so will not only increase your chances of success, but also help you to sleep better knowing that you're prepared for any emergency. You don't have to buy lots of insurance to reduce risks. You can reduce risks by carefully managing your business, the risks involved, and the costs of insurance. Here's how you can put this chapter into action.

_____ List the risks that your auto repair service faces in your location.

_____ Ask other business owners to recommend reputable and helpful insurance agents, attorneys, and accountants, who have experience with auto repair services.

_____ Identify your business' exposure to loss and list solutions to reduce exposure.

_____ Decide how you can eliminate the loss of your valuable accounts receivable and other records due to fire, theft, or other risk.

_____ Decide how you can reduce the risk of losing a key person, including yourself, to your business.

_____ Select a single insurance agent who can assist you in cost effectively managing your business risks.

_____ Decide how you can manage and reduce bad debts in your auto repair business.

The next chapter in this book tells you how to solve common business problems and effectively communicate the solution.

ABC Auto Repair Service

PAYMENT PAST DUE

123 Main Street, Yourtown USA

Dick Jones
777 Mountain Road
Yourtown USA 12345

DATE: June 30, 19xx

Comments: We appreciate your business, Mr. Jones, and want to continue your good credit. To do so, we must have a payment of at least $200 on this account by July 15.

Bill Smith

Statement of Account

Date	Invoice Number	Description	Amount	Total
April 14	92111	Engine Rebuild	$947.56	$947.56
April 14	Payment on Account		($200.00)	($200.00)
May 30	Payment on Account		($125.00)	($125.00)
June 25	Payment on Account		($75.00)	($75.00)
Amount Due Now			**Amount Remitted**	
$547.56				

Thank you for your prompt attention

In reviewing your account, we have determined that the above invoices have not been paid and are now past due. We would be most grateful for your prompt attention and remittance. If you have any questions or problems with this billing, please contact us immediately. If your remittance has already been sent out, please disregard this notice.

8-1 This Payment Past Due Notice gives the customer a specific date when payment is expected.

9

Solving business problems

Remember this: you are *not* paid to repair autos, but to solve automotive problems! The more efficiently you solve them, the better you will be paid. So this chapter can give you some practical help, proven by thousands of businesspeople like yourself, on how to solve common business problems. It will also present you with time-proven ways of solving communication problems.

Bear with me. I'll try to make this chapter not sound like a college course. But the fact is that reviewing the basics of effective problem-solving and communications as applied to your auto repair service can make your business run smoother and more profitably. Have I got your attention?

COMMON BUSINESS PROBLEMS

As the owner of your own auto repair business you deal with problems on a daily basis. So learning how to effectively solve problems can dramatically affect the growth and success of your business. Most business owners solve problems by intuition. By learning the "skill" of problem solving, just as you would learn the skill of automotive repair, you will be more comfortable solving problems and reduce the inherent stress of your job.

What is a problem? A problem is a situation that presents difficulty to your ability to move ahead. Here are a few examples:

- An electronic diagnostics computer doesn't function as it should.
- A part you need for a valve job is unavailable.
- An employee is undermining your authority at the job site.
- New business is down.
- A customer is complaining about shoddy workmanship.
- You're two payments behind on a lease and they've threatened to sue.

Where do problems come from? Problems arise from every facet of human and mechanical function, as well as from nature. Some problems we cause ourselves, like hiring an untrainable employee. Other problems are caused by forces beyond our control, such as shop damage caused by a storm. Problems are a natural, every-day occurrence of life. If mismanaged, problems cause tension and frustration that only compounds the situation. You must learn how to deal with problems in a logical, rational fashion.

STEPS TO SOLVING ANY PROBLEM

The solutions to some problems, such as how to plan next week's work schedule, are typically simple and require only a few moments of contemplation and planning. Some problems, such as how to increase income by $100,000 in the next six months, are more critical to your operation and will require more time and effort. In fact, for critical problems, you might want to set aside a full day to analyze the problem and find the best solutions.

Before a problem can be solved, you must first recognize that a problem exists. Here is where your approach to problem solving is crucial. Do not allow the problem to intimidate you. Don't take it personally. Approach it rationally and remind yourself that every problem is solvable if it is tackled appropriately.

Fear of failure can block your ability to think clearly. You can overcome this natural fear if you:

- Follow a workable procedure for finding solutions.
- Accept the fact that you can't foresee everything.
- Assume that the solution you select is your best option at the time.
- Accept the possibility that things might change and your solution fail.

Define the problem   Once you recognize that a problem exists, your next step is to identify or define the problem itself. Do so by asking yourself questions.

- What exactly happened?
- What started the problem?
- Did something occur that wasn't supposed to?
- Did something break that was suppose to operate?
- Were there unexpected results?

Determine the type   Then ask questions that help you identify the nature of the problem.

- Is this a person, equipment, or operational problem?
- What product or service does it involve?
- Is the problem tangible or intangible?
- Is the problem internal or external to the firm?

Evaluate the significance   How important is this problem to the scheme of things? Ask yourself the following.

- Is this problem disrupting operations?
- Is this problem hampering sales?
- Is this problem causing conflict among people?
- Is this problem affecting personnel and their productivity?

- Is this problem affecting business goals and, if so, which ones?
- Is this problem affecting customers, suppliers, subcontractors, or any other external people?

Estimate the frequency   Some problems are "100-year floods" that don't occur often enough to warrant extensive attention. Ask these questions.

- Is it a problem that occurred in the past and the main concern is to make certain that it doesn't occur again?
- Is it a problem that currently exists and the main concern is to clear up the situation?
- Is it a problem that might occur in the future and the basic concern is planning and taking action before the problem arises?

The answers to these questions can help you focus on the true problem. You can't effectively research the causes of a problem until you have a clear definition of the problem. Sometimes, shop owners/managers spend many hours on what they perceive as the problem only to learn, after seeking the causes, that something else was really the problem.

To appropriately identify the problem and its causes, you might need to do some research. If the solution is worthwhile to the goals of your business, invest the required time and resources. If it isn't, don't. Before you begin the search for a defined problem, however, consider what has previously been done by your firm (if anything) regarding this problem, what other firms have done, what knowledge you might need to acquire, what has been learned from past experience, and what do experts say about the problem. Make sure that as you travel the road to a solution, you don't trip on common roadblocks, some of which include:

- bad habits
- perceptions
- fears
- assumptions
- affinity
- procrastination
- reactiveness
- rashness
- sensitivities

At this point, you have a clear understanding and a definition or diagram of the problem. You understand what it is and maybe even why, but you have intentionally refrained from deciding what you should do about it. It's now time to look for a solution.

FINDING GOOD SOLUTIONS

There are a number of ways to find solutions. Try out each of them and select the best solution.

Analytical thinking This thinking method is based on analysis. It is the most conventional and logical of all the methods and follows a step-by-step pattern.

First, examine each cause of the problem. Then, for each cause, based on your direct knowledge and experience, list the solutions that logically would seem to solve the problem. Next, check the possible solutions you arrive at with the research you have compiled on how the problem was solved by others.

Association There are three types of associative thinking, a linking process either through similarity, difference, or contiguity. For example, contiguity finds solutions from things that are connected through proximity, sequence, and cause and effect. The process works like this. First, list as many parts of the problem as you can. Then, giving yourself a short time limit, list as many ideas that have either proximity, sequence, or related cause and effect to the ones you have listed. For example, a contiguous association might be:

> misplaced tools = cluttered workbench (proximity)
> misplaced tools = rushing (sequence)
> misplaced tools = irate customer (cause and effect)

Associative thinking taps the resources of the mind. It brings into focus options you might not have considered if you stuck to ideas only directly related to the problem. As a result of associative thinking, you might find other relationships embedded in the problem that will lead to a better solution. Using association might help you solve the problem of a shrinking marketplace by helping you discover related markets for your auto repair services.

Analogy This thinking method is a way to find solutions through comparisons. The process is based on comparing the different facets of the problem with other problems that might or might not have similar facets. An analogy might go like this:

> "Employees have been coming in late to work quite often. How can I get them to be at work on time? This to me is like soldiers being late for a battle. Would soldiers come late to a battle? Why not? Because their future as a soldier depends upon being there, and because there will be severe penalties for soldiers who are AWOL."

By comparing the situation of workers to the situation of soldiers, you might find a solution for a way to motivate employees to come to work on time.

Brainstorming This thinking method is based on a free, nonthreatening, anything-goes atmosphere. You can brainstorm alone or with a group of people. Most often a group of people from different departments of your firm or from diverse backgrounds is preferable. The process works like this. Explain the problem to the group and encourage each member to throw out as many ideas for solutions as he or she can think of no matter how ridiculous or far-fetched they might sound. Write down all the ideas on a large pad of paper, then discuss the ideas among the group, revise them, toss them out, combine and expand them. Based on the group's recognition of the effectiveness of each idea, select the best ones for closer review. For example, a group of all of your employees might throw out for consideration any thoughts they might have on how to increase sales or improve profits for the firm.

Intuition This mode of thinking is based on "hunches." It is not, as some think, irrational. Intuition or hunches are built on a strong foundation of facts and experiences that are buried somewhere in the subconscious. All the things you know and have experienced can lead you to believe that something might be true, although you've never actually experienced that reality. Use your intuition as much as possible, but check it against the reality of the situation. You have surely used intuition countless times to solve a particularly difficult auto repair problem.

SELECTING THE BEST SOLUTION

You've now developed a list of possible solutions. Go through this list and cross out those that obviously won't work. These ideas aren't wasted, for they impact on those ideas that remain. In other words, the best ideas you select might be revised using ideas that won't work by themselves.

Break the remaining solutions down into positive effects and negative effects. To do this, some auto repair business owners write each solution they are considering on a separate piece of paper. Below the solution they draw a vertical line down the center of the sheet, labeling one column "Advantages" and the other column "Disadvantages." Finally, they analyze each facet of the solution and its effect on the problem, listing each of the advantages and disadvantages they can think of.

One way to help you think of the advantages and disadvantages is to role-play each solution. Call in a few of your employees and play out each solution. Ask them for their reactions. Based on what you observe and on their feedback, you will have a better idea of the advantages and disadvantages of each solution you are considering.

After you complete this process for each primary solution, select those solutions that have the most advantages. At this point, you should be considering only two or three. In order to select the most appropriate solution from these, consider:

- Cost-effectiveness.
- Time constraints.
- Availability of manpower and materials.
- Your own intuition.

Before you actually implement the chosen solution, evaluate it. Ask yourself questions such as these:

- Are the objectives of the solution sound, clear, and simple?
- Will the solution achieve the objectives?
- What are the possibilities that it will fail and in what way?
- How can I reduce the possibility of failure?

TAKING ACTION

Finding the solution doesn't mean that the problem is solved. Now you need to design a plan of action so that the solution is carried out properly. Designing and implementing the plan of action is equally as important as finding the solution. The best solution can fail if it isn't well implemented. When designing the plan of action, consider the following.

- Who will be involved in the solution?
- How will they participate?
- Who will be affected by the solution?
- How will they be affected?
- What course of action will be taken?
- How should this course of action be presented to employees, customers, suppliers, and others?
- When will the action start and be completed?
- Where will this action happen?
- How will this action happen?
- What is needed to make it happen?

Design a plan-of-action chart including all the details you need to consider to implement the plan and when each phase should happen. Keep in mind, though, that the best plans have setbacks for any number of reasons. A key person might be out for illness or a supplier might ship critical parts late, or a change in the customer's plans might require that the timetable be changed.

As each phase of your plan of action is implemented, ask yourself whether your goals were achieved, how well they were achieved, and did it work smoothly. To check your own perceptions of the results, get as much feedback as possible from your managers and employees. What you might think is working might not be considered so by those closer to the action. Always remember that they are one of your most valuable tools in successfully carrying out your solution.

SOLVING COMMUNICATION PROBLEMS

So what does communication have to do with becoming a successful auto repair business owner? Plenty! In fact, without good communications you will soon not have your business. Your customers won't know what you can do for them or why your service is better than that of others, your banker won't know why you need the expansion loan, local regulators won't issue you required licenses and permits, employees won't know what you want them to do. Get the point? Communication is vital to the success of your business.

Of course, most businesspeople do communicate with customers, bankers, regulators, and employees. The problem is that many don't do it well enough to avoid problems, such as misunderstandings, incorrect specifications, hurt feelings, puzzling responses, inaccuracies, and delays. Powerful communications can:

- Change prospects into long-time clients.
- Appease disgruntled customers.
- Clearly direct unproductive employees.
- Gain support from powerful decision-makers.
- Simplify the training of new employees.
- Encourage customers to pay their bills swiftly.
- Help you negotiate better pricing from suppliers.

- Acquire low-cost funding from lenders.
- Improve community and media relations.
- Improve the effectiveness of your advertising.

Are you sold yet? Your auto repair business thoroughly depends on effective communications. It's actually the "secret" ingredient that separates experienced auto repair employees from successful auto repair service business owners.

WHY COMMUNICATION IS SO IMPORTANT

On a ledge in central Africa sits the smartest rock in the world. This rock not only understands the true meaning of life, it knows how to enhance the quality of life on this planet to a level far beyond any civilization that has ever lived. It understands the concepts of math beyond a hundred Einsteins, compassion greater than a thousand Mother Teresas, and the wisdom of a million Judge Wapners. Yet it can't talk. It can't write. It can't communicate with animate beings. So what good is it? It's good for skipping across ponds!

The point is that being successful requires communicating well with others. Communication is the key to your success as an auto repair service business owner, and as a person. Yet, the concept of communication is very simple. Any communication requires three things.

- A thought; some information that you want someone else to have or that you want from them.
- A transmission; a method of getting this thought from you to someone else.
- A receiver; someone whom you want to acquire your thought.

It's that simple. Basic communication is used every day of your life to:

- Tell an employee when and where to start a specific job;
- ask a supplier when the next shipment of parts will arrive;
- read a book about starting a successful auto repair business;
- order a hamburger-to-go at the drive-up window;
- call up an old friend to share some common experiences.

In each case, there is a thought (either a statement or a question), a transmission (oral speech, writing, or graphic image), and a receiver (employee, supplier, reader, restaurant clerk, or friend).

The thought(s) you want to transmit to a receiver might be a fact (the status of a job) or an emotion (expression of your feelings). By nature, business normally involves factual thoughts rather than emotions.

The transmission might be conveyed in person, over the phone, on a written fax, with a letter or invoice, with a diagram or drawing, or in a recorded message.

The receiver might get your message instantaneously, in a few moments over a fax machine, in a few days via the mail, or months or even years from now in a published document.

In each case, you must decide who is your receiver , what the receiver needs to know, how best to present the information to the receiver, and how soon.

Clear writing requires clear thinking. So what is "thinking?" It's simply the process of asking ourselves questions and then answering them. "How do I disassemble this short block? I know; I first . . . ." Or "How am I going to meet payroll this month? Let's see, my bank balance is $13,500 and I have $8700 in recurring bills . . . ."

You can clarify your thinking by becoming more aware of the questions you ask yourself. The better the question, the better the answer. "Do I want to know how to solve this specific problem, or all similar problems?" So the key to clear thinking is to ask questions of your questions, or redefine your question until it accurately states what you want to know. Then finding the answer becomes easier.

SAYING WHAT YOU MEAN

Every day, a successful auto repair service business owner speaks to many people in person or on the telephone. They are prospects, customers, suppliers, employees, other shop owners, government employees, bank employees, professionals, salespeople, agents, and others. He might speak to each in a different way with a distinct vocabulary. The words he uses to explain the problems of an automatic transmission are very different than those used to transact business at the bank.

So what's different? Why does a communicator speak differently to various people? Because each is a unique audience. Each needs different information and has a different vocabulary. For example, the terms valve, pipe, and plug mean different things to a plumber than they do to people in the auto repair trade.

The first rule of saying what you mean is to consider your audience. That is, consider your listener. This is such an obvious rule that we automatically follow it, most of the time. We walk into the bank and automatically switch our jargon to that understood by the audience: the teller, loan officer, or banker. If, on the way out of the bank, we see a customer, we automatically return to trade jargon, but only at the level the customer will probably understand. We don't get too technical. Then, seeing a friendly auto repair business owner in the parking lot, our vocabulary changes again, this time possibly to highly technical terms. In each case, we have automatically considered our audience.

However, it is the exceptions to this automatic consideration of the audience that makes the most trouble. A prospect calls you. If you begin speaking in highly technical terms, the prospect might be impressed, but he will more probably be confused (though he might never say so). Or the prospect who has extensive knowledge in your trade might keep up with you.

How can you know the prospect's level of understanding? By asking. You wouldn't embarrass him by asking, "How much of this do you understand?" But you will ask him, "Tell me about the problem you're trying to solve." Then, by listening to the response, you'll be able to determine the prospect's knowledge of auto repair and synchronize your vocabulary with his or hers.

Hint: You can always keep people talking by repeating their last few words in question form. He says, "I really need someone to re-bore the block." You respond, "Re-bore the block?" and he will probably continue feeding you clues to help you determine his knowledge. Remember that a good communicator is first a good listener.

Need

Once you've determined your audience's understanding of the problem and its solution, you can start asking more questions to find out what he needs. That is, is he looking for some technical information, for pricing, for an immediate solution, for a reason to buy from you, or for something else?

The best way to learn need is, again, to ask. Many auto repair services simply ask, "How can I help you?" and take their cue from the response. "Well, I'm not sure . . ." tells you to ask more questions until the problem is fully defined in the person's mind. "What I need is some pricing. . ." says that you need to review the benefits of your service and promise to work up an estimate. "I need someone to get my car out of the middle of the freeway. . ." says you need to jump in your truck and get over there.

In some cases, people will call you to pick your brain. "I have this problem. How can I solve it?" If it's a problem to which you sell the solution, don't give it away. This might sound unfair, but, with some research and trial-and-error, the caller can find the solution on their own. What he would pay you for is to save him the time and trouble. Let him do the work. You can simply explain that, "I would have to see the situation before I could give you a comprehensive answer." In summary, determine need. Ask yourself, what does this person need to know?

Presentation

How can you best present the solution to this person? If your audience is a prospective customer and he needs an estimate of costs for a specific job, your presentation is a quote or a bid. If your audience is a loan officer and she needs information about your business, your presentation is a thorough loan application. If your audience is a disgruntled customer and he wants a resolution to a problem he feels you caused, your presentation is an immediate and factual response and solution.

To easily present a solution, first define the problem. Once you've clearly defined the actual problem, the solution usually becomes obvious. For example, an engine rebuilding service owner says he's angry with your parts company because the parts for a critical job didn't arrive in time. So you begin asking questions: "Didn't arrive in time?" "When was it scheduled to arrive?" "Was someone there to receive the shipment?" "Is that a time that you normally receive shipments?"

By probing, you learn that their shipping dock is normally closed from 1 to 3 p.m on Friday afternoons, but that the shipper was not informed because you weren't informed. So the real problem is that the customer didn't tell you that the shipping dock would be closed during the part of the day on which he expected the shipment. The solution, quite obviously, is to resend the shipment when the dock will be open. You can present the solution by asking the exact hours when the dock is open and ensuring that the shipper follows them. Defining the problem doesn't blame anyone, it just makes sure that all the facts are used to develop a solution. It's nothing personal to you or to your customer. The best way to communicate or present a solution to someone is to: (1) know what they know (audience), and (2) know what they need to know (need). Understanding these two things allows you to easily present what your audience needs in a way they can understand.

Measurement

Communication is a loop. There must be a return path. In the case of communication, it's feedback in one of many forms. When you speak to someone in person, you can usually evaluate whether your audience understands what you say by watching their "body language": eye movement, hands and arms, smiles and frowns.

On the phone, it's more difficult to measure feedback. So you ask questions: "Does that make sense?" "Did I explain that clearly?" After such a clarifying question, leave a long pause for a response after the "yes" or "no." When you successfully communicate your thoughts, the listener will usually rephrase it in his own terms. If he doesn't, or if he repeats your own exact words back to you, consider that you might not have been sufficiently clear. Rephrase what you said. "That's right. To put it another way . . . ." So the four steps to saying what you mean are: know your audience, know what they need to know, give them what they need, and make sure they understand it.

WRITING WHAT YOU MEAN

In general, writing what you mean is the same as saying what you mean. The same four principles apply: audience, need, presentation, and measurement. But, of course, they are applied somewhat differently. The best and worst aspect of written communication is that it gives you time to come up with a response, and gives the reader time to ponder your response. So, even more than oral communications that drift away with the wind, written communications require more time and thought. For many, this is what's so intimidating about writing. The words are permanent. But this permanence is also what makes the written word so powerful. Write it once, clearly and accurately, and be done with it.

WRITING SECRETS

Here are the three steps to writing that are guaranteed to make you more comfortable and more successful with written communications:

- Prewrite
- Write
- Rewrite

That's it! No written document, including this book, is written in a single draft. All successful writing evolves through these three stages, by these or other names, once the audience, need, presentation, and measurement have been defined. In the coming pages, we'll cover these three stages, with examples, until you are comfortable with them, even enjoy them.

Prewrite   Prewriting is simply preparing to write. Make notes about the topic you want to cover, put them in a logical order, and look for ways to make your ideas as clear as possible. For example, if you need to write a letter to a customer about the Friday delivery problem mentioned earlier, first list the topics you want to cover.

- The dock was closed when delivery was made.
- The shipper didn't expect that dock would be closed.

- The customer didn't mention to you that dock would be closed.
- We're very sorry that the important delivery was missed.
- You are a valued customer and we apologize for the misunderstanding.
- The shipper agreed to attempt redelivery, if they are sure dock will be open.
- We want to make all of our customers happy with our service.
- In the future, we will specifically ask all customers for times that their dock will be open and keep them on record.

Once you have all the topics written down, put them in the logical order in which the *reader* wants to see them. Following our example, the order would be as follows.

1. We're very sorry that the important delivery was missed.
2. We want to make all of our customers happy with our service.
3. The dock was closed when the delivery was made.
4. The shipper agreed to attempt redelivery, if they are sure dock will be open.
5. The shipper didn't expect that the dock would be closed.
6. Customer didn't mention to you that dock would be closed.
7. In the future, we will specifically ask all customers for times that their dock will be open and keep them on record.
8. You are a valued customer and we apologize for the misunderstanding.

Finally, look for ways to make your ideas as clear as possible. Help your reader visualize the problem and the solution. Here are a couple of comments that you could weave into your letter to make it more visual.

- "I can fully imagine what you must have thought about our firm when Friday ended and your supplies hadn't arrived."
- "The delivery driver, Bob Haskins, has promised to make sure you get this shipment as quickly as possible."

How do you develop a list of topics that you want to cover in your written communication? Think about it. And thinking, as we discussed earlier, is merely asking questions and then answering them. Typical questions might include the following.

- What is the purpose of this correspondence?
- What does the reader want to know?
- What are the facts of this situation, in random order?
- What is the most logical order for these facts?
- What does the reader want to know first?
- What single point do I want to leave in the reader's mind?

Find the answers to these and related questions and your correspondence will be prewritten.

Write Now that you've prewritten what you want to say, the writing becomes easier. Elaborate on each point, in order. For example, the above outline started with:

1. We're very sorry that the important delivery was missed.

This is the first topic you want to cover. Amplify it like this:

"Bob, I'm very sorry that the important delivery on invoice #12345 was not made last Friday afternoon when you expected it. I can fully imagine what you must have thought about our firm when Friday ended and your parts hadn't arrived."

Then lead into the second point of our prewrite outline:

2. We want to make all of our customers happy with our service.

Continue the correspondence with,

"All of our customers are very important to us, and your business is especially important, Bob, because you were one of our first clients. If you're not happy with our service, then we're not happy."

Then bring the third point into your correspondence:

3. Dock was closed when delivery was made.

Say it more positively:

"The delivery driver arrived at your loading dock Friday afternoon at 2:30 p.m. with the shipment on his truck. Unfortunately, he discovered that deliveries weren't accepted between 1 and 3 p.m. on Fridays."

Then develop the fourth point:

4. Shipper agreed to attempt redelivery if they are sure dock will be open.

"The shipper called me later that day, but it was too late in the day to redeliver so he brought it back to the warehouse. He offered to redeliver the shipment at your convenience."

Get the point? Once you've prewritten your correspondence, the writing is easy. It's simply a matter of turning independent thoughts into smooth sentences. Don't worry about spelling, punctuation, or sentence structure at this point. Just develop each thought into a sentence or two.

Rewrite Now comes the cleanup. If you're not an adept speller, refer to a dictionary, a spelling computer, or a spell-checker in your computer's word-processing system. Don't worry too much about "proper English." The best English is conversational English, so read your sentences out loud and you will probably hear any major errors. If you're still uncomfortable with tenses and phrasing, ask someone with those skills to review your draft before you complete it.

You can also dress up your writing by adding transitions such as "However," "In addition," "By the way," "As we discussed," and others. They can make your correspondence sound more like conversation, as well as signal the reader that you are changing thoughts or want to emphasize a specific point.

One more point about writing: if you've decided to purchase and use a computer in your business, consider a word-processing program such as WordPerfect, Microsoft Write or Word, XyWrite, AmiPro, WordStar, or others. Writing on a word processor allows you to prewrite, write, and rewrite quickly and easily. You can readily move words, sentences, and paragraphs around until you are satisfied with them. Then you can store them on your computer so that you can reuse these well-written thoughts in future correspondence.

Some word processors include an outliner, a spell-checker, a thesaurus, and even a grammar checker. If yours doesn't include these features, they can be purchased separately and added to your system. A word processor lets you continually improve your written communications until they say exactly what you want them to say without retyping.

PROFITABLE NEGOTIATIONS

Many people fear the face-to-face confrontation of negotiating. They don't like to buy cars because they know that not negotiating the price is considered un-American. In fact, it is. Very few things are nonnegotiable. With just a little practice, you can actually enjoy negotiating with others.

The game

To remove any fear of negotiating, remember that it's just a game. You wouldn't be fearful of playing a checkers game or a basketball game. In fact, many products and services you purchase include a percentage of the price set aside for those who negotiate. It ranges from a couple of percent to 20 percent or more of the price. In most cases, the higher the price, the higher the available discount. Many larger ticket items, such as cars and houses, can be negotiated to a discount of 10 to 20 percent, even if the owner says "my price is firm."

You're not fearful of chess or many sports games because you understand the rules. There will always be unsportsmanlike players who break these rules, but the majority of players follow them. Here are a few of the rules of negotiating.

Don't negotiate unless you're willing to buy If you're looking at a $500 item and you offer $450, the seller might accept and you're stuck with something you don't want, or you have to explain that you weren't serious.

Don't fall in love There are few unique items in this world. If you can find it once, you can probably find it again. If you tell yourself that you must have this item, then you must have it, at any price.

Apologize for your low offer "I'm embarrassed to offer $200, but that's all I can pay for it." This doesn't say $200 is all you have or is all you will pay for it if necessary, so it still leaves you room to negotiate. A few sellers might walk away, but most will make a counteroffer that is lower than the original asking price . . . so you both win.

Don't be afraid to walk away Once you've determined what the product or service is worth to you, set a realistic limit that you will pay. If it isn't met, walk away. Some sellers might call you back and reopen negotiations, and others might let you go. Of course, you can always come back later and reopen negotiations yourself.

What products and services can you negotiate? Just about any of them. Suppliers will often negotiate prices or terms on items or orders valued over a few hundred dollars. Some subcontractors might negotiate their hourly fees if you can keep them busy during normally slow times. Car/truck dealers are notoriously adept negotiators, but you can often get the best deal by determining wholesale value (what they probably paid for the vehicle) and adding a standard commission and sales costs plus a little profit. Ask your banker for the wholesale blue book value for the vehicle you're considering.

The other side of the table

Learning how to negotiate with sellers can also help you when you face customers who want to negotiate. Set up your own pricing structure with this in mind. But always ask for a trade. That is, if a customer asks for a 5 percent discount, you might want to give it to him if he pays cash in advance. For a 10 percent, you might ask for cash in advance and a letter of recommendation from his firm when the job is done. The rule is to never give away a discount; trade it for something you want, even a token. Most important, never sell your services for less than they cost you to furnish.

YOUR SUCCESS ACTION LIST

Your job is to solve problems and to communicate the solution to others. This chapter describes how successful auto repair service business owners use these valuable tools to make their business more profitable, and less stressful. You can do the same. Here's how you can put this chapter into action.

_____ Select a problem your starting or operating business now faces and develop the best solution by:

1. defining the problem;
2. determining the type of problem;
3. evaluating its significance; and
4. estimating frequency.

_____ Use each type of solution-finder (analytical, association, analogy, brainstorming, intuition) to develop as many potential solutions as possible.

_____ Select the best solution and take action.

_____ Write the solution out so that all users will clearly understand the problem, the chosen solution, and how they will participate in the implementation of the solution.

_____ Be prepared to negotiate your solution.

Chapter 10 tells you how to find and keep good employees that will enhance your auto repair service.

10
Finding and keeping good employees

Your experience as an employee can be valuable as you find and keep good employees. Remember what it's like to work for someone else and be sensitive to the needs and goals of your employees.

This chapter includes ideas and guidelines from many other successful auto repair service owners and businesspeople on how to manage employees for mutual profit. You'll learn how to draw the most qualified applicants and how to verify their skills. You'll learn how to set wages, select a benefits package, and manage the largest asset, and expense, your auto repair service has—your employees.

FINDING GOOD EMPLOYEES

To get the right person for the job you must decide what kind of skill is needed to perform the job. Once you know what it takes to do the job, you can match the applicant's skills and experience to the job's requirements. This step will probably come easy for you if you're hiring an auto repair worker, but how about office help or other support positions?

The first step to analyzing a job is to describe it. Suppose that, as the owner of a growing auto repair business, you decide to hire someone to relieve you of some of your administrative or sales duties. Look at the many functions you perform and decide what are your stronger and weaker areas.

Suppose you decide that you need help in the office. The phone is always ringing. Letters that need answering are piling up. Insurance claims must be typed and mailed so you can get paid.

Once you have a job description on paper, decide what skills the person must have to fill the job. What is the lowest skill level you will accept? In this example, let's assume that you decide initially to hire a secretary, but discover that secretaries are scarce and expensive. Likewise, in your area, stenographers are almost as hard to find and nearly as expensive as secretaries. Perhaps you could get by with a typist. Hiring a typist might be both easier and cheaper than hiring a secretary or stenographer. Many high school students are well qualified typists, and many are seeking part-time work.

When you start looking for someone to fill your job, make sure you describe exactly what you want. As an "office manager," what do you want this person to do? Answer the telephone and take messages? Contact you at the job site? Type correspondence? Write correspondence? Sort mail? Pay bills? Prepare bills for payment? Keep accounting records? Produce invoices? Mail monthly statements? Manage collection of past-due accounts? Read trade journals and mark important articles for you? Order parts and materials? Manage payroll? Prepare the books for your accountant? Make quarterly tax payments? Make good coffee?

FINDING JOB APPLICANTS

Once you know the types of skills you need from your new employee, you are ready to contact sources that can help you recruit job applicants.

If you are a union shop, work with the union to find skilled journeyman and apprentice workers. An advantage to apprentices is that their pay ranges from 35 to 85 percent of the wage of a journeyman, depending on the local union contract, the apprenticeship program, and the time served in the apprenticeship.

Each state has an employment service (Department of Employment, Unemployment Bureau, or Employment Security Agency). All are affiliated with the United States Employment Service, and local offices are ready to help businesses locate qualified applicants. The state employment service can screen applicants for you by giving aptitude tests (if any are available for the skills you need). Passing scores indicate the applicant's ability to learn the work. So, be as specific as you can about the skills you want.

Private employment agencies can also help you recruit candidates. However, the employee or the employer must pay a fee to the private agency for its services. This fee can be the equivalent of from one month to as much as one year of the employee's salary.

Another source of applicants is a "Help Wanted" sign in your shop window. Of course, a lot of unqualified applicants might inquire about the job, and you cannot simultaneously interview an applicant and talk on the phone to a customer.

Newspaper advertisements are another source of applicants. You reach a large group of job seekers, and if you used a blind box address you can screen their applications at your convenience. If you list an office phone number, you might end up on the phone with an applicant instead of with a customer.

Job applicants are readily available from local schools. The local high school might have a distributive or cooperative education department where the students work in your office part time while taking trade or business courses at school. Many part-time students continue with their employer after they finish school. Consider local and regional business schools as well. The students are often more mature and more motivated than high school students.

You might also find job applicants by contacting friends, neighbors, customers, suppliers, current employees, local associations, service clubs, or even a nearby armed forces base where people are leaving the service. However, don't overlook the problems of such recruiting. What happens to the goodwill of these sources if they recommend a friend whom you do not hire, or if you have to fire the person they recommend?

Your choice of recruitment method depends on what you're looking for, your location, and your method of managing your business. You have many sources available to you. A combination might serve you best. The important thing is to find the right applicant with the correct skills for the job you want to fill, whatever the source.

CERTIFICATIONS

The National Institute for Automotive Service Excellence at 13505 Dulles Technology Dr., Herndon, VA 22071, 703-713-3800, offers a certification program for automotive technicians. Over 300,000 men and women are currently certified as ASE Automobile Technicians. Another 30,000 are ASE Collision Repair Technicians, over 34,000 are ASE Medium/Heavy Truck Technicians, and more than 3000 are ASE Engine Machinists.

Technicians are certified in specializations. ASE Automobile Technicians can be certified in engine repair, automatic transmission/transaxle, manual drive train and axles, suspension and steering, brakes, electrical systems, heating and air conditioning, or engine performance. A technician who becomes certified in all of these areas becomes an ASE Master Automobile Technician. About 25 percent of all ASE Automobile Technicians earn the Master Automobile Technician designation. There is a similar program for Master Truck Technicians.

What does it take to earn ASE certification? A technician must have at least two years of relevant hands-on work experience as well as pass an exam conducted twice a year at 500 locations. If certified, the technician must re-test every five years for recertification in order to ensure that they keep up with changing technology.

Certification programs such as the one developed by the National Institute for Automotive Service Excellence can greatly assist you in selecting qualified professionals for your shop.

LABOR LAWS

As you begin the search for qualified employees, there are certain laws, federal and state, that come into play. Your local state employment office can help you learn the requirements of these laws.

The Social Security Act of 1935, as amended is concerned with employment insurance laws as well as retirement insurance. The Fair Labor Standards Act of 1938, as amended establishes minimum wages, overtime pay, recordkeeping, and child labor standards for most businesses. The Occupational Safety and Health Act (OSHA) of 1970 is concerned with safety and health in the workplace and covers almost all employers. There are specific standards, regulations, and reporting requirements that must be met.

Other laws might impact your business as well. Contact your local state employment office to determine the requirements for hiring disadvantaged workers, federal service contracts for work on public buildings or other public projects, employee pension and welfare benefit plans, and the garnishment of employee's wages.

In addition, the *Immigration Reform and Control Act of 1986* prohibits the employment of illegal aliens. Employers must require every employee to fill out the Employment Eligibility Verification Form (Form I9) within three days of the date of hire (if hired after November 7, 1987). Fines are levied for noncompliance. For more information, contact the nearest office of the Immigration and Naturalization Service.

THE APPLICATION FORM

The hardest part of the hiring process, once you've listed the required skills, is to find and hire the right employee. You need some method of screening the applicants and selecting the best one for the position.

The application form (FIGS. 10-1a through 10-1c) is a tool that you can use to make your tasks of interviewing and selection easier. The form should have blank spaces for all the facts you need as a basis for judging the applicants.

ABC Auto Repair Service

EMPLOYMENT APPLICATION

123 Main Street, Yourtown USA 12345

Position Applied For Automotive Mechanic	Type of Employment Full Time ☑ Summer ☐ Part Time ☐ Temporary ☐	Date 30 Jun 19xx

Name of Applicant (please indicate how you wish to be addressed)

Surname Johnson	First Name Robert	Initial (s) L.

Address (No., Street, City, State, Zip Code)
987 River Road, Yourtown, USA 12345

Social Security Number 123-45-6789	Telephone Number (Home) 234-8282	Business 234-9870

Previous Address in the United States
666 Main Street, Apt. 3-A, Yourtown, USA, 12345

Some positions in the company require that staff be bonded.
Are you bondable?   YES ☑   NO ☐
Have you ever been bonded? YES ☑   NO ☐

Are you legally entitled to work in the United States? ☑ YES ☐ NO	Are you willing to relocate? ☑ YES ☐ NO

Do you have a valid driver's licence?   Class
☑ YES   ☐ NO

Education

Secondary School attended and location. Yourtown High School Yourtown USA	Highest grade successfully completed. 12th		Year Graduated 1979

University attended and location.	No. of years completed	Year graduated	Degrees

Major subjects of specialization.
Auto Mechanics, Industrial Arts

Community College attended and location. Yourtown Community College Yourtown USA	No. of years completed 2	Year graduated 1981	Degrees Associate of Arts

Major subjects of specialization.
Automotive Mechanics, Transmission Service, Auto Body

Other Educational Training/ Courses.
ASE Engine Repair, Automatic Transmission/Transaxle, Brake courses

Office/ Secretarial Applications

Skill /Aptitude	Years of experience	Words per minute	List secretarial training courses completed and any other training which maybe helpful in considering your application.
Typing			
Shorthand			

10-1a Employment Application: page 1

EMPLOYMENT HISTORY (List present or most recent positions first)

1. Name of Employer
Bill Murray Buick

Address   No.   Street   City
789 Main St., Yourtown, USA

Type of Business
New Car Sales and Service

Department
Service Department

Your Position
Apprentice Mechanic

Duties Perform tune-ups, lubrication and oil changes, pick up and delivery for first year, then earned opportunity to perform more complex repairs on engines, transmissions, and differentials including front-wheel drive cars.

Name and Position of Immediate Supervisor
Frank Murray, Service Department Supervisor

Date Employed (Day, Mo, Yr)	Date Left (Day, Mo, Yr)	Starting Salary	Final Salary
19 Nov 1981	1 Apr 1988	$750.00	$1,600.00

Reason for leaving

Bill Murray Buick went out of business

2. Name of Employer
Jim's Performance Motors

Address   No.   Street   City
987 Main St., Yourtown, USA

Type of Business
Automotive Performance Services

Department
Service

Your Position
Tune-up Specialist

Duties Perform engine tune-ups on high-performance and racing cars in shop and on traveling pit crew. Race cars won numerous regional titles and national circuits.

Name and Position of Immediate Supervisor
Jim Loggan

Date Employed (Day, Mo, Yr)	Date Left (Day, Mo, Yr)	Starting Salary	Final Salary
1 Apr 1988		$1,800.00	$2,950.00

Reason for leaving

Still employed. Leaving to reduce time away from family. Jim Loggan is aware of my leaving and offers an excellent reference.

3. Name of Employer

Address   No.   Street   City

Type of Business

Department

Your Position

Duties

Name and Position of Immediate Supervisor

Date Employed (Day, Mo, Yr)	Date Left (Day, Mo, Yr)	Starting Salary	Final Salary

Reason for leaving

MAY WE ASK YOUR PRESENT EMPLOYER FOR A REFERENCE   ☑ YES   ☐ NO

REFERENCES (Please do not list relatives or former employers)

Name	Occupation	Address
Martin Franklin	College Instructor	654 River St., Yourtown
John Jones	Baker/Kiwanis President	333 Main St., Yourtown
Ben Hopper	Pastor	567 Main St., Yourtown

Whom do you know in this company?
Mike Jenkins, Service Manager
Yon Killok, Mechanic

10-1b Employment Application: page 2

Scholarships

Activities/ Interests (Student, Professional, Community, etc)
Yourtown Kiwanis, vice president

Publication, patents and thesis subjects

Languages (spoken, written, read) Note fluency

Other interests or hobbies
Fishing

Special talents

Medical — Do you agree to take a medical exam at company expense
related to the essential requirements of the position   ☑ YES   ☐ NO

We appreciate your interest in seeking employment with us - please feel free to make any additional remarks in the space provided below or attach any additional information that would be helpful in evaluating your qualifications.

Additional Remarks

Earned ASE Certification in Engine Repair, Automatic Transmission/Transaxle, Brakes, and Engine Performance. Working toward ASE Master Automobile Technician designation.

Successful high performance mechanic who wants to work in a reputable auto repair garage in Yourtown.

Please Read Carefully

I hereby certify that to the best of my knowledge and belief the answers given by me to the foregoing questions and all statements made by me in the application are correct.

If employed, I agree that all material created and produced whether in written, graphic or broadcasting form, all inventions new or changes in processes developed during my employment are the exclusive property of the company to use and/or sell and that subsequent to my employment with this company I will not disclose, use or reveal any confidential information related to the company without first obtaining written consent from an officer of the company.

I hereby apply for employment upon the basis and understanding that such employment may be terminated at any time upon notice given to me personally or sent to my last known address.

I consent to   ABC Auto Repair Service _____ obtaining such personal and job-related information as required in connection with this application
for employment

_____   _____
Date   Signature of applicant

This application form complies with all Human Rights Legislation.

10-1c Employment Application: page 3

You want a fairly complete application so you can get sufficient information. However, keep the form as simple as you can. The form can be photocopied as needed. Have the applicants fill out the application before you talk to them. It makes an excellent starting point for the interview. It is also a written record of experience and former employers' names and addresses.

The Civil Rights Act of 1964 prohibits discrimination in employment practices because of race, religion, sexual persuasion, gender, or national origin. Public Law 90-202 prohibits discrimination on the basis of age with respect to individuals who are between 40 and 70 years of age. Federal laws also prohibit discrimination against the physically handicapped. Again, your state employment office can help you understand the laws regarding applicants and employment. In addition, firms like G. Neil, located at 720 International Parkway, Sunrise, FL 33345, offer catalogs of human relations supplies, such as job applications, personnel folders, labor-law posters, attendance controllers, employee awards, and related materials.

When an applicant has had work experience, other references are typically not as important. However, if the level of work experience is limited, additional references might be obtained from other individuals, such as school counselors who might be able to offer objective information.

Personal references are almost useless as an applicant would only list people who have a kind word for them. Some employers use them to open a discussion. "What would this reference say were your greatest skills and traits?" "What would this reference say were skills and traits that you needed to work on?"

THE INTERVIEW

The objective of the job interview is to find out as much information as you can about the job applicant's work background, especially work habits and skills. Your major task is to get the applicants to talk about themselves and about their work habits. The best way to go about this is to ask each applicant specific questions.

- What did you do on your last job?
- How did you do it?
- Why was it done?
- What were the results?

As you go along, evaluate the applicants' replies. Do they know what they are talking about? Are they evasive or unskilled in the job tasks? Can they account for discrepancies in their employment record?

When the interview is over, ask the applicant to check back with you later, if you think you might be interested in that applicant. Never commit yourself until you have interviewed all likely applicants. You want to be sure that you select the best available applicant for the job. Document any negative factors. You might be sued.

Next, verify the information you've obtained. A previous employer is usually the best source. Sometimes a previous employer will give information over the phone. But, if you have the time, it is usually best to request the information in writing and get a written reply. Of course, never contact a present employer without permission from the applicant.

To help ensure a prompt reply, ask previous employers a few specific questions about the applicant that can be answered with a yes or no or with a very short answer.

- How long did the employee work for you?
- Was his or her work: poor, average, or excellent?
- Why did the employee leave your employment?

Also make sure that you include a self-addressed, stamped envelope for their reply.

After you have verified the information on all your applicants, you're ready to make your selection. The right employee can help you make money. The wrong employee can cost you much wasted time and materials, and might even drive away your customers. Be sure that once you've decided on the most appropriate applicant, you document in writing why you selected a specific applicant (FIG. 10-2) and why you did not select other applicants. Make sure that all decisions and comments are relative to job requirements and not other factors. Then, if you are challenged about your fair employment practices, you have the documentation that can keep you from being sued or paying large fines.

DEVELOPING A USEFUL PERSONNEL POLICY

More and more, the government is requiring written personnel policies, even for the smallest firms. A written personnel policy manual can make your life, as an owner/manager of an auto repair service, easier as well. Fortunately, there are specific books and computer programs that can help you write your personnel policies to conform with current laws, as well as make the task easier. Or you can hire a personnel specialist to help you develop and document your policy.

WRITING THE POLICY MANUAL

The first rule of writing personnel policies is to know yourself. Know your business. Know your own personal abilities and weaknesses, and try to anticipate how you will deal with the situations that you expect to arise in the daily operation of your auto repair business.

Then, formulate your policies in writing. Include all matters that would affect employees, such as wages, promotions, vacations, time off, grievances, fringe benefits, and even retirement policies.

Once you've developed your personnel policies, write down the policy on all matters that affect your employees and give each one a copy. For a small auto repair service office, this statement might consist of just one or two typed pages. Matters such as these shouldn't be left to whim: hours of work, time, recordkeeping, paid holidays, vacations, dress regulations, wage payment system, overtime, separation procedure, severance pay, pension and retirement plan, hospitalization and medical care benefits, and grievance procedures.

Employment and training procedures must be established so that you have a better chance of getting the job done the way you want it done. Your policy manual should probably cover policy decisions in the following areas.

123 Main Street, Yourtown USA

Date June 30, 19xx

Social Security Number 123-45-6789	Employee Number 17		Sex	Worker's Comp.	Job Cat.
Birth Date (YY MM DD) January 9, 1961	Code Reason Desc. Rehire ☐ New Hire ☒		Employment Date (YY MM DD) July 1, 19xx		Fair Non exempt ☐ Exempt ☐

Name (Last Name, First Name, Middle Initial) Robert L. Johnson
Legal Address (Street, Apt. No., City, State and Zip Code) 987 River Road, Yourtown USA 12345
Mailing Address (Street, Apt. No., City, State and Zip Code) Same
Bulk Mailing Address (No., P.O Box Address) (Street, City, State and Zip Code) Same
Check Mailing Address (Street, Apt. No., City, State and Zip Code) Same
Department Name (City, State and Zip Code are also needed)

Emergency Contact Name Linda Johnson	Relationship Wife		Telephone 234-8282
Marital Status Single ☐ Married ☒	Home Phone No. 234-8282	Review/ Raise date	Annual Salary $ 36,000.00
Salary Date July 1, 19xx	Code Reason Desc. Rehire ☐ New Hire ☒	Hourly Rate 18.00	Pay Period Hours 40 Hrs
Job Date July 1, 19xx	Reason Rehire ☐ New Hire ☐	Job Code	Job Title Shop Forman
Salary Grade $3.00	Location Code	Location Code Description	
Requisition Number	Addition ☐ Replacement ☒	Person Replaced Bob Smithers	

REHIRES ONLY

Previous Hire Date YY/ MM/ DD	Previous Termination Date YY/MM/DD	Term Code

COMMENTS

Extensive high-performance experience. Working toward ASE Master Automotive Technician designation.

APPROVALS

Operations Administrator/Immediate Supervisor	Date	PAYROLL USE ONLY
Department Head/V P	Date	
Human resources	Date	
Human resources	Date	

10-2 This New Hire/Rehire Personnel Action form records your hiring decisions.

Hours Unless dictated by a labor contract, indicate the number of hours to be worked per week, the number of days per week, evening and holiday work, and the time and method of payment for both regular and overtime work. Unnecessary payment of overtime at premium rates is a source of needless expense. By planning ahead, you might be able to organize your employees' work to keep overtime to a minimum. When peak periods do occur, you can often handle them by using part-time help paid at regular rates. Use weekly or monthly time reports (FIG. 10-3 and FIG. 10-4) to track hours worked by employees.

WEEKLY TIME REPORT

ABC Auto Repair Service

123 Main Street, Yourtown USA 12345

LOCATION / ORG. UNIT   DATE June 30, 19xx

NAME	HOURS	CLASSIFICATION	DESCRIPTION OF WORK
Bill Franklin	42	Mechanic, Journeyman	Auto repairs, primarily engine and drive train
Jim Jackson	32	Mechanic, Apprentice	Auto repairs, tune-ups, lubrication, oil changes, parts delivery
Fran Mitchell	40	Office Manager	Telephone, bookkeeping, payroll, records
Roger Reed	45	Shop Forman	Quote pricing, manage jobs, some repair as available

REMARKS

The undersigned employee certifies that the above and foregoing is the actual, correct number of hours worked by him/her on the day stated, and that he/she has not been told or instructed by anyone having authority over him/her to incorrectly state the number of hours actually worked.

Employee's Signature_____

Supervisor's Signature_____

10-3 Keep a Weekly Time Report on your employees.

Compensation Most of your employees will be paid a salary or commission competitive with the pay offered by other similar local firms. Try to relate the incentive to both your goals and the goals of your employees. Whatever plan and level of compensation you use, be sure each employee understands it completely.

Probationary period Define the period (usually 30, 60, or 90 days) during which a new employee can be dismissed without a hearing on the cause, if allowed by local laws.

Benefits You might consider offering your employees free life insurance, health insurance, pension plan, and tuition payments at schools and colleges. You might also look into joining with other auto repair services in a group disability plan and a group workers' compensation insurance plan. Such a plan might mean a consider-

ABC Auto Repair Service

123 Main Street, Yourtown USA 12345

PERIOD END	MONTH	DAY	YEAR	PERSONNEL #	NAME	DIV
	06	30	xx	12	Bill Franklin	Shop

TIME DISTRIBUTION FOR PERIOD

Description of Work	1 / 16	2 / 17	3 / 18	4 / 19	5 / 20	6 / 21	7 / 22	8 / 23	9 / 24	10 / 25	11 / 26	12 / 27	13 / 28	14 / 29	15 / 30	/ 31	Total Hours
Ryerson: valve job		6	2														8
Murphy: engine rebuild			7	4		3											14
Jake's Trucking: fleet service				2	7	4					6		3				22
		1	3						4								8
Morgan Racing: high-performance						2							5				7
tune-ups					3							3					6
Simpson: engine rebuild									8	2	1	1					12
	4																4
Rowley: transmission repair		2	6	3	8												19
Batterson: engine rebuild					7			6	4	4	1						22
Morgan Racing: engine rebuild												8	9	6	6	1	30
Holiday																	
Personal Illness - Approved								8									8
Overtime																	
												Total Hours				160

10-4 Summarize hours on Monthly Time Sheet.

List of Expenses and Dollar Value (attach receipts)				Overtime Approved By	Time Report Audited
Description	$	Description	$		
		Total Expenses		PAGE OF	

able savings in your premium costs. Indicate when benefits begin: upon employment, the first day of the month following employment, upon completion of a specific number of hours of work, etc.

Vacations Your policy manual should answer: How long will vacations be? Will you specify the time of the year they can be taken? With or without pay? How does an employee schedule vacation time? What is your policy if vacation time goes unused or if additional time is requested?

Time off Will you allow employees time off for personal reasons, emergencies in the family, holidays, Saturday or Sunday holidays?

Training You must make sure that each employee is given adequate training for the job. In a small auto repair office, the training responsibility normally falls to the owner/manager. But, if you have supervisors, each one should recognize the importance of being a good teacher and should schedule time to teach or review the requirements of the job with new employees.

Retirement What are your plans for retirement benefits such as social security insurance, pension plans, and annuity plan insurance?

Grievances You might expect conflicts with employees without regard for the quality of the employment you offer. The best course of action is to plan for them and establish a procedure for handling grievances. Consider the employees' rights to demand review and establish provisions for third-party arbitration. If you hire through a union, this will be spelled out in your labor contract.

Promotion You will want to consider such promotion matters as normal increases of wages and salaries, changes to job titles, and the effects that your business' growth will have on your employees and their careers.

Personnel review Will you periodically review your employee's performance? If so, what factors will you consider? Will you make salary adjustments or training recommendations?

Termination Even though this is a distasteful matter to many business owners, it would be wise to have a written policy regarding layoffs, seniority rights, severance pay, and the conditions that warrant summary discharge.

DETERMINING WAGES

Pay administration is a management tool that enables you to control personnel cost, increase employee morale, and reduce work force turnover. A formal pay system provides a means of rewarding individuals for their contributions to the success of your firm, while making sure that your firm receives a fair return on its investment in employee pay.

If you are hiring union members, the local labor union can assist you in defining job descriptions and establishing pay levels and incentives.

There are two good reasons to establish a fair employee pay plan: your business and your employees. A formal pay plan, one that lets employees know where they stand and where they can go as far as take-home pay is concerned, won't solve your employee relations problems. It can, however, remove one of those areas of doubt and rumor that might keep your work force anxious and unhappy, and less loyal and more mobile than you'd like them to be.

What's in it for you? Let's face it, in an auto repair business good employees make the difference between success and failure. Many people enjoy a good "mystery," but not when it's about how their pay is established. Employees who work under a pay plan they understand can see that it's fair and consistent rather than at the whim of the owner. They know what to expect and what they can hope to earn in the future. So a good pay plan can help you recruit, keep, and motivate employees. It can help you build a solid foundation for a successful business.

Most auto repair services pay employees on a commission such as 50:50 or 60:40 depending on other duties. Others pay a base salary and partial commission. Still others pay an hourly wage or a weekly or monthly salary.

OVERTIME

In most cases, overtime should not be required, as the typical job is bid based on a normal workday. However, as business increases seasonally or as modified schedules require, you might want to consider overtime. First consider your employment policy or union requirements regarding payment for overtime hours. Depending on the standard workday and the number of hours required beyond that day, overtime can typically cost from 25 to as much as 200 percent more than standard pay.

In addition, efficiency decreases as overtime increases. By how much? One source has developed a table of overtime efficiency rates that, with five 10-hour days on the same job, the efficiency rate for the last two hours of the day are reduced to 87.5 percent. With five 12-hour days on the same job, the efficiency rate for the last four hours of the day are reduced to 75 percent. If the worker of five 12-hour days must move to another job after 8 hours, the efficiency rate for the 4 hours at the second job drop to 68.8 percent. The point is that employee costs go up and efficiency goes down during overtime.

If overtime is required to complete a job, make sure that you consider the costs of both overtime pay and reduced efficiency as you bid, schedule, and manage the job. And make sure that your employee handbook communicates your policies regarding overtime.

WRITING THE PAY PLAN

As your auto repair business grows beyond a single employee, take time to consider a formal pay plan. Developing a written pay plan doesn't have to cost you a lot of time and money. In fact, an elaborate plan is more difficult to put into practice, communicate, and manage.

The most important aspect of setting up a formal pay administration plan is to get acceptance, understanding, and the support of your management and supervisory employees. Of course, for a small auto repair office, that's you. The steps to setting up a successful pay plan are:

- Define the jobs.
- Evaluate the jobs.
- Price the jobs.
- Install the plan.
- Communicate the plan to employees.
- Appraise employee performance under the plan.

Defining jobs

Unless you know each job's specifications and requirements, you can't compare them for pay purposes. It's no surprise, therefore, that the initial step to installing a formal pay plan is preparing a job description for each position.

You might be able to write these job descriptions yourself, since in many small businesses the owner-manager at one time or another has worked at just about every job. However, the best and easiest way to put together such job information is simply to ask employees to describe their jobs. Ask supervisors, if you have them, to review these descriptions. Prepare a simple form to be filled out by the employee or by someone, such as a supervisor, interviewing the employee. The form should include:

- job title
- reporting relationship
- specifications
- primary function
- main duties (by importance and percent of time spent)
- other duties
- job requirements (training, experience, responsibilities, unusual working conditions)

It will probably take some time to prepare job descriptions from the information you get from your employees, but what you learn might have other uses besides comparing jobs for pay purposes. For one thing, you might discover that some employees are not doing what you thought they were, or what they were hired to do. You might find you want to make some changes in their work routines. The information might also be useful for hiring, training, and developing employees; realigning duties in your firm; comparing job data for salary surveys; assuring compliance with various employment practice and pay rate laws; and evaluating job performance based on assigned duties.

Evaluating jobs

Nobody yet has come up with a precise way of deciding exactly how much a particular job is worth to a company. Human judgment is the only way to put a dollar value on work. A good job evaluation method for smaller firms is called simple ranking.

Under the simple-ranking system, job descriptions are compared against each other. They are ranked according to difficulty and responsibility. Using your judgment, you end up with an array of jobs that shows the relative value of each position to the company.

After you rank the job descriptions by value to the firm, the next step is to group jobs that are similar in scope and responsibility into the same pay grade. Then you arrange these groups in a series of pay levels from highest to lowest. The number of pay levels depends on the total number of jobs and types of work in your organization, but for a small firm, 6 to 12 pay levels is the typical range to cover everyone from the janitor to the president.

Pricing jobs

So far, you've looked only inside the company itself. To put an accurate dollar value on each of your pay levels, look outside at the going rates for similar work in your area. Since you have ranked and grouped your jobs in pay levels, you won't have to survey each job. Survey those on each level that are easiest to describe and are most common in the industry.

A survey of who's paying how much for what in your locality is the best way to find out how much you ought to pay for each of your jobs. You probably have neither the time nor the money to make such a survey yourself. That shouldn't be a problem; you should be able to get the data you need from sources such as a local auto repair service association, a union local, the local chamber of commerce, major firms in your area, or from national sources such as the Automotive Service Association, Convenient Automotive Services Institute, Society of Collision Repair Specialists, the U.S. Bureau of Labor Statistics (Department of Labor, 441 G St N.W., Room 2421, Washington DC 20212), or the American Management Association (135 West 50th St., New York NY 10020).

After you are satisfied that you are comparing apples to apples, compute an average rate for each job and enter it on a worksheet. The average rates in the figure are purely arbitrary and for example only.

You might need to adjust the average rates somewhat to keep a sufficient difference between pay levels to separate them. The going rates you find for each pay level can then become the midpoints of your pay-level ranges. You can, of course, set your midpoints above or below the survey averages based on your firm's ability to pay, the length of your work week, the type and value of your firm's benefits program, and the local job market.

Then build a pay range for each pay level, with a minimum, a midpoint, and a maximum. Typically, the minimum rate in a level is 85 percent of the midpoint rate, and the maximum rate is 115 percent of the midpoint. With this arrangement, a new employee can increase his or her earnings by 30 percent without a job change, thus having performance incentives even if the employee is not promoted.

Such a pay range enables you to tell where your employees' pay and pay potential stand in relation to the market rates for their kinds of work. It should show you at a glance where you need to make changes to achieve rates that are fair within your organization and pay that's competitive with similar businesses in your community. With a planned pay structure, you can tie the individual rates of pay to job performance and contribution to company goals while providing enough flexibility to handle special situations.

IMPLEMENTING THE PLAN

At this point you have a "general plan," but you don't, of course, pay in general. You pay each employee individually. You must now consider how the plan will be administered to provide for individual pay increases. When administering the pay-increase feature of your plan, you can use several approaches.

- Merit increases, granted to recognize performance and contribution.
- Promotion increases for employees assigned to different jobs in higher pay levels.

- Progression to minimum for employees who are below the minimum or hiring rate for the pay level.
- Probationary increases for newer employees who have attained the necessary skills and experience to function effectively.
- Tenure increases for time with the company.
- General increases, granted employees to maintain real earnings as economic factors require and to keep pay competitive.

These are the most common approaches, but there are many variations. Most annual increases are made for cost of living, tenure, or employment market reasons. Obviously, you might use several, all, or combinations of the various increase methods.

COMMUNICATING THE PLAN

After you've put your pay administration plan into place you have to consider how to tell employees about it. Setting up a good pay administration program is almost useless if you don't communicate it to your employees.

How you tell them is your decision. Some of the more successful methods include personal letters to each employees, and staff meetings to explain the plan and answer general questions. However you tell your employees, you must clearly, honestly, and openly explain the way the plan works. This is a prime opportunity for you to enhance good relations with your employees. Be sure that your current employees understand the plan. Explaining the plan to new hires is also essential, as well as reviewing the plan periodically with all employees to handle questions and concerns.

APPRAISING YOUR EMPLOYEES

The majority of employees in the labor force work under a merit-increase pay system, though most of their pay increases result from other factors. This approach involves periodic review and appraisal of how well employees perform their assigned duties.

An effective employee appraisal plan improves two-way communication between the manager and the employee. It also relates pay to work performance and results, while showing the employee how they can improve by helping them understand job responsibilities and expectations. An employee appraisal plan also provides a standardized approach to evaluating job performance. Large shops require a formal approach while the employee appraisal at smaller shops is usually more informal.

Such a performance review helps not only the employee whose work is being appraised, but it also helps the manager doing the appraising to gain insight into the organization. An open exchange between employee and manager can show the manager where improvements in equipment, procedures, or other factors might improve employee performance. Try to foster a climate in which employees can discuss progress and problems informally at any time throughout the year.

To get the best results, use a standardized written form for appraisals. An appraisal form should cover the results achieved, quality of performance, volume of work, effectiveness in working with others in the firm and with customers and suppliers, initiative, job knowledge, and dependability.

To keep your pay administration plan in tune with the times, review it at least annually. Make adjustments where necessary and don't forget to communicate your changes to all personnel. This isn't the kind of plan that can be set up and then forgotten.

During your annual review, ask yourself if the plan is working for you. That's the most important question. Are you getting the kind of employees you want or are you just making do? What is the employee turnover rate? Do employees seem to care about the business? Most importantly, does your pay administration plan help you achieve the objectives of your business?

MANAGING EMPLOYEE BENEFITS

Employee benefits play an important role in the lives of employees and their families, and they have a significant financial impact on your business. Auto repair services cannot be competitive employers if they don't develop a comprehensive benefit program. However, if not managed, an employee-benefit program can quickly eat up a small firm's profits.

A comprehensive employee-benefit program can be broken down into four components: legally required benefits, health and welfare benefits, retirement benefits, and prerequisites.

Legally required benefit plans are mandated by law and the systems necessary to administer such plans are well established. These plans include social security insurance (FICA), workers' compensation insurance, and unemployment compensation insurance (FUTA).

Health and welfare benefits and retirement benefits can be viewed as benefits provided to work in conjunction with statutory benefits to protect employees from financial hazards such as illness, disability, death, and retirement. Health and welfare plans are perhaps the most visible of all the benefit program components. They include medical care, dental care, vision care, short-term disability, long-term disability, life insurance, accidental death and dismemberment insurance, dependent care, and legal assistance.

Retirement plans are established to help ensure that employees are able to maintain their accustomed standard of living upon retirement. Retirement benefit plans basically fall into two categories: defined-contribution plans that provide employees with an account balance at retirement, and defined-benefit plans that provide employees with a projected amount of income at retirement.

Prerequisite benefits are any other benefits an employer promises such as a company automobile or truck, professional association or club membership, paid tuition, sabbatical, extra vacation time, personal expense account, credit cards, financial counseling services, or other benefits of employment.

SELECTING AN EMPLOYEE-BENEFIT PROGRAM

Designing and implementing an employee-benefit program can be a complicated process. Many small businesses contract with employee-benefit consulting firms, insurance companies, specialized attorneys, or accounting firms to assist in this task.

As you establish your program, either by yourself or with a professional, ask yourself questions such as these.

- What should the program accomplish in the long run?
- What is the maximum amount you can afford to spend on a program?
- Are you capable and knowledgeable enough to administer the program?
- What type of program will best fit the needs of your employees?
- Should you involve your employees in the design and selection of the benefit program? If so, how much and at what stage?

Health and welfare plans

When you purchase a health and welfare plan, select a professional whose clientele is made up primarily of small businesses. In fact, if you can find one in your area, select one that is used and recommended by other auto repair services. Your insurer needs to be aware of the special problems that face small businesses, especially in your trade. Generous plans that look attractive and logical today might become a financial burden for your growing company. Remember that it is much easier to add benefits than it is to take them away.

Medical plans are usually the greatest concern of employers and employees. There are essentially two kinds of traditional medical plans. Major medical plans cover 100 percent of hospital and inpatient surgical expense as well as a percentage (typically 80 percent) of all other covered expenses. Comprehensive medical plans cover a percentage (again, generally 80 percent) of all medical expenses.

With both types of plans, the employee is usually required to pay part of the premium, particularly for dependents, as well as a deductible. Deductibles often range from $100 to $200 for single coverage, and from $200 to $1000 per person for family coverage.

A comprehensive medical plan is typically less expensive because more of the cost is shifted to the employee. Any plan you design should include features to contain your costs.

As an alternative to a traditional medical plan, an employer might contract with a health maintenance organization (HMO) to provide employees with medical services. The main difference between a traditional medical plan and an HMO is that the traditional plan allows employees to choose their medical providers, while HMOs often provide medical services at specified clinics or through "preferred" doctors and hospitals. HMOs trade this flexibility for lower costs that are often passed on to the employee through reduced or eliminated deductibles or lower rates.

If your auto repair firm has 25 or more employees, you might be legally required to offer your employees the option of coverage under an HMO. Discuss current requirements with your insurer.

Disability insurance is an important but often overlooked benefit for small businesses. Disability insurance prevents a drain of financial resources to support a principal in the event that he or she cannot continue working.

Group life insurance is a benefit employees have come to expect in many regions and trades. Such insurance is usually a multiple of an employee's salary. Be aware that an amount of insurance over a legally specified amount is subject to taxation as income to the employee.

Recent legislation provides that employers who maintain medical and dental plans must provide certain employees the opportunity to continue coverage if they otherwise become ineligible through employment termination or other causes. In addition, new rules state that if a firm's health and welfare plan discriminates in favor of key employees, the benefits to those employees are taxable as income. Talk to your plan administrator about current laws and requirements.

Retirement plans

Retirement benefit plans are either "qualified" or "unqualified." A plan is qualified if it meets certain standards mandated by law. It is beneficial to maintain a qualified retirement plan because contributions are currently deductible, earnings on plan assets are tax-deferred, benefits earned are not considered taxable income until received, and certain distributions are eligible for special tax treatment.

Of the various qualified plans, profit-sharing plans, 401(k) plans, and defined-benefit plans are the most popular.

Profit-sharing plans A profit-sharing plan is a defined-contribution plan in which the sponsoring employer has agreed to contribute a discretionary or set amount to the plan. Any contributions made to the plan are generally allocated *pro rata* to each participant's plan account based on compensation. The sponsoring employer makes no promise as to the dollar amount a participant will receive at retirement. The focus in a profit-sharing plan, and in defined-contribution plans, is on the contribution. What a participant receives at retirement is a direct function of the contributions made to the plan and the earnings on such contributions during the participant's employment with the plan sponsor. At retirement, profit-sharing plan participants receive an amount equal to the balance in their account. Profit-sharing plans are favored by employers because they give employers the ability to retain discretion when determining the amount of the contribution made to the plan.

401(k) plans Another type of defined contribution is the 401(k) plan. In a 401(k) plan, participants agree to defer a portion of their pre-tax salary as a contribution to the plan. In addition, the sponsoring employer might decide to match all or a portion of the participant deferrals. The employer might even decide to make a profit-sharing contribution to the plan. As described earlier, the focus is on the contribution to the plan. At retirement, participants receive an amount equal to their account balance. Special nondiscrimination tests apply to 401(k) plans that might reduce the amount of deferrals highly compensated employees are allowed to make and that somewhat complicate plan administration. The 401(k) plans are popular because they allow employees the ability to save for retirement with pre-tax dollars, and they can be designed to be relatively inexpensive.

Defined-benefit plans In direct contrast to a defined-contribution plan, a defined-benefit plan promises participants a benefit specified by a formula in the plan. The focus of a defined-benefit plan is the retirement benefit provided instead of the contribution made. Plan sponsors must contribute to the actuarially determined amounts necessary to meet the dollar amounts promised to participants. Generally, benefits are paid at retirement over the remainder of the employee's life, so a defined-benefit plan guarantees a certain flow of income at retirement.

Selecting the right plans

As you can see, certain plans are more suitable for auto repair services than others based on the employer's financial situation and the demographics of the employee group. Employers who are not confident of their future income might not want to start a defined-benefit plan that requires a specific level of contributions. However, if your employees are fairly young, a profit-sharing plan or 401(k) plan might result in a more significant and more appreciated benefit than a defined-benefit plan. The 401(k) plans are very popular now that IRAs have been virtually eliminated. However, the nondiscrimination tests make it more difficult for small businesses to maintain 401(k) plans. If your work force is composed mainly of older employees, a defined-benefit plan will be more beneficial to them, but more expensive for you to maintain.

Remember that while a qualified plan has many positive aspects, the qualified retirement plan area is complicated and well monitored by the government. Make sure you have adequate counsel before you decide on the most appropriate plan for your business.

You can also set up your own retirement plan as a self-employed business owner, called a Keogh or HR 10 plan. For more information on Keoghs and SEPs (Simplified Employee Pension plans), request Publication 560, *Retirement Plans for the Self-Employed*, from your regional IRS office. There's no charge.

HIRING TEMPORARY HELP

How does your auto repair business cope with unexpected personnel shortages? Many businesses face this question whether the cause is seasonal peaking, several employees on sick leave, or an unexpected increase in business. For some skills, many auto repair services hire and use subcontractors. But for office work, a growing number hire help through temporary personnel services. In fact, many new auto repair services start their business employing part-time temporary office personnel instead of hiring full-time employees.

A temporary personnel service, listed in your phone book's yellow pages under Employment Contractors-Temporary Help, is not an employment agency. Like many service firms, it hires people as its own employees and assigns them to companies requesting assistance. This means that when you use a service, you are not hiring an employee, you are buying the use of their time. The temporary personnel firm is responsible for payroll, bookkeeping, tax deductions, workers' compensation insurance, fringe benefits, and all other similar costs connected with the employee. You are relieved of the burden of recruiting, interviewing, screening, and basic skill training.

Most national temporary personnel companies also offer performance guarantees and fidelity bonding at no added cost to their clients. They also relieve you of the need for government forms and for reporting withholding tax, social security insurance, and unemployment compensation insurance.

If you need temporary personnel for a period of six months or more, it's usually more cost-effective to hire a full-time employee. Also, if the task requires skills or training beyond basic office skills, it might cost you less to pay overtime to an employee with those skills.

The key to the successful use of temporary employees is to plan what type of help you need, how much, and when. The more accurate the information you give to the temporary service firm improves their ability to supply you with the correct person for your needs.

Before your temporary employee arrives on the job, there are a few things you should do. First, appoint one of your permanent employees to supervise the temporary employee and check on the progress of the work. Be sure this supervisor understands the job to be done and what the responsibilities are. Next, let your permanent staff know that you are taking on extra help and that it will be temporary. Explain why the extra help is needed and ask them to cooperate with the new employee in anyway possible.

Have everything ready before the temporary employee arrives. The work to be done should be organized and laid out so that the employee can begin producing with a minimum of time spent adjusting to the job and the surroundings. Also, don't set up schedules that are impossible to complete within the time you allot. Try to stay within the time limits you gave the temporary help service, but plan to extend the time period if necessary rather than hurry the employee.

Finally, furnish detailed instructions. Describe your type of business and the services you offer. Help the temp feel comfortable and a part of your team. Most temporary employees have broad business experience and can easily adapt to your requirements, if they know what these are.

HIRING A SERVICE MANAGER

If you've been your own service manager, you might want to consider hiring a service manager when your business expands. This person can take this task from you and let you get on with other things. Unfortunately, most auto repair services don't know how to hire a good service manager. Here are some ideas.

There are three main types of service managers. The first is the order handler. A knowledgeable person with a pleasant personality is a good choice for this job, maybe an employee who has worked in the automotive repair field but now must move to a desk job for whatever reason.

The second type is the order taker. Technical knowledge, again, is important. However, this position requires that the service manager know and apply some salesmanship skills. A prospect might stop by the shop and request an estimate. The order taker asks, for example, if there are other needed repairs that can be done at the same time.

The third type of service manager is the order getter. This position requires someone who knows people and how to sell to them. In fact, sales skills are often as important as technical knowledge. An order getter develops and qualifies prospects, ranks them by interest and opportunity, then works with them in order to develop them into customers. An active service manager finds ways to get more people to come to your business first.

So how do you hire a service manager? First you determine which type you need: order handler, order taker, or order getter. Then consider your budget. The more creative the service manager, the more he or she must be paid. Many auto repair services offer order getters a base salary plus a commission. Terms are quite negotiable. Don't make the mistake that many business managers make. Don't complain if you write a commission check that's larger than your own salary. Remember that every sales dollar is another potential profit dollar for you.

What should you look for in an order getter? Common sense, maturity, intelligence, tact, a positive attitude, personal hygiene, and stability. Your service manager must be a people person.

YOUR SUCCESS ACTION LIST

Your auto repair service will succeed or fail largely on how you manage your employees. This vital chapter includes information on selecting, hiring, managing, and compensating shop, office, and sales employees.

The next and final chapter offers advanced management techniques to help your auto repair service business grow. Here's how you can put Chapter 10 into action.

_____ Write a job description for each of the employees you now have or expect to have and list the requirements for each job.

_____ Contact your local state employment office to make sure that you are aware of all employment laws that affect your business.

_____ Select a stock employment application form that meets your requirements, is legal, and makes the hiring process easier.

_____ Make a list of questions to ask during an employment interview.

_____ Begin writing your business' personnel policy.

_____ Establish wages and a pay plan for specific jobs in your auto repair business.

_____ Select and implement an employee-benefits program with the help of your accountant, attorney, insurance agent, and/or trade association.

_____ Decide whether to use temporary help and, if so, for what jobs.

_____ Decide whether to hire a sales staff and, if so, what type and size.

11
Expanding your business

As noted in Chapter 1, success is a journey rather than a destination. Success is getting up every morning—Monday through Sunday—to do what you enjoy. Unfortunately, as a business grows, it sometimes takes the owner away from his or her original dream and pleasures. What was once fun is now work. The purpose of this chapter is to help you maintain your founding focus while expanding your auto repair service to a point where it is also reasonably profitable and secure. Because, for many long-time auto repair service owners, it is the business rather than the trade that becomes a frustration.

In this chapter, we'll cover making sure that your process still works well, managing through rotten times, using management techniques that work for bigger businesses, ensuring business continuation, applying time and stress management, and, finally, planning for retirement.

WHAT WORKS FOR YOU?

Even though there are hundreds of worthwhile tips for expanding your auto repair business within this book, there is one primary rule that supersedes all others: Do what works best for you. That is, if your business is growing through telephone marketing while other auto repair services are using direct mail, do what works for you. You're certainly wiser to at least try the other methods, but there are so many variables among local markets, customer types, client needs, and your own skills and personality, that the "best" way to do something is relative. What works well for you might not work at all for someone else.

That doesn't mean that you should always follow the easiest path. A good business manager continually looks for new and better ways to complete the "process" discussed earlier. It might be purchasing a new computer program that automates credit collections, or searching for a niche market that isn't being served. But remember, just because something is new doesn't always mean that it is better. Be aggressive in your learning and conservative in your changing. Know what works for you.

One way to know what works is to continually rethink how you manage your business and serve your customers. Remember that to "think" is simply to ask yourself questions, then answer them. And the better the question, the better the answer.

So, as you go about your daily business, ask yourself: How can I do this job better, more efficiently, faster, more profitably, safer, or with more quality?

- How can I better handle incoming calls from prospects who want an accurate repair quote in a hurry?
- How can I get more prospects to call me for a quote without spending too much money on advertising and promotion?
- How can I get my employees to stop spending so much time at the coffee machine and more time at the rack?
- How can I encourage my banker to extend me more credit during the slower business months?
- How can I find out if customers are happy or unhappy with my service?
- How can I get my customers to tell others about my service in a positive way?
- How can I ensure that my employees are working as safely as possible?
- How can I reduce my insurance costs without increasing my risk?
- How can I cut costs without cutting my quality of service?

A successful manager is always rethinking the way he or she does everything from maintaining an office to purchasing equipment to serving customers. To make your business grow, you must rethink your business every day.

One more tip: if you're a better tradesman than you are a business manager, hire a manager. If you become a better business manager, hire a tradesman to do the work. Do what you do best, and what you enjoy most.

MAKING SURE IT WORKS

Here is a seeming contradiction to the above rule: If it ain't broke, break it! Actually, the two rules work together. Do what works for you, but make sure it's really working. To test its strength, try to break it from time to time. Here's what I mean. New customers are coming to you faster than you can handle them, so you take some time to plan what you'll do when the customers aren't coming at all. Or you've set up a front office that smoothly handles incoming calls, handles messages timely, and manages the paperwork without problems; consider what you'll do if this gem-of-an-office-manager decides to move to the competition or to leave the area. What would you do to ensure that valuable records aren't lost, that proven procedures are documented, that your next office manager is as efficient as the one you have? Plan now as if it already happened, because it will. Murphy owned an auto repair shop!

MANAGING BUSINESS RECESSIONS

No businesses are truly recession proof. All businesses have cycles where sales become easier or harder to make. Auto repair services are subject to the same business cycle that most businesses face. Even so, there are steps you can take to minimize the market's down-swing and extend its up-swing.

First, determine the business cycle for your market. Review income and financial records from prior years, or check with the local chamber of commerce or regional trade association. Draw a chart that illustrates the local business cycle. In your region, it might be that most of the market for your service occurs in the spring and summer. Or maybe in the winter and fall. Or the cycle might be fairly level throughout the year, but alternate years might fluctuate up or down. The first step to coping with recessionary periods in the local business cycle is to determine exactly what and when that cycle is.

The next step is to plan for it. That is, if you're coming up to a typically slower period, determine what you need to do. In past years, how much has income dropped? For how long? Can you find income sources in other specialities where the cycle is moving up? What expenses can you cut back? Do you have an employee who would like a seasonal layoff so he can catch up on other interests.

Maybe you need to dramatically cut back on your expenses and debts for this period. If so, list them out now, determine which will naturally diminish and which will need to be reduced.

One successful auto repair service owner, while in a busy period, decided that times would be much slower six months hence. So he talked with his bank and other creditors and offered to prepay debts and expenses now so he could cut back payments later. It worked. When times got rougher, he reduced his expenses and wintered the problem.

If you aren't in your slow season yet, you can also talk to your banker about building a line of credit now that can help you get through the tougher times ahead.

One more option for those who are facing a downturn in auto repair business: trade out your services. That is, if your bank or a major creditor is beginning to pressure you, offer to perform repair services for them in lieu of partial or complete payment. Even if they don't require your service now, you can either promise future services as required or learn if they have other customers who might wish to hire or trade. Many creditors would rather work out a trade than absorb a bad debt. Of course, much depends on your relationship with them.

Some creditors, such as the IRS and other governmental agencies, will not consider service trades. However, they can sometimes develop terms for a businessperson who has an otherwise good financial record and the opportunity for growth once the local economy turns around. But don't expect compassion; its purely business.

Another source for cash to tide you through a recession is available from a second mortgage on your shop, your home, or other large asset. Speak with your lender about this opportunity. Even if you decide not to take out a second mortgage, you will be ready if and when you need to do so.

One more thing: consider widening your market. That is, travel to a nearby metropolitan area and study whether you can expand your services to reach it. If so, you can pick up additional sales by either subcontracting your services or by promoting your services in the expanded market. It certainly beats starving at home.

USING ADVANCED MANAGEMENT TECHNIQUES

The "big boys"—your larger competitors—probably got so with the help of what is called "strategic planning." Strategic planning is a process that helps you assess the current business environment, redefine your company's mission or purpose, decide where you want your business to be in three to five years, recognize your firm's strengths and weaknesses, and map out a course to take your firm from where you are to where you want to be.

Why should you spend the many hours it takes to develop a strategic plan for your business? Because you want to succeed in business. Technology and the fast pace of change are making business management more complex. Strategic planning helps you foresee and react quickly to market changes and opportunities, and identify areas in which your business lags behind. Also, competition is becoming tougher. In most cases, small businesses find themselves competing with much larger companies, ones that know the benefits of strategic planning and practice it. The strategic planning process involves your employees, your banker, your accountant, and possibly your attorney, helping each to feel more a part of your team.

The strategic planning process begins with an assessment of the current economic situation. First, examine factors outside of your company that can affect it's performance. You're looking for forecasts on the national, regional, local, and your industry's business economy. Sources include business trade publications such as the *Wall Street Journal*, industrial trade journals, the United States Department of Commerce (for their 12 leading economic indicators and other figures), local and regional chambers of commerce, and industry trade associations, listed earlier.

Next comes the planning session with key employees and independent advisers. Present your written summary of economic forecasts, then ask everyone to put on their creativity caps. Have lots of writing pads, flip charts, or a large writing board for recording *any* ideas. All ideas are equally important and valid.

This group of people is your SWOT Team. Together you will list your firm's strengths, weaknesses, opportunities, and threats. Try to list at least 10 items in each category. Here are some idea-starting examples.

- Strengths:

    ~Our company is well known in our field.
    ~We have developed excellent suppliers.
    ~Our financial credit rating is good.
    ~We have a highly qualified and efficient staff.

- Weaknesses:

    ~Our regional economy is in a recession.
    ~Some employees don't work as part of the team.
    ~Our recordkeeping system is too cumbersome.
    ~We cannot always respond fast to market changes.

- Opportunities:

    ~Our major competitor will probably be out of business within a year.
    ~Our major parts supplier is offering additional discounts for which we can easily qualify.
    ~Most of our customers can purchase additional services from us if we let them know of availability.
    ~Installing a new telephone system would improve sales and enhance relations with our current customers.

- Threats:

~A new competitor is cutting prices to attract market share.

~A new competitor has lured away two of our employees by offering better pay.

Get the picture? Before you decide where you want the company to be in a few years, you must know where it has been, where it is now, and what speed bumps you should expect. Make sure that everything is down in writing, even the "dumb" ideas, before you leave your meeting.

REFINING YOUR MISSION STATEMENT AND OBJECTIVES

An organization's mission statement describes its purpose. You developed a preliminary mission statement earlier in this book when you set up your business notebook. Now look at how it can be refined to clarify where you want the firm to go and why.

A mission statement is typically short—a single sentence or paragraph in length. It can include any or all of the following: reason for the firm, the products or services offered, the market and clients served, and the intended direction of the firm. Here are some examples.

- "The ABC Auto Repair Service provides economical auto repair in the northeast section of Ourtown."

- "Our goal is simple: we want to be the best auto repair service in this part of the state."

- "ABC Auto Repair Service's goal is to provide the highest quality auto repair to high-income clients in Smith County. We intend to capitalize on our reputation for quality to expand into related services within three years."

From the mission statement and your strategic planning sessions, develop a list of 5 to 10 key result areas (KRAs). Typical KRAs include:

- Increasing revenues.
- Improving profitability.
- Enhancing credit and collections policies.
- Keeping pace or outdistancing the competition.
- Improving efficiency.
- Increasing level of service offered to customers.
- Capitalizing on emerging trends.
- Utilizing newer technology to improve operations.
- Improving labor relations.
- Improving internal relations.
- Improving relations with suppliers.
- Enhancing our image through publicity and advertising.
- Capitalizing on our physical facilities.
- Improving organizational structure.
- Arranging for the sale or transfer of the business.

Obviously, this list is not complete. Nor should you include all of these noble KRAs on your list. Pick a few that are most appropriate to your mission statement and make them your goals.

The next step to strategic planning is to define specific strategic and tactical objectives for each of your KRAs. A strategic objective indicates what you want to accomplish in measurable terms, such as "increase revenues from existing customers by $6000 per month by December 31." The tactical objective then lists the short-term objectives or steps needed to meet the strategic objective. In the example, tactical objectives might include the following.

- Identify services now offered that could be cross-sold to existing customers.
- Determine which service can most easily be cross-sold.
- Determine the best method of selling these services to existing customers: telemarketing, direct mail, or automatic maintenance services.

Next, establish a budget for accomplishing these objectives. If you're expecting to earn $6000 in additional sales and you typically allocate 20 percent of your costs to sales, your budget might be up to $1200 per month. Or you might need to establish a budget to set up the process without expecting to receive offsetting income for a short period of time.

Finally, and just as important, set up a monitoring system to ensure that your strategic plan is on target and reaching its goals. Many successful auto repair businesses dedicate a portion of scheduled management meetings to reviewing progress on the firm's strategic plan.

Establishing a strategic plan for your auto repair business might seem like a lot of work. But remember that it can save you time and make you money by keeping your business focused. Big business uses strategic planning because, in many cases, it is a major reason why they became big.

ENSURING THE CONTINUATION OF YOUR BUSINESS

The auto repair business you've started, nourished, managed, and expanded has become a part of you. For many firms, the owner is the business and vice versa. So what happens to your auto repair business when you or your partner dies or is disabled? That's up to you.

Life insurance and good planning can provide significant amounts of cash to help employees and family members cushion the financial impact of the death or retirement of the owner/manager of a sole proprietorship, partnership, or a closely-held corporation. It can also help attract and retain valuable employees.

Sole proprietorships

The personal skills, reputation, and management ability of the sole proprietor help to make the business successful. Without these human-life values the business is worth only the liquidation value of the tangible assets.

The sole proprietor's personal and business assets are one and the same. When death occurs, the loss can become a financial disaster for the proprietor's estate and fatal to the business. The business that was producing a good living for the owner and his family will become a defunct business. What are the options?

Family continuation The business might be transferred to a capable family member as a gift through provisions in the proprietor's will or by a sale provided through a prearranged purchase agreement effective at death. Cash is needed to offset losses to the business caused by the owner's death, to equalize the value of bequests made to other family members if the transfer is a gift, and to provide the sale price if the transfer is through sale.

New owner If the buyer is a key employee, competitor, or other person, the business might be transferred at death, based on a prearranged sale agreement. However, cash is needed to provide a "business continuation fund" to meet expenses and perhaps to offset losses until the business adjusts to the new management.

Liquidation If future management is not available then the business must be liquidated. Cash is needed to offset the difference between the business' going-concern value and its auction-block liquidation value to provide a fund for income replacement to the family and to pay outstanding business debts.

Partnerships

Unless there is a written agreement to the contrary, the death of a partner automatically dissolves the firm. In the absence of such an agreement, surviving partners have no right to buy the deceased's partnership interest. Surviving partners cannot assume the goodwill or take over the assets without consent of the deceased's estate. If the deceased was in debt to the partnership, the estate must settle the account in full and in cash.

The surviving partners act as liquidating trustees. They have exclusive possession of firm property but no right to carry on the business. If the business is continued, the surviving partners must share all profits with the deceased's estate and are liable for all losses. They must convert everything into cash at the best price obtainable. They must make an accounting to the deceased's estate and divide the proceeds with the estate. They must liquidate themselves out of their business and income.

What are the options a business has on the death of a partner.

Liquidation If the surviving partner and deceased's heirs do nothing, the business is liquidated, resulting in "auction price" value for the salable assets. The business might receive nothing for goodwill. This is a disastrous solution for both the dead partner's family and the surviving partners. It means termination of jobs for the surviving partners and employees.

Reorganization The surviving partners might attempt to reorganize the partnership by taking the heirs into the partnership. But if heirs are incapable of working, the survivors must do all the work and share the profits. The surviving partners can also accept a new partner picked by the heirs. Or the surviving partners can sell their interest in the business to the heirs. Or they can buy out the interest now controlled by the deceased partner's heirs.

Of course, there are some preparations that can be made prior to the death of a partner that can make a reorganization smoother. Buy and sell agreements funded with life insurance should be entered into while all partners are alive. Such an agreement, drafted by an attorney, typically includes a commitment by each partner not to dispose of his or her interest without first offering it at an agreed sale price to the partnership. The agreement also includes a provision for the partnership to buy a deceased partner's interest. The funding of the purchase typically will be from the proceeds of a life insurance policy written for that specific purpose.

Corporations

The death of a stockholder who has been active in the operation of a closely-held corporation allows the business entity to continue its legal structure, but not its personal structure. The interests of the heirs of the deceased inevitably come in conflict with the interests of the surviving associates.

What options are available to surviving stockholders?

Retention of stock by heirs The deceased's family might retain the stock interest. If the heirs have a majority interest, they might choose to become personally involved in management in order to receive income. Or they might choose to remain inactive, elect a new board of directors and force the company to pay dividends. In either case, the surviving stockholders might lose a voice in management and possibly their jobs, while the deceased's family might become heirs to a business on the brink of failure. If the heirs have a minority interest and are not employed by the surviving associates, their only means of receiving an income from the corporation will be through dividends.

Sale of stock by heirs After the death of a stockholder, the deceased's heirs or estate might offer to sell the stock interest to the surviving stockholders. Or an outside buyer might be interested in purchasing stock in the corporation. While all of the interested parties are alive, they can enter into a binding buy-and-sell agreement funded with life insurance. This is done with a *Stockholder's Buy and Sell Agreement* drawn up with the assistance of your corporate attorney and accountant.

Key employees

Many growing firms develop key employees who are assets that the firm cannot afford to be without. Even though these key employees might not own an interest in the firm, they are nonetheless valuable to its continuation. So what happens if a key employee dies?

Auto repair services who have key employees should consider life insurance payable to the firm on the death or disability of one of these human assets. How much life insurance? It should be an amount sufficient to offset financial losses during the readjustment period, to retain good credit standing, to assure customers and suppliers that the company will continue as usual. In addition, key-employee insurance could retire loans, mortgages, bonds, attract and train a successor, or carry out ongoing plans for expansion and new developments.

Talk to your insurance agent about the appropriate policy for insuring your business against the loss of a proprietor, a partner, a stockholder, or a key employee. It's one of the costs of growth.

EFFECTIVELY MANAGING YOUR TIME

A growing auto repair business might seem to take up at least 24 hours of your day. Maybe more. Don't let it! Some auto repair business owners spend most of their day fighting fires. Others let the fires burn each other out. The smart auto repair owner manages available time by prioritizing the jobs to be done. Those that are vital to the success of the business get done first. Important jobs come next. Then those that are of limited value fill up the remainder of his time, if there is any.

Many successful auto repair service owners start their day with a planning session of up to a half hour. In this time, the owner/manager plans out the events of his day to ensure that the vital jobs get done and the important jobs are handled as time is available. He or she might schedule "chatter" time with employees or customers, but will ensure that the discussions stay mostly on business or at least on personal topics that can help forge a better business relationship.

How can an auto repair service business owner ensure that his time is well managed? First, organize work space so that important papers don't get lost and unimportant papers do. Make a rule that you will avoid handling papers more than once. If you pick up a piece of paper, make a decision regarding it right then if possible.

Set up a regular work schedule. It might be from 7 am to 6 pm or 8 to 5 or 6 to 6. Whatever it is, try to stick to it. If you manage your time well, you will be able to. If you have one time of the day that seems more productive for you than others, plan your most important functions around it.

What about travel and waiting time? Take work with you in a briefcase or purchase a cellular phone or laptop computer that you can use to stay productive every minute. As your time-management skills improve you'll learn how to do more than one thing at a time. You might be making job notes or talking with a key employee or gathering information on an upcoming bid while you're waiting to talk with an inspector or a customer.

Meetings seem to be one of the biggest time wasters. But you can change this by organizing all of your meetings. Meetings, to be productive, must have a purpose or agenda and a time limit. Even if you didn't call the meeting, if you see that it has no focus or structure you can step in and say, "I have another appointment in an hour. What topics do we have to cover in this meeting?" Then list those topics as the agenda.

One more time management tip: use one of the popular time-management planning systems to help you get the most out of your day. They include *Day Timer* (Day Timers, Inc.) and *Day Runner* (Harper House, Inc.). These and other systems give you a place to record appointments, daily to-do lists, special projects and their steps, as well as a contact book for names and addresses. If you spend most of your time in the office at a computer, there are numerous contact management and scheduling programs that can help you manage your time. If you use a portable computer, you can install these programs on it and carry this information wherever you go.

Time and stress are closely related. The lack of time to do what you need to do often increases personal stress. How do you manage both? Here are some ideas from successful auto repair service owners.

Plan your time and establish priorities on a daily "to do" list. Decide what your prime time is and do your most important or difficult tasks then. Set business hours, specific times when you are at work and times when you turn on the answering machine because you are on duty but off call. You, your customers, and your family will appreciate knowing your set routine, even though you know that for special events or emergencies you can break that schedule.

Notice what your four or five big time-wasters are and learn techniques to eliminate them or compensate for them. Some common ones are:

- Telephone interruptions.
- Visitors.
- Socializing.
- Excessive paperwork.
- Lack of policies and procedures.
- Procrastination.
- Failure to delegate.
- Unclear objectives.
- Poor scheduling.
- Lack of self-discipline.
- Lack of skill in a needed area.

Stay in contact with people. As you move from a tradesperson to an auto repair business owner, you will naturally spend more time in "the office." Make sure that you get out and talk with your customers, your employees, and for social events. This can help your morale if you feel isolated. Just as important, your contacts will appreciate your visibility and your interest in sharing time with them.

Build a fitness program into your day. As an active mechanic you might have gotten plenty of exercise doing your daily job. However, as a business manager you might not, unless you take time for fitness. Many successful businesspeople exercise in order to think creatively because physical activity sends oxygen to the brain and helps the mind function better. With regular exercise your health will improve, your stress level will go down, and your trim look will inspire people to have confidence in your abilities.

If you're working from your home, give your business as much of a separate and distinct identity as possible. Although you might save a few dollars by using the dining room table as a desk and a cardboard box as a file cabinet, the stress and strain of operating without proper space and supplies can take its toll. Have a separate room or area for your business, with a separate entrance if customers or suppliers visit. Consider soundproofing this area so your family won't be bothered by your noise and vice versa. In addition to the psychological and physical comfort of having a separate room for your home office, the IRS requires it in order for you to make a legitimate claim for tax deductions.

Finally, take care of your major business asset: You. Being the boss can be exciting, fulfilling, and rewarding. It can also be lonely, stressful, and demanding. Learn to balance your professional and personal life. Go on vacation. Get a weekly massage. Join a health club. Take a class in meditation or spiritual studies. Attend a business owner's breakfast club. Your business depends on you to be at your best.

HAVE FUN!

The primary reason you started your own business was to increase your opportunities to enjoy life. You wanted to offer a needed service, you wanted to help others, you wanted to extend your skills in auto repair and in business, you wanted to be able to afford the better things of life. However, you didn't want to spend your entire waking time working. In fact, you might get so caught up in the chase for success that you miss the opportunities that success brings along the way.

Those who have found success in the auto repair and other fields will tell you that success is often empty if it isn't shared with others. And that doesn't mean waiting until a successful destination, say at $1 million net worth, is reached. It means sharing success with others along the way, on a day-to-day basis. Maybe, for you, this means sharing your success with your close family, or a few close friends, or even some humanity-serving organization in which you believe. In any case, consider that your financial success will mean more to you if you can use it to bring physical, emotional, or spiritual success to others.

Manage your life outside your business as you do your time at the business. Look for ways to help others. Find methods of giving yourself the things you most enjoy, whether time with friends, time with hobbies, time with competitive sports, time alone, or all of the above. Especially, take time to recharge your batteries. You will use lots of personal energy to start, manage, and expand your auto repair business. Make sure you take the time to re-energize yourself.

PULLING THE PLUG

The failure rate of new businesses is very high. It lowers as your auto repair service matures. The longer you are in business, the greater the chance you will continue in business.

However, your auto repair business can fail at any time. Most fail because they don't have a functioning recordkeeping system. They aren't even sure exactly when or how they fail, they just do. So a key element to continued success is to maintain good records and learn how to manage by them.

But there might come a time when business conditions require that you throw in the towel. If you're not making sufficient profit or are reducing your capital to losses ratio, you will soon be in financial trouble. What to do?

First, cut overhead as much as possible. The sooner this is done, the longer your business can survive, maybe long enough to find a solution. Next, sell unused or inefficient assets. Of course, you must maintain your working tools. But maybe you can move your office to a less expensive location, even back home.

Talk with your creditors about the situation and what you plan to do. Some might be very helpful and offer a workable solution: an extension of credit, assistance in finding additional contracts, or even purchase of stock in your business.

Finally, as necessary, talk with your attorney about your legal obligations and options. No one wants to declare bankruptcy, but it might be necessary. Or you might decide to set up a payment schedule for all debts and return to the work force as an employee.

There is no shame in failing to succeed, just in failing to try. If there are things you've learned from the experience, you can use them to increase your worth to an employer. Who better to manage an auto repair business than one who has *learned* what *doesn't* work.

RETIREMENT

When should you retire from your profitable auto repair business? When you want to.

When to retire

Some auto repair service owners hold off retiring until they are no longer physically able to work their trade. Others make plans to retire when they are 65 or even 62 years of age. Still others give their business 10 or 20 years to grow, then sell it to semi-retire or to move to a different trade. Some work their children into the business, then gradually turn it over to them.

How to retire

Some successful auto repair business owners sell their shares to a partner or to another corporation. Others sell or give their equity in the business to a son or son-in-law. A few simply liquidate their assets and keep the proceeds. Some sell out to key employees or to competitors.

The business can be sold outright for cash, earning the owner a cash settlement for his equity. Or the seller can "carry the paper" or sell it on a contract with a down payment and monthly payments for a specified term. In this case, buyers often require the seller to sign a "noncompetition" contract that says the seller can't go to work for a competing auto repair service or start another auto repair firm in the same market.

YOUR SUCCESS ACTION LIST

Expanding your successful auto repair service can be as much fun as starting it, or it can be your worst nightmare. Decide what works best for you, make sure that it works well, plan for the inevitable downturn in business, apply advanced management skills, do what you can to ensure a long life for your business, manage your time well, and start planning for a well-earned and well-healed retirement. Here's how you can put this chapter into action.

_____ Take pride in what you do.

_____ Enjoy your life.

Appendix

Cash Receipts Register

PERIOD ENDING:

Date	Check Number	Account Number	Amount	Name

A-1 Cash receipts register.

Cash Disbursements Register

PERIOD ENDING:

Date	Check Number	Account Number	Amount	Name

A-2 Cash disbursements register.

Cash Flow Forecast

| DATE: |
| FOR TIME PERIOD: |
| APPROVED BY: |
| PREPARED BY: |

	Date:		Date:		Date:	
	ESTIMATE	ACTUAL	ESTIMATE	ACTUAL	ESTIMATE	ACTUAL
Opening Balance						
Collections From Trade						
Misc. Cash Receipts						
TOTAL CASH AVAILABLE						
DISBURSEMENTS						
Payroll						
Trade Payables						
Other						
Capital Expenses						
Income Tax						
Bank Loan Payment						
TOTAL DISBURSEMENTS						
Ending Balance						
Less Minimum Balance						
CASH AVAILABLE						

FOR INTERNAL USE ONLY

A-3 Cash flow forecast.

Date:

Code	Description	Unit Cost

A-4 Price list.

Quotation Form

Date:

Quote #

Client:

Materials

Quantity	Description	Cost Per Unit	Total
		Total Cost:	

Labor

	Hours	Description	Cost Per Hour	Total
REGULAR				
OVERTIME				
			Total Cost:	

GRAND TOTAL

_____   _____
Authorized Signature   Date

A-5 Quotation form.

Date:
Page: No.   of
Material /Equipment:
RFQ. #:
By:

Bidder:								Quotation Closing Date:		
Date of Quotation:								Requisition Value:		
Quotation Reference No.:								Jobsite Date:		
Location of Manufacturer:								Mode of Shipment:		
Bid Validity Date:								Required At:		
ITEM	QTY	BRIEF DESCRIPTION	$	$	$	$	$	SELECTED VENDOR(S):		
								Reason for Selection:		
								☐ Specifications	☐ Delivery	
								☐ Only Source	☐ Other	
								Comments:		
TOTAL PRICE										
FOB Point										
In-Land Freight								APPROVALS	FULL SIGNATURE	DATE
Acceptance of Company General Conditions										
Bidders Acceptance of Guarantee Required										
Firm Price /Maximum Escalation										
Terms of Payment										
Estimated Total Cost Recommended Items										
Delivery Time - Weeks /Months										
Meets Specifications - Yes /No										

A-6 Quote summary.

PROPOSAL

NUMBER

DATE

Proposal Submitted to:

Job Site Information:

NAME

JOB NAME

ADDRESS

JOB LOCATION

CITY   STATE   ZIP CODE

JOB PHONE

We hereby submit specifications and estimates for:

We hereby propose to furnish material and labor -complete in accordance with the above specifications for

_____ dollars $ _____

Payment to be made as follows:

_____

_____

_____

All matter is guaranteed to be as specified. All work to be completed in a workmanlike manner according to standard practices. Any alternation or deviation from above specifications involving extra costs will be executed only upon written orders, and will become an extra charge over and above the estimate. All agreements contingent upon strikes, accidents, or delays beyond Our Company. Owner is to carry necessary insurance. Our Company workers are fully covered by Workman's Compensation Insurance.

Authorized Signature

X _____

Note: This proposal may be withdrawn by us if not accepted within _____ days

Acceptance of Proposal. The above prices and specifications are satisfactory and hereby accepted. You are authorized to do the work as specified. Payment will be made as outlined above.

X _____
Signature

X _____
Signature

_____
Date of Acceptance

A-7 Proposal.

CUSTOMER ORDER NUMBER

NAME

ADDRESS

CITY   STATE   ZIP

LOCATION

TELEPHONE NUMBER

DATE OF ORDER

JOB NUMBER   JOB NAME   JOB LOCATION

DATE STARTED   TERMS   ORDER TAKEN BY

PARTS AND MATERIALS

Quantity	Description	Price	Amount
		TOTAL MATERIALS	

SUBLET REPAIRS

Quantity	Sublet Repairs	Price	Amount
		TOTAL SUBLET REPAIRS	

LABOR

Hours	Labor	Rate	Amount
		TOTAL LABOR	

Description of work done.

SUBTOTAL

TAX   %

TOTAL

WORK ORDER BY

I hereby acknowledge the satisfactory completion of work done.

A-8 Work order.

ORDER FORM

Date _____

SOLD TO:	SHIPPING ADDRESS:

Order Number: _____ Salesperson: _____

Telephone: _____ Ship Via: _____ Date: _____

Quantity	Description	Unit Price	Amount

TERMS

- ☐ Cash
- ☐ COD
- ☐ On Account
- ☐ MC / Visa / Amex - Card Number # _____
  Expiry date _____
  Name on Card _____

Subtotal	
Delivery Charge	
TOTAL	
% Sales Tax	
Balance Due	

A-9 Order form.

JOB EXPENSE RECORD

DATE

JOB NUMBER #	CLIENT	TELEPHONE NUMBER #
	STARTING DATE	COMPLETION DATE
JOB DESCRIPTION		

MATERIALS

DATE	ITEM	Net Cost	Mark-up	Total Cost
	Total			

LABOR

DATE	Name	Hours	Rate	Net Cost	Mark-up	Total Cost
		Total				

MISCELLANEOUS EXPENSES

DATE	DESCRIPTION	AMOUNT
	Total	

	Net Cost	Mark-up	Total Cost
Total Materials			
Total Labor			
Total Miscellaneous			
Grand Total			

A-10 Job expense record.

CUSTOMER SERVICE EXPENSE REPORT

(To be submitted to the Service Department, immediately after trip)

NAME:		REPORT DATE:
CUSTOMER:		JOB ORDER:
PRODUCT:		DEPARTMENT:

LABOR

LABOR	SUN	MON	TUES	WED	THURS	FRI	SAT
Normal Hours *							
Overtime							
Travel **							

*include travel time during normal weekday working hours. **List travel time outside normal working hours, Saturday, Sunday and Holidays.

MATERIALS
(List all materials left at Customer's Facility)

MODEL DESCRIPTION	PART NUMBER	QUANTITY	SERIAL NUMBERS	UNIT COST*	TOTAL COST*

*To be completed by Sales   **TOTAL MATERIAL COST** | |

EXPENSES
List total expenses and attach copy of expense report _____

COMMENTS (List details of any special cost agreement with the customer)

COSTING
(To be completed by Sales)

LABOR	TOTAL HOURS	HOURLY RATE	COST
STRAIGHT TIME			
1 1/2 TIME			
DOUBLE TIME			
TOTAL LABOR			
TOTAL EXPENSES			
TOTAL MATERIAL			
TOTAL COST			

CUSTOMER CHARGES
(To be completed by Sales)
COMMENTS: _____

A-11   Customer service expense report.

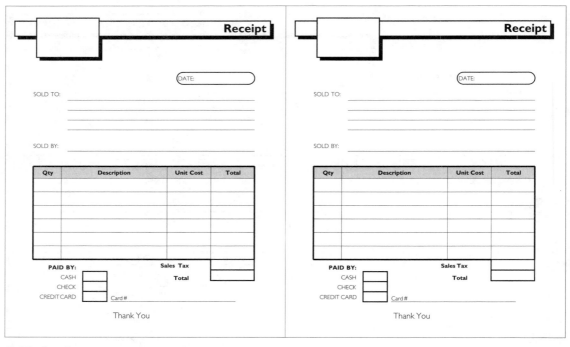

A-12 Receipts.

Invoice

| DATE: |
| INVOICE: |
| P.O. #: |
| SALESPERSON: |

SOLD TO:

SHIP TO:

Qty Ordered	Qty Shipped	Description	Price	Total
			Subtotal	
			Sales Tax	
			Total	

A-13 Invoice.

CREDIT APPLICATION

DATE:

BUSINESS INFORMATION	DESCRIPTION OF BUSINESS		
NAME OF BUSINESS	NO. OF EMPLOYEES	CREDIT REQUESTED	TYPE OF BUSINESS
LEGAL (IF DIFFERENT)	IN BUSINESS SINCE		
ADDRESS	BUSINESS STRUCTURE		
CITY	☐ CORPORATION ☐ PARTNERSHIP ☐ PROPRIETORSHIP ☐ DIVISION/SUBSIDIARY NAME OF PARENT COMPANY _____ HOW LONG IN BUSINESS _____		

STATE	ZIP	PHONE

COMPANY PRINCIPALS RESPONSIBLE FOR BUSINESS TRANSACTIONS

NAME :	TITLE:	ADDRESS:	PHONE:
NAME:	TITLE:	ADDRESS:	PHONE:
NAME:	TITLE:	ADDRESS:	PHONE:

BANK REFERENCES

NAME OF BANK	NAME TO CONTACT
BRANCH	ADDRESS
CHECKING ACCOUNT NO.	TELEPHONE NUMBER

TRADE REFERENCES

FIRM NAME	CONTACT NAME	TELEPHONE NUMBER	ACCOUNT OPEN SINCE

CONFIRMATION OF INFORMATION ACCURACY AND RELEASE OF AUTHORITY TO VERIFY

I hereby certify that the information in this credit application is correct. The information included in this credit application is for use by the above firm in determining the amount and conditions of credit to be extended. I understand that this firm may also utilize the other sources of credit which it considers necessary in making this determination. Further I hereby authorize the bank and trade references listed in this credit application to release the information necessary to assist this firm in establishing a line of credit.

X _____

SIGNATURE   TITLE   DATE

POLICY STATEMENT: INITIAL ORDER FROM NEW ACCOUNTS WILL NOT BE PROCESSED UNLESS ACCOMPANIED BY THE ABOVE REQUESTED INFORMATION.
TERMS: NET 30 DAYS FROM DATE OF INVOICE UNLESS OTHERWISE STATED.

A-14 Credit application.

A FRIENDLY REMINDER

No doubt you have overlooked payment, but if you have mailed your payment, please accept our thanks. If you have not mailed your payment, please take a moment now to complete this form and return it along with your check. Thank You.

Account No.		**Amount Due**	
NAME			
ADDRESS			
CITY	STATE		ZIP CODE

No.
Date 1st Notice

Due Date

Customer Report:

☐ PAYMENT ENCLOSED
☐ PAYMENT ALREADY MAILED

Date _____ No._____

PAYMENT PAST DUE

Second Notice: If there is a reason for not paying this due amount please let us know. Your account is seriously overdue. Please complete this form and mail with your check today. Your credit is important.

Account No.		**Amount Due**	
NAME			
ADDRESS			
CITY	STATE		ZIP CODE

No.
Date 1st Notice
Date 2nd Notice

Due Date

Customer Report:

☐ PAYMENT ENCLOSED
☐ PAYMENT ALREADY MAILED

Date _____ No._____

FINAL NOTICE!

After repeated requests to convince you to pay, we must now notify you that if we do not receive your payment in the next ten days from this notice, we will start collection proceedings to ensure recovery. We urge you to send your check now.

Account No.		**Amount Due**	
NAME			
ADDRESS			
CITY	STATE		ZIP CODE

No.
Date 1st Notice
Date 2nd Notice
Date

Due Date

Customer Report:

☐ PAYMENT ENCLOSED
☐ PAYMENT ALREADY MAILED

Date _____ No._____

A-15 Account reminders.

PAYMENT PAST DUE

DATE:

Comments:

Statement of Account

Date	Invoice Number	Description	Amount	Total
Amount Due Now			**Amount Remitted**	

Thank you for your prompt attention

In reviewing your account, we have determined that the above invoices have not been paid and are now past due. We would be most grateful for your prompt attention and remittance. If you have any questions or problems with this billing, please contact us immediately. If your remittance has already been sent out, please disregard this notice.

A-16 Payment past due.

Period Ending:

Invoice Date	Invoice #	Acct #	Customer Name	30 days	60 days	90+ days	Total
			TOTALS				

GRAND TOTAL DUE

A-17 Aging of accounts receivable.

Period Ending:

Invoice Date	Invoice #	Acct #	Account Name	30 days	60 days	90+ days	Total
				TOTALS			
				GRAND TOTAL DUE			

A-18 Aging of accounts payable.

| Date: |
| Debit No: |
| Purchase Order Number: |
| Account Number: |

VENDOR'S		
INVOICE DATE	**INVOICE NO.**	**PACKING NO.**

Attention: CREDIT MANAGER

TO DEBIT YOUR ACCOUNT AS FOLLOWS:

☐ ERROR IN PRICE BILLED:

You billed $ _____ each

Purchase Order reads $ _____ each

Difference $ _____ @ No. of pieces _____ $ _____

☐ SETUP CHARGE - BILLED IN ERROR:

NOTE: *The above amount will not be paid until authorized by our buyer, and that any correspondance on the matter should be directed to*
_____ *, Purchasing Department.*
When authorization has been approved, you must re-bill the Debit Memo amount.

☐ ERROR IN QUANTITY BILLED:

You billed _____

We received _____

Difference _____

Unit Price _____ $ _____

☐ OTHER:

Taxes, Purchase Order states: non taxable $ _____

Freight charge, Purchase Order states: FOB $ _____

We Debit $ _____

Signed _____
ACCOUNTS PAYABLE

A-19 Debit memorandum.

OFFICE SUPPLIES/ EQUIPMENT REQUISITION FORM

REQUESTED BY/ DATE

APPROVED BY

REQUEST **NUMBER**

STOCK NUMBER	QUANTITY ORDERED	QUANTITY SHIPPED	BACK ORDERED	DESCRIPTION	DATE SHIPPED	DATE REC.	VENDOR & P.O. NUMBER (PURCHASING ONLY)

Amount   Date

On Line Supply Charges
(Purchasing Only)

Amount   Date

On Line Supply Credits
(Purchasing Only)

Requisitioned Items Shipped By

Requisitioned Items Received By

A-20   Office supplies/equipment requisition form.

Inventory

Date	
Page	of

Department :

Location :

Item#	Qty	Description	Price	Total
			TOTAL	

Priced By:	Called By:
Checked By:	Entered By:

A-21 Inventory form.

Requisition Number: _____
This number must appear on quotation and all related correspondence. This is not an order.

Date:

RETURN QUOTE TO:

NAME

COMPANY

ADDRESS

CITY   STATE   ZIP   TELEPHONE #

QUOTE TO US BY:

REQUESTED TERMS:

REQUESTED F.O.B:

Item	Quantity Ordered	Description	Unit Count	Unit Price	Total Amount

Authorized Signature _____

Date _____

A-22 Request for quote.

REQUISITION ON PURCHASING DEPARTMENT

DATE:

VENDOR		DIVISION:		OFFICE	
		DEPARTMENT		ADDRESS CODE	
Vendor Code:		SHIP PREPAID		VIA	F.O.B.

SHIP TO:

☐ ADD
☐ ALLOW

Shipper Encharge:

☐ TAX EXEMPT   ☐ SERVICES - NONTAXABLE

Req. No.	Project Description	Project Number	Job Number	Account No.

Item	Catalog No.	Quantity (Units)	Description	Unit Price	Shipping Date	Date Required

Intended Use of Material:

SUGGESTED VENDOR REQUESTED BY:

REMARKS

APPROVED BY:

MANAGER	DEPARTMENT HEAD	EXECUTIVE	PURCHASING AGENT	BUYER

A-23 Requisition on purchasing department.

Purchased From: _____
_____
_____
_____

Ship To: _____
_____
_____
_____

Requisition By: _____
P.O. Number: _____
Date: _____
Ship Via: _____
F.O.B.: _____
Issued By: _____
Date Issued: _____

Quantity	Code	Description	Unit Cost	Total
			TOTAL	

Terms and Conditions

_____   _____
DATE   AUTHORIZED SIGNATURE

A-24 Purchase order.

TIME PERIOD FROM: TO:

P.O.#	Date	Issued To	For	Contact	Total

A-25 Purchase order log.

Date

Requesting User		
Extension	Org. Name	Org. Unit No.

INTENDED USE Briefly describe your intended use of the requested item.	
BENEFITS or SAVINGS List the benefits or cost savings which justify the request.	
SOFTWARE List software capabilities required.	
EQUIPMENT List equipment capabilities required.	
ACCESS Is access to other computers required?	
USERS List intended users that will need training.	

Requesting User Approval	Date
Organizational Signature Authority	Date

A-26 Enduser equipment/software request.

TRAVEL REQUEST FORM

NAME:

DEPARTMENT:

EXTENSION NUMBER:

HOME PHONE:

PURPOSE OF TRIP:

FROM	TO	DEPARTURE DATE	TIME	ARRIVAL DATE	TIME

ROUTING (for travel desk only)

From	To	Dep. Time	Flight #	Arr. time	Flight #	Hotel Reservation	Reserve Car?
							☐ YES ☐ NO
							☐ YES ☐ NO
							☐ YES ☐ NO
							☐ YES ☐ NO
							☐ YES ☐ NO
							☐ YES ☐ NO
							☐ YES ☐ NO
							☐ YES ☐ NO
							☐ YES ☐ NO
							☐ YES ☐ NO
							☐ YES ☐ NO
							☐ YES ☐ NO

SPECIAL TRAVEL ARRANGEMENTS

_____
EMPLOYEE SIGNATURE

Date: _____

_____
MANAGER SIGNATURE

A-27 Travel request form.

TRAVEL RESERVATION WORKSHEET

| Made By: |
| Travel Agent: |
| Accepted: |
| On: |

Employee Name:	Department:
Trip Origin:	Destination:
Departure Date:	Return Date:
Flight Reservation:	Class:

AIRLINE	FLIGHT	DATE	FROM	TO	TIME	
					DEP.	
					ARR.	
					DEP.	
					ARR.	
					DEP.	
					ARR.	
					DEP.	
					ARR.	
					DEP.	
					ARR.	
					DEP.	
					ARR.	

HOTEL ACCOMMODATIONS:

CAR RENTAL:

SPECIAL INSTRUCTIONS:

REASON FOR TRIP:

RESERVATIONS APPROVED BY: _____ **DATE:** _____
EMPLOYEE

_____
SUPERVISOR

A-28 Travel reservation worksheet.

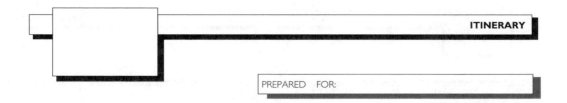

PREPARED   FOR:

DATE	LOCAL TIME		CITY	FLIGHT	ACCOMMODATIONS & APPOINTMENTS
	DEP				
	ARR				
	DEP				
	ARR				
	DEP				
	ARR				
	DEP				
	ARR				
	DEP				
	ARR				
	DEP				
	ARR				
	DEP				
	ARR				
	DEP				
	ARR				
	DEP				
	ARR				
	DEP				
	ARR				
	DEP				
	ARR				
	DEP				
	ARR				
	DEP				
	ARR				
	DEP				
	ARR				
	DEP				
	ARR				
	DEP				
	ARR				
	DEP				
	ARR				
	DEP				
	ARR				

A-29   Itinerary.

EXPENSE REPORT

Attach
Receipts

EXPENSE ACCOUNT OF:					For Period From:						To:		

DATE	TRAVELLED		MI/KM	TRANS-PORT.	HOTEL	MEALS			PHONE	PARKING	MISC.	DAILY TOTAL
	FROM	TO				BKFST.	LUNCH	DINNER			EXPLAIN BELOW*	
SAT												
SUN												
MON												
TUES												
WED												
THURS												
FRI												
TOTALS												

* EXPLANATION

_____
_____
_____
_____
_____
_____

ELAPSED BUSINESS MILES/KILOMETERS

Previous Total _____
Current Week _____
Total to Date _____
CREDIT CARD BILLS _____

Bus. MI/KM
_____ @ _____ = _____

TOTAL EXPENSE _____
Less Advance _____
Balance _____
☐ Claimed   ☐ Refunded

Signature of Claimant:
Approved by:
Date:

A-30 Expense report.

AUTOMOBILE TRAVEL LOG

Monthly Summary Sheet

Date:

AUTOMOBILE INFORMATION

Make of Auto: _____

Year & Model: _____

Vehicle I.D. Number: _____

Driver of Vehicle: _____

Odometer   End of month: _____

                  Beginning of month: _____

Total Miles Driven: _____

Qualified Business Miles Driven: _____

Allowable Reimbursement Rate: _____ x $_____ /mi

Total Expense $ _____

YEAR TO DATE - INFORMATION

	BUSINESS MILES	TOTAL MILES
Prior YTD		
Current Month		
New YTD		

DATE: _____

SIGNATURE : _____

APPROVAL : _____

A-31 Automobile travel log.

TELEPHONE CALL RECORD

TIME PERIOD FROM: _____ TO: _____

Date	Caller	Call To	Company and Location	Code	Phone #	Charges

NOTES OR COMMENTS:

A-32   Telephone call record.

Phone Message

Date:
Time:

For:
From:
Company:
Number:

Telephoned ☐   Will Call Back ☐
Please Call ☐   Returned Call ☐

Message:

Taken By :

Phone Message

Date:
Time:

For:
From:
Company:
Number:

Telephoned ☐   Will Call Back ☐
Please Call ☐   Returned Call ☐

Message:

Taken By :

Phone Message

Date:
Time:

For:
From:
Company:
Number:

Telephoned ☐   Will Call Back ☐
Please Call ☐   Returned Call ☐

Message:

Taken By :

Phone Message

Date:
Time:

For:
From:
Company:
Number:

Telephoned ☐   Will Call Back ☐
Please Call ☐   Returned Call ☐

Message:

Taken By :

A-33 Phone messages.

INTER
OFFICE
MEMO

Date:

To:

From:

Subject:

Comments

A-34 Interoffice memos.

FAX COVER

To:

Company Name:

Fax Number:

From:

Description:

Number of pages (including cover):
Date sent: Time sent:
If there are any problems receiving this transmission please call:

A-35   Cartoon fax cover sheet.

F A X   C O V E R   S H E E T

To:

Company Name:

Fax Number:

From:

Description:

Number of pages (including cover):
Date sent:
Time sent:

If there are any problems receiving
this transmission please call:

A-36 Fax cover sheet.

JOB APPLICATION

Date:

Social Security Number

Name: _____ Telephone: _____
      LAST   FIRST   INITIAL

Address: _____
         STREET

_____
CITY   STATE   ZIP

Education History

Institution	Name & Location	Grade Completed: Diploma/ Degree
High School		
University / College		
Other (Day / Night)		

Employment History (most current first)

Employer :	Your Job Title:
Address :	Duties:
	Reason for Leaving:
Phone:	Salary:
	Employment from : to:

Employer:	Your Job Title:
Address:	Duties:
	Reason for Leaving:
Phone:	Salary:
	Employment from : to:

Employer:	Your Job Title:
Address:	Duties:
	Reason for Leaving:
Phone:	Salary:
	Employment from : to:

JOB APPLICATION Page 1.

A-37a Job application—page 1.

References

	Name	Occupation	Telephone
1			
2			
3			

Skills

○   ○

○   ○

○   ○

○   ○

○   ○ Other explain:

Date Available

Hours Available

Salary Expected

Position Applied For:

Shift Desired:

☐ Day

☐ Night

☐ Afternoon

☐ Any Shift

The information provided on this application is accurate to the best of my knowledge and subject to verification by this company. I understand that proof of age may be required upon employment. I understand I must truthfully answer all the questions on this application. I also understand that if I do not, I may be refused employment, or separated if I am a current company employee. While employed by this company I agree not to engage in any other business or employment without the consent of this company.

If employment results from this application, I understand that additional personal data or a physical examination may be required if I am eligible for benefits. I authorize all previous employers to furnish this company with any information they may have regarding my employment and my reason for leaving, and I release my prior employers and this company from all liability for and damage resulting from the information provided.

I fully understand that if I am not bondable by a surety company, this company may be unable to offer employment.

SIGNATURE: _____ DATE: _____

JOB APPLICATION Page 2.

A-37b Job application—page 2.

EMPLOYMENT APPLICATION

Position Applied For	Type of Employment		Date
	Full Time ☐ Summer ☐		
	Part Time ☐ Temporary ☐		

Name of Applicant (please indicate how you wish to be addressed)

Surname	First Name	Initial(s)

Address (No., Street, City, State, Zip Code)

Social Security Number	Telephone Number (Home) Business

Previous Address In the United States

Some positions in the company require that staff be bonded.

Are you bondable?   YES ☐   NO ☐

Have you ever been bonded? YES ☐   NO ☐

Are you legally entitled to work in the United States? ☐ YES ☐ NO	Are you willing to relocate? ☐ YES ☐ NO

Do you have a valid driver's licence?   ☐ YES   ☐ NO   Class

Education

Secondary School attended and location.	Highest grade successfully completed.		Year Graduated

University attended and location.	No. of years completed	Year graduated	Degrees

Major subjects of specialization.

Community College attended and location.	No. of years completed	Year graduated	Degrees

Major subjects of specialization.

Other Educational Training/ Courses.

Office/ Secretarial Applications

Skill /Aptitude	Years of experience	Words per minute	List secretarial training courses completed and any other training which maybe helpful in considering your application.
Typing			
Shorthand			

EMPLOYMENT APPLICATION Page 1.

A-38a Employment application—page 1.

EMPLOYMENT HISTORY (List present or most recent positions first)

1. Name of Employer	Address	No.	Street	City

Type of Business	Department	Your Position

Duties

Name and Position of Immediate Supervisor

Date Employed (Day, Mo, Yr)	Date Left (Day, Mo, Yr)	Starting Salary	Final Salary

Reason for leaving

2. Name of Employer	Address	No.	Street	City

Type of Business	Department	Your Position

Duties

Name and Position of Immediate Supervisor

Date Employed (Day, Mo, Yr)	Date Left (Day, Mo, Yr)	Starting Salary	Final Salary

Reason for leaving

3. Name of Employer	Address	No.	Street	City

Type of Business	Department	Your Position

Duties

Name and Position of Immediate Supervisor

Date Employed (Day, Mo, Yr)	Date Left (Day, Mo, Yr)	Starting Salary	Final Salary

Reason for leaving

MAY WE ASK YOUR PRESENT EMPLOYER FOR A REFERENCE ☐ YES ☐ NO

REFERENCES (Please do not list relatives or former employers)

Name	Occupation	Address

Whom do you know in this company?

A-38b Employment application—page 2.

Scholarships

Activities/ Interests (Student, Professional, Community, etc)

Publication, patents and thesis subjects

Languages (spoken, written, read) Note fluency

Other interests or hobbies

Special talents

Medical   Do you agree to take a medical exam at company expense   ☐ YES   ☐ NO
related to the essential requirements of the position

We appreciate your interest in seeking employment with us - please feel free to make any additional remarks in the space provided below or attach any additional information that would be helpful in evaluating your qualifications.

Additional   Remarks

Please Read Carefully

I hereby certify that to the best of my knowledge and belief the answers given by me to the foregoing questions and all statements made by me in the application are correct.

If employed, I agree that all material created and produced whether in written, graphic or broadcasting form, all inventions new or changes in processes developed during my employment are the exclusive property of the company to use and/or sell and that subsequent to my employment with this company I will not disclose, use or reveal any confidential information related to the company without first obtaining written consent from an officer of the company.

I hereby apply for employment upon the basis and understanding that such employment may be terminated at any time upon notice given to me personally or sent to my last known address.

I consent to _____ obtaining such personal and job-related information as required in connection with this application
for employment

_____   _____
Date   Signature of applicant

This application form complies with all Human Rights Legislation.

A-38c Employment application—page 3.

NEW HIRE / REHIRE PERSONNEL ACTION

Date _____

Social Security Number	Employee Number	Sex	Worker's Comp.	Job Cat.
Birth Date (YY MM DD)	Code Reason Desc. Rehire ☐ New Hire ☐	Employment Date (YY MM DD)		Fair Non exempt ☐ Exempt ☐

Name (Last Name, First Name, Middle Initial)
Legal Address (Street, Apt. No., City, State and Zip Code)
Mailing Address (Street, Apt. No., City, State and Zip Code)
Bulk Mailing Address (No., P.O. Box Address) (Street, City, State and Zip Code)
Check Mailing Address (Street, Apt. No., City, State and Zip Code)
Department Name (City, State and Zip Code are also needed)

Emergency Contact Name	Relationship	Telephone

Marital Status Single ☐ Married ☐	Home Phone No.	Review/ Raise date	Annual Salary $

Salary Date	Code Reason Desc. Rehire ☐ New Hire ☐	Hourly Rate	Pay Period Hours _____ Hrs
Job Date	Reason Rehire ☐ New Hire ☐	Job Code	Job Title
Salary Grade	Location Code	Location Code Description	
Requisition Number	Addition ☐ Replacement ☐ Person Replaced		

REHIRES ONLY

Previous Hire Date YY/MM/DD	Previous Termination Date YY/MM/DD	Term Code

COMMENTS

APPROVALS

Operations Administrator/Immediate Supervisor	Date	PAYROLL USE ONLY
Department Head / V P	Date	
Human resources	Date	
Human resources	Date	

A-39 New hire/rehire personnel action.

PERFORMACE REPORT

EMPLOYEE: | DATE:

EVALUATE EMPLOYEE FROM 1-5 AND COMMENT IN SPACE PROVIDED

Team Player		
Meets Deadlines		
Organizational Skills		
Communication Skills		

Employer's Comments

Agreed Objectives

Date of Next Evaluation:

X _____
Signed
Employee

X _____
Interviewer

A-40 Performance report.

DATE:

TERRITORY:

SALES AND PROFIT	FORECAST	ACTUAL
Gross Sales		
Gross Profit		
% Gross Profit		
Net Profit		
% Net Profit to Gross Sales		

SELLING COST		
Salary		
Commision		
Auto Expense		
Travel Expense		
Telephone Expense		
Entertainment Expense		
Other Expense		

ACTIVITY		
Total Days Worked		
Number of Calls Made		
Average Number of Calls per Day		

ACCOUNT INFORMATION		
Number of New Accounts		
Number of Accounts Lost		
Number of Accounts at End of Period		
Number of Potential Accounts		

Prepared by: _____

A-41 Salesperson's analysis.

Name/Firm	City, State, Zip Code	Code	Phone

A-42 Telephone and address directory.

LOCATION/ORG. UNIT			DATE
NAME	HOURS	CLASSIFICATION	DESCRIPTION OF WORK

REMARKS

The undersigned employee certifies that the above and foregoing is the actual, correct number of hours worked by him/her on the day stated, and that he/she has not been told or instructed by anyone having authority over him/her to incorrectly state the number of hours actually worked.

Employee's Signature _____

Supervisor's Signature _____

A-43 Weekly time report.

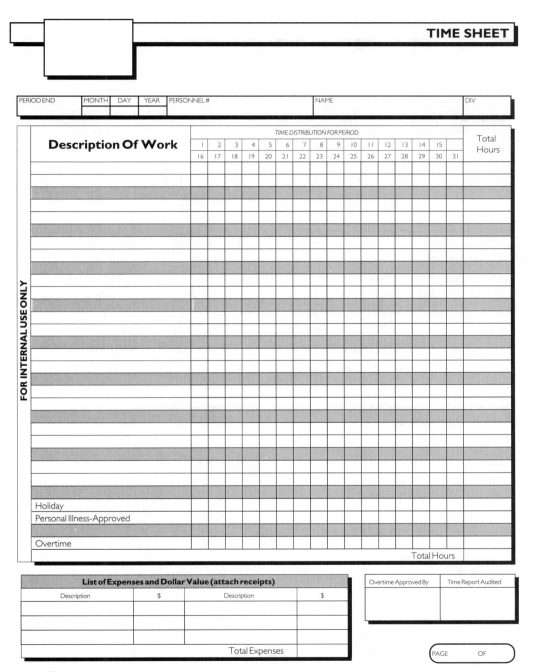

TIME SHEET

PERIOD END	MONTH	DAY	YEAR	PERSONNEL #	NAME	DIV

Description Of Work — TIME DISTRIBUTION FOR PERIOD

	1	2	3	4	5	6	7	8	9	10	11	12	13	14	15	Total Hours
	16	17	18	19	20	21	22	23	24	25	26	27	28	29	30	31

FOR INTERNAL USE ONLY

Holiday

Personal Illness-Approved

Overtime

Total Hours

List of Expenses and Dollar Value (attach receipts)

Description	$	Description	$
		Total Expenses	

Overtime Approved By	Time Report Audited

PAGE   OF

A-44 Time sheet.

PERSON:

FROM:

TO:

PRIORITIES	Monday	Tuesday	Wednesday	Thursday	Friday	Saturday	Sunday
1							
2							
3							
4							
5							

A-45 Monthly activity planner.

DAY OF THE WEEK:
MONTH AND YEAR:

TIME	TO DO	NOTES
8:00–9:00		
9:00–10:00		
10:00–11:00		
11:00–12:00		
12:00–1:00		
1:00–2:00		
2:00–3:00		
3:00–4:00		
4:00–5:00		
5:00–6:00		
6:00–7:00		
7:00–8:00		
8:00–9:00		
9:00–10:00		
10:00–11:00		
11:00–12:00		

A-46 Daily planner.

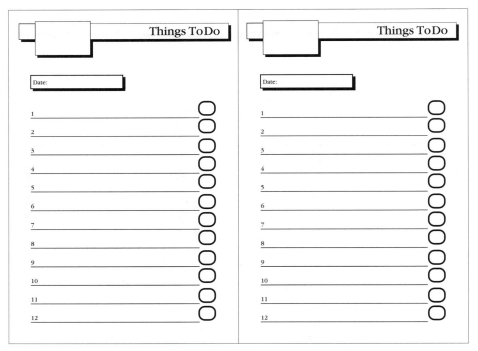

A-47 Things to do.

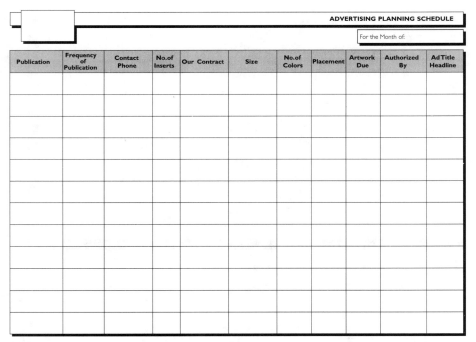

A-48 Advertising planning schedule.

Index

About the author

Author Dan Ramsey is the author of 40 other books on business, automotive, and related topics since 1962, including *Electrical Contractor: Start and Run a Money-Making Business* (TAB Books/McGraw-Hill, 1993) and *Painting Contractor: Start and Run a Money-Making Business* (TAB Books/McGraw-Hill, 1993).

Ramsey holds a Bachelor of Science degree from Eastern Oregon State College in General Studies emphasizing Business and Communications. He is President of Communication Solutions, a consulting service solving business problems through efficient communications. He is also a member of The National Association of Home and Workshop Writers.

Richard Day, technical consultant and author of the book's foreword, worked as an auto mechanic for several dealerships before opening his own auto repair shop in the early 1950s. Rich's three-bay auto shop did many tune-ups, brake jobs, and general troubleshooting.

Rich later gave up auto repair for writing and editing, lending his broad automotive and transportation trade experience to his craft. He has since written some 19 books including *How To Service and Repair Your Own Car*, and two do-it-yourself auto repair books, *Automechanics* and *Engine Tuning*, both educational books for high school auto-mechanic courses.

One of Rich's books on a nonautomotive subject won the National Association of Home and Workshop Writers/Stanley Tools Do-It-Yourself Book Award as best book of 1992.

Rich served for many years as consulting editor, home and shop for the prestigious *Popular Science* magazine. In that capacity he wrote numerous illustrated articles on do-it-yourself auto repair subjects, including doing a valve job, servicing disc brakes, using air tools, working with feedback carburetors, servicing automatic chokes, caring for cooling systems, servicing exhaust systems, and troubleshooting alternators. Rich also researched and wrote a 16-page *Popular Science* special report on automotive braking systems.

Rich has retired as an author and lives with his wife in their owner-built wilderness cabin on a mountainside in Southern California. They have formed a corporation to produce and market video tapes on many of the same subjects that Rich covered in his books and articles over the years.

Rich is a fellow member with Dan Ramsey of the National Association of Home and Workshop Writers, as well as a past president. He is currently director.